Temperament
and Development

Temperament

and

Development

ALEXANDER THOMAS, M.D.

Professor of Psychiatry
New York University Medical Center

and

STELLA CHESS, M.D.

Professor of Child Psychiatry
New York University Medical Center

BRUNNER / MAZEL, *Publishers* • New York

Library of Congress Cataloging in Publication Data

Thomas, Alexander, 1914-
    Temperament and development.

    Includes bibliographical references and index.
    1. Temperament.   2. Developmental psychology.
I.   Chess, Stella, joint author.   II. Title.
BF798.T47   618.9'28'9071   76-49428
ISBN 0-87630-139-1

Copyright © 1977 by Alexander Thomas and Stella Chess
Published by
BRUNNER/MAZEL, INC.
19 Union Square West, New York, N. Y. 10003

MANUFACTURED IN THE UNITED STATES OF AMERICA

Contents

Foreword

Man's increased understanding of himself and his world has been a major ingredient in the history of human society. The chief intellectual characteristic of this history has been man's ability to increasingly remove himself from the concrete experience of the phenomenological "here and now" and place himself in an abstracted world of concepts and logic. This cognitive component of evolution is a double-edged sword, however, for at the same time that it has fostered technological advances it has produced social alienation.

Definitions of alienation have been topics of major philosophical disputes which cannot be briefly elaborated. Rousseau's description of the noble savage will serve for our example. As long as man stayed at a primitive level he did not differentiate himself as an object or self separate from his world of experience with other objects and selves. The consequence of this lack of separation was a oneness with the world in which complete empathy was experienced for the feelings of others. For Rousseau, civilization taught man higher cognitive functions, such as categorizing and labeling, which permitted man to set himself apart from the rest of the world. Once man could label objects as separate and distinct from himself, he lost his primitive empathic feelings of unity with those objects. Once an object or person is given a label different from one's own, there is no need to treat it as one would treat oneself. The alienation produced by civilization was between the world of categories and labels and the world of creatures living together in an undifferentiated symbiosis.

The present volume is an attempt to recreate that initial empathic symbiosis between man and his world. This unity is not a regression to primitive beginnings but rather based on the civilized ability to use categories and labels. The relevance of categories and labels to understanding human development is prominently found in the nature-nurture controversy. The use of labels enables us to convert a biological unity of an organism and its surroundings into a logical separation between constitution and environment. Once the organism is logically isolated from its world, we can then go further and assign the organism to one of a variety of logical categories. For example, when we label a child as retarded, hyperactive, autistic, or, more simply, rotten, we imply that there is something objectively unique about that child that allows such categorization. How children achieve these statuses is a major subject of discussion. The primacy of nature or nurture in this matter has been a question for debate ever since Plato and Aristotle first raised the issue over 2500 years ago.

When the New York Longitudinal Study was conceived in the 1950s, the authors were concerned that environmental influences were given too much credit in determining the growth and development of a child's personality. They felt that the importance of constitutional determinants was severely underemphasized and that a corrective was necessary to the strong "nurture" emphasis found in the then dominant learning and psychoanalytic theories of development. Aside from theoretical issues these authors had a humanistic concern. They felt that, from the environmentalist perspective, parents had to take undeserved blame for any deviancy in the behavior of their children.

The position taken in this volume provides a new logic for reintegrating the concepts of constitution and environment into a model which incorporates the dynamism of our biological and psychological reality. The developmental process is one in which an organism from conception is enmeshed in an interactive environment. From the biochemical world that interacts with the genetic material in the fertilized egg to the social and psychological world that interacts with the wakening consciousness of the newborn child, there is no separation between organism and environment in the real world. It is only in the minds of men abstracted from the real world that such a separation can occur.

When the child's personality is seen to be the outcome of an interactive process in which his or her characteristics are only one of the multitude of ingredients in the social context of development, then labels applied to the child alone or to the environment alone do not serve to help us to understand development. But if we cannot label and categorize, what role is left for science? What at first glance may seem a pessimistic message for science is at the same time an optimistic one for humanism, and as we look further we shall see that it is in reality an optimistic one for science as well.

The pessimistic message is aimed at those who perceive in development simple outcomes derived from simple beginnings, with direct causal chains leading from antecedent to consequent. The message is that such continuities are few and far between, if they exist at all. Development must be characterized as a complex interplay between the contemporary characteristics of the child and the contemporary characteristics of his or her environment. Moreover, the two sets of characteristics are in part a result of their previous interplay, while at the same time their current interplay is producing new characteristics in both child and environment. To feel distressed at the complexity of influences which affect the growth of the child is to be distressed at the uniqueness of being a living creature, especially the uniqueness of being human.

The optimistic message is aimed at those who are not prepared to doom children to unalterable fates. Whether these destinies were presumed to be determined by genetic endowment, constitutional defects, psychosexual trauma, or deviant child-rearing, the fact that these predestinations cannot be documented permits the hope that positive developmental outcomes can occur despite the most profound early distortions.

The purported failures of parents at rearing their children and of scientists at not being able to adequately explain these failures must be seen relative to where we are as a civilization. It is true that a dependence on categories and labels abstracted from real people has limited our understanding of the continual dynamic interaction of child, caregiver, and society, but it also has permitted a level of adaptability, achievement, and comfort which transcends that reached by any other species on earth. What is now necessary is a resynthesis of man and his world which would not deny categories but utilize them in a new integration. This book is such an effort. The data reported demonstrate in concrete terms how uniquely individual children relate to their uniquely individual contexts to reach uniquely individual outcomes. These developmental outcomes can be understood and explained but not predicted or determined. Children with similar constitutions may end up quite differently while children with different constitutions may end up quite the same. Only by accepting the complexity of the social system can we approximate a scientific understanding of human development.

In closing, I would like to propose a seeming anachronism. The theme of this book is to deny the separability of constitution and environment. Neither the nature nor the nurture approach is scientifically or humanistically valid. Despite this thesis I feel a necessity to propose a new environmentalism which accepts indivisibleness of the child-environment system but at the same time places the major responsibility for a child's outcome on the environment.

The New York Longitudinal Study, by focusing on infant individuality, has been able to demonstrate that certain children with "difficult temperaments" produce problems for parents such that they are unable to appropriately cope with the child. In many of these situations the parent-child interaction has produced deviant developmental outcomes. The New York group further argues that the responsibility for such deviant outcomes cannot be placed on either the parent or the child. The child cannot be blamed for his or her constitutional uniqueness and the parent cannot be blamed for using socially acceptable child-rearing norms which will not work with their particular child. But is this saying enough? Is no one guilty? Perhaps before reading this book we are all innocent, but what about after? Once we are aware of the interactive problems presented by children of certain temperaments, are we to blame if we do not provide the necessary caretaking adaptations?

I would argue that we may not be guilty but we are responsible. It is true that the child is an important ingredient in any interaction, but the child is the most vulnerable and the least adaptive ingredient. One cannot ask infants to alter their temperaments in order not to upset their parents. One *can* ask parents to alter their child-rearing techniques in order not to produce developmental tensions in their child. But now we open Pandora's box. Is the inability of parents to adaptively respond to the temperament of their child merely due to the fact that they haven't read the reports on the New York Longitudinal Study? Clearly not! In a complex modern society the interaction of parents with their children is only one of the potentially demanding and stressful interactions in which they are involved. The social, economic, and emotional stresses produced by a civilization undergoing its own development have an important impact on the individual's ability to adapt in any single sphere such as child-rearing.

The message of this book is that one cannot place blame on either parent or child for life's problems. The message should not be that we are uninvolved with these problems, or that we are not responsible for these problems. Ultimately we are responsible—if not as individuals, or as parents, then as a society. So it is as a society that we should promote the educational, social, and emotional resources to permit the parental adaptations demanded by the temperament concept.

ARNOLD J. SAMEROFF, PH.D.
Professor of Psychology and Pediatrics
University of Rochester

Preface

For many years we have been engaged in the study of temperament and its significance for normal and deviant psychological development. The research methodology we developed was necessarily elaborate and detailed. The goals of our research also required the use of the longitudinal method of study. Although they are expensive and time-consuming, longitudinal studies are required to identify specific characteristics of temperament in individual infants and to gather data on the vicissitudes of these temperamental attributes in each child over time and their influence on the developmental course.

These methodological demands were unavoidable in the initial studies that we undertook, but they inhibited many other investigators from utilizing our concepts and protocols for their own projects. Increasingly, we have been asked to develop more manageable research protocols. At the same time a number of investigators have pursued studies related to our own work and made significant contributions to our knowledge of the nature of temperament and its functional significance.

The present volume, therefore, has several objectives:

1) To summarize our findings and concepts to date.

2) To summarize and relate the results of other temperament studies to our own work.
3) To provide short questionnaires for the identification of temperamental characteristics in individual children.
4) To outline the practical implications of temperament for parents, teachers, pediatricians and mental health professionals.
5) To explore some of the theoretical implications of the temperament-environment interactional process for concepts of the origins and dynamics of personality structure and the nature of the developmental process.

Our own anterospective longitudinal studies have also resulted in a number of interesting psychological and psychiatric findings not directly related to the phenomenon of temperament. These have been reported extensively in a number of professional publications. Since the present volume focuses on the issue of temperament and its significance, these other findings and considerations will not be discussed directly here except as they relate to the main theme of the present volume.

Our longitudinal studies could not have been possible without the complete and continuous cooperation of the parents who have responded unstintingly and cheerfully over the years to our demands on their time and energies. Their children, also, have participated freely and easily as they have reached adolescence and we have made independent requests for their participation. We are grateful, also, to the many teachers and directors of nursery and elementary schools who inconvenienced themselves beyond the call of duty to make us welcome, to provide the opportunity to observe the children in school settings, and to submit to detailed interviews about their pupils.

Our previous major publications on temperament had the co-authorship of Dr. Herbert Birch, who was both our active colleague in these studies and a dear close friend. Dr. Birch was an outstanding figure in the international research community who was at the height of his enormously productive and creative career at the time of his sudden death in 1973. His passing has been a great loss, not only to his family, friends and colleagues, but to society at large, because of his central concern, namely the link between research and broad social questions. Those of us who had the opportunity to work with

Herb Birch and know him personally can never forget the stimulation, imaginativeness and profound intelligence he brought to any discussion.

Our co-workers have been numerous, and all have been consistently and thoughtfully devoted to their responsibilities and tasks. Their full commitment to the research has made possible the success of our longitudinal studies. Their number is too great for individual acknowledgment in this brief preface.

We do owe a special debt of appreciation to Dr. Sam Korn, who has carried the senior responsibility for data analysis in all our projects for over 15 years. Dr. Korn has been no mere statistician, though his expertise and sophistication in this area are indeed impressive. He has contributed significantly to the conceptualization of research issues, the planning of programs of work, the supervision of ongoing data collection, and the interpretation of the results of data analysis. His incisive critique of the first manuscript draft was of great value in our final revisions of this book.

Our thanks are extended to Martha Cameron, who worked intensively and intelligently over the many editorial issues in this volume. Her contribution extended far beyond routine copy editing and bibliographic research to include highly professional and skillful editing and content evaluation.

Our longitudinal studies were initially aided financially by several private sources. Since 1960 we have received major support from the National Institute of Mental Health (MH-3614, 5-0359-4-11, and 26414), together with additional support from the National Institute of Child Health and Human Development, the Office of Education and the Children's Bureau of the Department of Health, Education and Welfare, the Health Research Council and the Foundation for Child Development. Most recently, additional financial support has come from the Children's Fund of the Okun Foundation. The views expressed in this volume are, of course, entirely the authors' and should in no way be construed as reflecting the opinions of any of the agencies that have given our studies financial support.

A. T.
S. C.

Historical

background

All of us who have responsibility for child-care, whether as parents, teachers, nurses, pediatricians, psychiatrists or psychologists, share one fundamental belief. We are all convinced that the child's environment—his conditions of life, relationships with his parents and other family members, the extrafamilial socio-cultural setting—has a decisive influence in shaping his physical and psychological development.

This conviction is based on a host of scientific studies over many decades, on empirical experience, and on the various theoretical concepts of the developmental process. One theory may emphasize motivational forces and psychodynamic defenses, as in psychoanalysis, or conditioning, perception and cognition, as in learning theory, or social determinants, as in various sociological theories, or the processes of accommodation-assimilation, as in Piaget's formulation. But all these and other concepts agree that individual differences in personality development result from differences in environmental stimuli and life experiences. All agree in rejecting the static, mechanical beliefs of past centuries which conceived of development as the mere unfolding and elaboration of fixed characteristics already present in the newborn infant.

1

To say that environment is a decisive factor in individual psychological development is quite different from the supposition that it is the *only* determinant. However, from the 1920s on through the 1950s, environmental determinism became an increasingly dominant trend in both the professional literature and in teaching (1, 2). This trend was not limited to any one school of thought. It was manifest both in those inquiries basing themselves on psychoanalytic conceptualizations and in those deriving from various positions in academic psychology. The role of organismic characteristics received some attention, mainly through the view that developmental level was a fundamental factor in structuring tht child's reactions to his environment. However, the concept of developmental level in the main referred to general laws of responsiveness and to the time sequences in which universals in personality organization were achieved, but not to the issue of individuality or uniqueness of functioning.

It is true that Freud had asserted that "each individual ego is endowed from the beginning with its own peculiar dispositions and tendencies" (3), and that in the 1930s two pioneer workers in child development, Gesell (4) and Shirley (5) had reported significant individual differences in the behavioral characteristics of infants. However, neither they nor their followers explored in any systematic fashion the influence such characteristics might have on developmental course. In the 1940s and 1950s, a number of studies did appear which reported observations of individual differences in infants and young children in specific, discrete areas of functioning, such as: motility (6); perceptual responses (7); sleeping and feeding patterns (8); drive endowment (9); quality and intensity of emotional tone (10); social responsiveness (11); autonomic response patterns (12, 13, 14); biochemical individuality (15, 16); and electroencephalographic patterns (17). However, no long-term investigations were reported on the relationship between these findings in early life and the later course of psychological development. Following a different direction, Pavlov and his students (18) had classified different types of nervous systems according to the balance between excitation and inhibition, and had attempted to explain features of both normal and abnormal behavioral states on this basis. However, these explanations were mainly speculative and lacked human behavioral and clinical confirmatory data.

By the early 1950s the environmentalist view was firmly in the ascendancy and considered to be antithetical to any emphasis on an organismic contribution to individual psychological development. Thus, when we began to explore the possible significance of the infant's own intrinsic behavioral style on later development, our psychiatric colleagues with few exceptions assumed we were returning to some outdated and discredited constitutionalist view. Polite unconvinced nods met our insistence that the polarization of constitution and environment as mutually exclusive forces was artificial and mechanical, that the influence of constitution could not be understood without a simultaneous consideration of the influence of environment, and vice versa. Even the reference to the authority of modern biology, with its resolution of this age-old dispute of nature versus nurture by the recognition that growth and development were at all times the product of a constantly evolving interactive process between heredity and environment, failed to be persuasive. Psychoanalytic colleagues were also critical of the importance we gave to psychological attributes of the young child which were not derived from motivational forces or drive states.

Our ideas received a totally different reception among pediatricians. From their own practical experience they knew that babies were different at birth and that these differences influenced the manner in which the infant responded to specific child-care practices and to illness or other special events. They welcomed and encouraged our plan to do a systematic study of behavioral individuality in early childhood and explore the significance of such individual differences for psychological development. Several of these pediatricians were actively helpful to us in gathering a study sample and encouraging parents to participate in our project.

Our decision to launch this study of behavioral individuality derived from a number of considerations.

1) Like innumerable other parents, we were struck by the clearly evident individual differences in our children, even in the first few weeks of life. There were differences in the regularity of biological

functions such as sleep and hunger, in levels of motor activity, in the intensity of laughter or crying, in the initial reactions to new stimuli, in the ease with which the baby's reactions could be modified. Other individual characteristics also appeared to be present, but were more subtle and less easily definable in their expression. We noticed similar individual differences in the young children of our relatives and friends. Furthermore, in many, though not all of these children, there appeared to be a remarkable persistence of at least some of these characteristics of individuality as they grew older.

2) As clinicians, we were repeatedly impressed by our inability to make a direct correlation between environmental influences, such as parental attitudes and practices, and the child's psychological development. There was no question, of course, that these influences played an important role in the child's life, and we, like other clinicians, devoted much effort to trying to persuade parents and others to provide a healthier environment for children. However, we saw many, many instances in which psychopathology in a child occurred even with good parents, or in which a child's development pursued a consistently healthy direction, even into adult life, in the face of severe parental disturbance, family disorganization, and social stress.

Furthermore, even in cases where parental dysfunction was obviously responsible for the child's behavior problems, there was no consistent pattern between the parental approach and the specific pathology manifested by the child. For example, some children responded to domineering, authoritarian treatment by becoming anxious and submissive, while others became defiant and negativistic. Freud himself commented on this puzzling phenomenon. In a rarely quoted statement, he observed that:

> So long as we trace the development [of a mental process] backwards, the connection appears continuous, and we feel we have gained an insight which is completely satisfactory and even exhaustive. But if we proceed the reverse way, if we start from the premise inferred from the analysis and try to follow up the final result, then we no longer get the impression of an inevitable sequence of events, which could not have been otherwise determined. We notice at once that there might be another result, and that we might have been just as well able to understand and explain the latter (19).

The longer we worked with disturbed children and adults the more we became convinced that many behavioral phenomena which were conventionally attributed to purposive-motivational factors might be better understood if they were viewed as non-motivational behavioral styles. An adult who is shy in new social situations might be anxious and insecure. On the other hand, he might be self-confident but have the temperamental characteristic of adapting slowly to new situations. A child who dawdles in the morning and is chronically late to school might be avoiding school because of a learning problem. He might, on the other hand, be a child with high distractibility and low persistence who is easily diverted from a task or routine by extraneous stimuli. Such differential clinical judgments could have important consequences for psychiatric diagnosis and treatment (20, 21).

3) As mental health professionals we became increasingly concerned at the dominant professional ideology of the time, in which the causation of all child psychopathology, from simple behavior problems to juvenile delinquency to schizophrenia itself, was laid at the doorstep of the mother. (A more recent addition to this catalogue of sins occurred in the late 1960s and early 1970s, when some professionals ascribed the rebellion and anti-establishment attitudes of many college students to an excessively permissive upbringing by their parents (22).) The guilt and anxiety created in mothers whose children had even minor behavioral deviations were enormous. As stated by the President of Barnard College in the early 1950s,

> All the experts seem to be saying to young parents: Even the most innocent appearing act or a carelessly spoken word may "harm" a child or "damage" his future happiness. You hurt them by comparing them and praising them for being special. You hurt them by being too affectionate to them and by not being affectionate enough (23).

We ourselves have called this ideology the "Mal de Mère" syndrome (24).

Time after time it was clear that pointing the finger of blame at the mother had devastating psychological effects on her. The guilt and anxiety also distorted the mother's judgment, patience and flexibility in dealing with her child's problems, so that the reproach led in effect to a self-fulfilling prophecy. And yet, in so many cases we could see little evidence that the mother was completely or even partially responsible for her child's difficulties!

4) Finally, a review of the literature revealed that there was considerable skepticism of this exclusively environmentalist view (25, 26). The specific research studies and reviews of the literature questioning the earlier assumptions of exclusive intra- and extra-familial environmental determinants of child development have swelled with each passing year (27, 28).

With these considerations and concerns increasingly in mind, we began, in the early 1950s, to explore various research approaches to a systematic study of individual differences in children and their significance for the developmental process. By 1956 we launched our first longitudinal study.

REFERENCES

1. G. W. Allport, "European and American Theories of Personality," *Perspectives in Personality Theory*, eds., H. P. David and H. von Bracken (New York: Basic Books, 1961), pp. 324.
2. A. M. Rose, ed., *Mental Health and Mental Disorder* (New York: W. W. Norton and Co., Inc., 1955).
3. S. Freud, "Analysis, Terminable and Interminable," *Collected Papers*, 5:316 (London: Hogarth Press, 1950).
4. A. Gesell and L. B. Ames, "Early Evidences of Individuality in the Human Infant," *J. Genetic Psychol.*, 47:339 (1937).
5. M. M. Shirley, *The First Two Years: A Study of Twenty-Five Babies* (Minneapolis: University of Minnesota Press, 1931 and 1933).
6. M. Fries and P. Woolf, "Some Hypotheses on the Role of the Congenital Activity Type in Personality Development," *Psychoanalytic Study of the Child*, 8:48 (1953).
7. P. Bergman and S. Escalona, "Unusual Sensitivities in Very Young Children," *Psychoanalytic Study of the Child*, 3-4:33 (1949).
8. S. Escalona and Others, "Emotional Development in the First Year of Life," *Problems of Infancy and Childhood* (New York: Josiah Macy, Jr. Foundation, 1953), p. 11.
9. A. Alpert, P. W. Neubauer, and A. P. Weil, "Unusual Variation in Drive Endowment," *Psychoanalytic Study of the Child*, 11:125 (1956).
10. R. Meili, "A Longitudinal Study of Personality Development," *Dynamic Psychopathology in Childhood*, eds., L. Jessner and E. Pavenstedt (New York: Grune and Stratton, 1959), pp. 106-123. (This is a summary of a monographic report, "Anfange der Charakterentwicklung," Bern: Hans Hunber, 1957).
11. A. Gesell, *op. cit.*

12. W. H. Bridger and M. F. Reiser, "Psychophysiologic Studies of the Neonate," *Psychosomat. Med.*, 21:265 (1959).
13. H. J. Grossman and N. Y. Greenberg, "Psychosomatic Differentiation in Infancy," *Psychosomat. Med.*, 19:293 (1957).
14. J. B. Richmond and S. L. Lustman, "Automatic Function in the Neonate," *Psychosomat. Med.*, 17:269 (1955).
15. I. A. Mirsky, "Psychoanalysis and the Biological Sciences," *Twenty Years of Psychoanalysis*, eds., F. Alexander and H. Ross (New York: W. W. Norton, 1953), pp. 155-176.
16. R. V. Williams, *Biochemical Individuality*. (New York: John Wiley & Sons, 1956).
17. G. Walter, "Electroencephalographic Development of Children," *Discussion on Child Development*, I, eds., J. M. Tanner and B. Inhelder (New York: International Univ. Press, 1953), 132-160.
18. I. P. Pavlov, *Conditioned Reflexes: An Investigation of the Physiological Activity of the Cerebral Cortex*, trans. and ed., G. V. Anrep (London: Oxford University Press, 1927).
19. S. Freud, *Collected Papers*, 2:226 (London: Hogarth Press, 1950).
20. S. Chess and A. Thomas, "The Importance of Non-motivational Behavior Patterns in Psychiatric Diagnosis and Treatment," *Psychiatric Quarterly*, 33:326-334 (1959).
21. A. Thomas, "Purpose vs. Consequence in the Analysis of Behavior," *Am. J. Psychotherapy*, 24:49 (1970).
22. B. Bettelheim, "Children Must Learn to Fear," *New York Times Sunday Magazine*, April 13, 1969.
23. H. Bruch, "Parent Education, or the Illusion of Omnipotence," *American J. of Orthopsychiatry*, 24:723 (1954).
24. S. Chess, "Mal de Mère," *American J. of Orthopsychiatry*, 34:613 (1964).
25. H. Orlansky, "Infant Care and Personality," *Psychological Bulletin*, 46:1 (1949).
26. E. H. Klatskin, E. B. Jackson, and L. C. Wilkin, "The Influence of Degree of Flexibility in Maternal Child Care Practices on Early Child Behavior," *American J. Orthopsychiatry*, 26:79 (1956).
27. H. R. Beiser, "Discrepancies in the Symptomatology of Parents and Children," *Journal of the American Academy of Child Psychiatry*, 3:457 (1964).
28. H. R. Schaffer and P. E. Emerson, "The Development of Social Attachments in Infancy," *Monographs of the Society for Research in Child Development*, 29:3, 72 (1964).

2

Theoretical

and operational

framework

In our first publications we used the terms "primary reaction pattern" and "initial reactivity" to designate the characteristics of behavioral individuality that are identified in early infancy and childhood (1, 2). The terms "primary" and "initial" emphasized the early appearance of these individual differences in infancy and the lack of evidence that they were secondary to postnatal environmental influences. The designations "reaction patterns" and "reactivity" were meant to emphasize the relationship of these behavioral phenomena to environmental stimuli.

However, as our studies progressed we came to feel that these terms were too narrow and mechanical. It could be argued that "primary" and "initial" should be reserved for prenatal or perinatal behaviors or to whatever underlying factors, whether genetic, endocrine, neurophysiological, or psychophysiological, might be causative for these individual differences. The designation "reactive" tends to imply a passive, secondary role for these early behavioral characteristics, rather than the active independent manner in which they interact with environmental stimuli and demands. For this reason we turned to the term temperament, which had already been utilized by some other workers to designate similar behavioral phenomena (3, 4).

8

Temperament may best be viewed as a general term referring to the *how* of behavior. It differs from ability, which is concerned with the *what* and *how well* of behaving, and from motivation, which accounts for *why a person* does what he is doing. Temperament, by contrast, concerns the *way* in which an individual behaves. Two children may dress themselves with equal skillfulness or ride a bicycle with the same dexterity and have the same motives for engaging in these activities. Two adolescents may display similar learning ability and intellectual interests and their academic goals may coincide. Two adults may show the same technical expertness in their work and have the same reason for devoting themselves to their jobs. Yet, these two children, adolescents or adults may differ significantly with regard to the quickness with which they move, the ease with which they approach a new physical environment, social situation or task, the intensity and character of their mood expression, and the effort required by others to distract them when they are absorbed in an activity.

Temperament can be equated to the term *behavioral style*. Each refers to the *how* rather than the *what* (abilities and content) or the *why* (motivations) of behavior. In this definition, temperament is a phenomenologic term and has no implications as to etiology or immutability. On the contrary, like any other characteristic of the organism—whether it be height, weight, intellectual competence, perceptual skills—temperament is influenced by environmental factors in its expression and even in its nature as development proceeds.

Through our longitudinal research we were able to identify and study nine categories and three constellations of temperament, which we will describe at length in the following chapter. These, of course, do not exhaust all of the possibilities.

Abrams and Neubauer have described a characteristic which they label Person- or Thing-Orientedness, defined as "individual variation in development characterized by an inclination in orientedness either toward the animate or toward the inanimate world. This variant becomes manifest at the second month of life. It casts its impressions on the surrounds, on the continuing developmental process, and on certain aspects of character formation" (5). Graham and his associates, in a British study of children three to eight years of age, confirmed a number of our findings on temperament, and added an additional characteristic, which they labeled "fastidiousness" (6). Using our criteria for categories of temperament, Scholom factored out three main temperamental categories. The first is labeled Mood, comprised of approach, adaptability, mood and threshold; the second is Consistency, comprised of rhythmicity, persistence and attention span; the third is Energy Level, comprised of activity level, intensity and distractibility (7). In our own research group, Hertzig *et al.* analyzed the stylistic characteristics of the responses of three-year-old children to task demands of a standard I.Q. test and derived a number of response characteristics by an inductive analysis of the data (8).

It can be expected that future investigators will identify additional categories of behavioral style, which reflect the *how,* rather than the *what* or *why* of behavior. To avoid confusion of terms, the term *temperament* will refer to those stylistic characteristics which are evident in the early infancy period, while the broader term *behavioral style* will include characteristics or trends which appear in later childhood or adult life.

Our study of temperament was at all times predicated on a firm commitment to an interactionist concept of the developmental process (9). In other words, temperament is never considered by itself, but always in its relationship to, or interaction with, the individual's abilities and motives and external environmental stresses and opportunities. This interactive process produces certain consequences in behavior, which then interact with recurrent and new features of the environment to reinforce certain previous patterns, or attenuate some, or produce new behavioral characteristics, or all three. To analyze this constantly evolving process of development requires the view that new behaviors or personality attributes that appear at new age-stage developmental periods may represent older patterns in new form, as is commonly assumed, but may also constitute the emergence of qualitatively new psychological characteristics. This leads to the concept that the developmental process may show discontinuities as well as continuities, a formulation which has recently been emphasized in a review by Sameroff (10). (Sameroff

uses the term "transactional" as equivalent to the term "interactionist.") The general formulation of the interactionist position is ele-
gantly stated by Schneirla and Rosenblatt (11):

> Behavior is typified by reciprocal stimulative relationships. . . .
> Mammalian behavioral development is best conceived as a
> unitary system of processes changing progressively under the
> influence of an intimate interrelationship of factors of matura-
> tion and of experience—with maturation defined as the devel-
> opmental contribution of tissue growth and differentiation and
> their secondary processes, experience as the effects of stimula-
> tion and its organic traces on behavior.

Such an interactionist approach had several fundamental implications for our data-gathering and data-analysis methods. It required
that information on behavioral style be at all times gathered within
the specific context of the environmental situation in which it
occurred. Thus, a child's intensity of reaction, approach or withdrawal to a new situation, or degree of distractibility could not be
understood without a knowledge of the environmental situation
within which the child's response occurred. In similar fashion, a
parent's reaction to a child and her child-care attitudes and practices
could not be adequately evaluated without a simultaneous consideration of the child's temperamental characteristics and their influence
on the parent.

In analyzing the nature of the temperament-environment interactive process we have found the evolutionary concept of "goodness
of fit," as elaborated by Henderson (12), and the related ideas of
consonance and dissonance to be very useful. Goodness of fit results
when the properties of the environment and its expectations and
demands are in accord with the organism's own capacities, characteristics, and style of behaving. When this *consonance* between organism
and environment is present, optimal development in a progressive direction is possible. Conversely, poorness of fit involves discrepancies
and *dissonances* between environmental opportunities and demands
and the capacities and characteristics of the organism, so that distorted development and maladaptive functioning occur. Goodness
of fit is never an abstraction, but is always goodness of fit in terms

of the values and demands of a given culture or socioeconomic group.

This concept of goodness of fit is similar to that employed by Kagan in studying perceptual schemata in infants and their interaction with new environmental stimuli. He emphasizes that excessive stress and distress will depend on a discrepancy from an established scheme and not from the novelty or change in stimulation as such. "The emphasis is placed on the relation between his schemata and the events in the new environment, not on the absolute variability or intensity of the new situation. . . . If disruption is seen as a product of lack of congruence between schema and environment, one examines the distinctive qualities of the environment" (13).

It should be stated that goodness of fit does not imply an absence of stress and conflict. Quite the contrary. They are inevitable concomitants of the developmental process, in which new expectations and demands for change and progressively higher levels of functioning occur continuously as the child grows older. Demands, stresses and conflicts, when consonant with the child's developmental potentials and capacities for mastery, may be constructive in their consequences and should not be considered as an inevitable cause of behavioral disturbance. The issue involved in disturbed behavioral functioning is rather one of *excessive* stress resulting from poorness of fit and dissonance between environmental expectation and demands and the capacities of the child at a particular level of development.

Within this theoretical framework, the data-gathering procedures we developed had a number of objectives:

1) The behavioral data for each child at any age should be gathered from a wide range of daily activities. This assures that judgments of temperament would not have to rely on single or special situations in which the child's typical behavioral style might be distorted by some special influence.

2) Descriptions of the child's behavior should be linked to the environmental context at all times. Thus, if a mother reported that her child cried when put to bed at night, the next question would be "What did you do when he cried?" Then, "How did he react to what

you did?" Then, "What did you do then?" and so on until the sequence of interaction was completed.

3) Inasmuch as it would have been both impractical and expensive for an observer to live in the subject's home for a long period of time, we decided to use detailed parental reports of the child's behavior as a primary source of data for the early childhood period. This reliance on parental reports has been questioned by some who prefer data-gathering by direct observational methods (14). However, direct observations have their own methodological problems (15). The choice should not be determined by any *a priori* preference for one methodological method over another, but by the requirements of the specific research projects. For our study, the need to gather information on the young child's behavior in many situations of daily living and on the sequence of behavioral responses over hours and even days required the use of the parent as a primary data-gathering source. At older age periods, as the child's functioning outside the home increased, it became possible to utilize other sources of information besides the parent.

To insure accuracy and completeness in the parents' reports, emphasis should be put on descriptions of events and behaviors close in time to the interview. Furthermore, since distortion of parental reports appears to be markedly influenced by the degree of specificity and objectivity of the questions asked (16, 17, 18), our interview protocols at all times requested descriptions of concrete objective behaviors rather than judgments of complex motives and other subjective states. Similar descriptions were requested from teachers or other informants who were interviewed at later stages of the study, and from staff members who made direct observations in school situations and standard psychological test procedures. The validity of parental reports obtained in this manner was confirmed by comparison with the description of the child's behavior done by two trained independent observers in the home in 18 cases (19). The accuracy of parental descriptive and objective reports of their infants' behavior has been confirmed by other research workers (20).

4) The identification of temperamental individuality and its influence on psychological development requires an anterospective longi-

tudinal study starting in early infancy. Cross-sectional studies are considerably more economical and markedly less time-consuming, but their effectiveness is primarily limited to the delineation of group trends and comparisons. As stated by Kodlin and Thompson, "the cross-sectional approach can never satisfy the objective of a study which requires the measurement of the change in a trait through time in a given individual" (21). An anterospective study in which parents report behavior occurring in the immediate past is necessary to avoid the distortions of retrospective recall which can arise for a number of reasons (22, 23, 24, 25, 26). Wenar has summarized this problem of retrospective recall: "A good deal of past research has leaned heavily on the slenderest of reeds. It may well be that mothers' histories mislead more often than they illuminate and, as yet, we are in a poor position to know when they are doing one or the other" (27). In addition, starting the study in early infancy made it easier to distinguish temperamental aspects of behavior from motivational and psychodynamic phenomena which become increasingly significant in shaping behavior as the individual grows older.

5) In order to minimize the influence of sociocultural variability a homogeneous population should be studied. At a later date we did study the influence of some of these environmental factors by means of intergroup comparisons of different homogeneous sociocultural groups. The use of such a homogeneous group does not, of course, eliminate differences in environmental influences. The study protocols gave appropriate attention to such phenomena as trauma, unusual events and idiosyncratic parental attitudes. In a heterogeneous group it would have been more difficult to decide whether observed individual differences in behavior resulted from differences in temperament or differences in sociocultural background.

6) Data analysis should involve both quantitative and qualitative techniques. Our data-gathering procedures emphasized specific descriptions of behavior which, in addition to other advantages, could be subjected to item scoring. This made it possible to exploit the data by statistical and other quantitative techniques. Judgment is involved in the development of categories and the establishment of scoring criteria and methods. Once these are established, however,

quantitative procedures must of necessity be routine. The demand for reliability in scoring limits the possibility of the full utilization of the available information or the assignment of special functional significance to some single unusual behavioral item. The rigors of quantitative methods of data treatment also often preclude the identification of meaningful subtleties in the developmental course of individual children. It therefore becomes desirable to supplement the routine quantitative methods of scoring and analysis by qualitative judgmental methods. We have pursued such analyses through intensive culling of all the records available on the child from all the various sources of data, followed by judgmental evaluations by senior research staff members. Different issues require different proportions of quantitative and qualitative methods, and the relative emphasis is best determined in the course of the study of specific issues.

Finally, we set the goals of our longitudinal studies so that the role of temperament in psychological development could be investigated systematically. These goals included:

a) The development of a method for classifying behavioral individuality in early infancy in terms of objectively describable and reliably rated categories of temperament.

b) The study of consistencies and inconsistencies of these early characteristics in the course of development.

c) The analysis of the pertinence of early temperament to later psychological individuality.

d) The dynamic of temperament in the mastery of environmental demands and expectations at succeeding age-stage levels of development.

e) The identification of those children who develop behavior disorders, and the analysis of the ontogenesis and course of these disorders in terms of a continuously evolving child-environment interactional process.

REFERENCES

1. S. Chess, A. Thomas, H. G. Birch and M. Hertzig, "A Longitudinal Study of Primary Reaction Patterns in Children," *Comprehensive Psychiatry*, 1:8: 103-112 (1960).

2. A. Thomas, S. Chess, H. G. Birch, M. Hertzig and S. Korn, *Behavioral Individuality in Early Childhood* (New York: New York University Press, 1963).
3. J. P. Guilford, *Personality* (New York: McGraw-Hill, 1959).
4. R. B. Cattell, *Personality: A Systematic and Factual Study* (New York: McGraw-Hill, 1950).
5. S. Abrams and P. B. Neubauer, "Object Orientedness: The Person or The Thing." Presented at the meeting of the Psychoanalytic Association of New York, January, 1975.
6. P. Graham, M. Rutter and S. George, "Temperamental Characteristics as Predictors of Behavior Disorders in Children," *Am. J. Orthopsychiat.*, 43:328-339 (1973).
7. A. H. Scholom, "The Relationship of Infant and Parent Temperament to the Prediction of Child Adjustment." Doctoral dissertation, Michigan State University, 1975.
8. M. E. Hertzig, H. G. Birch, A. Thomas and O. A. Mendez, "Class and Ethnic Differences in the Responsiveness of Preschool Children to Cognitive Demands," *Monographs of the Society for Research in Child Development*, 33:1-69 (1968).
9. A. Thomas and S. Chess, "Behavioral Individuality in Childhood," *Development and Evolution of Behavior*, eds., L. R. Aronson, E. Tobach, D. S. Lehrman and J. S. Rosenblatt (San Francisco: W. H. Freeman and Co., 1970), pp. 529-541.
10. A. J. Sameroff, "Early Influences on Development: Fact or Fancy?" *Merrill-Palmer Quarterly*, 20:275-301 (1975).
11. T. C. Schneirla and J. S. Rosenblatt, "Behavioral Organization and Genesis of the Social Bond in Insects and Mammals," *Am. J. Orthopsychiatr.*, 31:223-253 (1961).
12. L. J. Henderson, *The Fitness of the Environment* (New York: Macmillan Co., 1913).
13. J. Kagan, *Change and Continuity in Infancy* (New York: John Wiley and Sons, 1971), p. 11.
14. L. J. Stone, H. T. Smith and L. B. Murphy, eds., *The Competent Infant* (New York: Basic Books, 1973), p. 16.
15. F. D. Horowitz, ed., *Review of Child Development Research* (Chicago: University of Chicago Press, 1975), IV:470.
16. E. A. Haggard, A. Brekstad and A. G. Skard, "On the reliability of the Anamnestic Interview," *J. Abnormal and Social Psychology*, 61:311 (1960).
17. K. E. Goddard, G. Broder and C. Wenar, "Reliability of Pediatric Histories. A Preliminary Study," *Pediatrics*, 28:1011 (1961).
18. M. K. Pyles, H. R. Stoltz and J. W. MacFarlane, "The Accuracy of Mothers' Reports on Birth and Development Data," *Child Development*, 6:165 (1935).
19. A. Thomas *et. al., op. cit.*, p. 54.
20. A. Costello, "Are Mothers Stimulating?" *Child Alive*, ed., R. Lewin (London: Temple Smith, 1975), pp. 45-46.
21. D. Kodlin and D. J. Thompson, "An Appraisal of the Longitudinal Approach to Studies of Growth and Development," *Monographs of the Society for Research in Child Development*, 23:1:8 (1958).
22. E. A. Haggard *et al., op. cit.*
23. K. E. Goddard *et al., op. cit.*
24. M. K. Pyles *et al., op. cit.*

25. L. Robbins, "The Accuracy of Parental Recall of Aspects of Child Development and Child Rearing Practices," *J. Abnormal Soc. Psychol.*, 66:261 (1963).
26. S. Chess, A. Thomas and H. G. Birch, "Distortions in Developmental Reporting Made by Parents of Behaviorally Disturbed Children," *J. Am. Acad. Child Psychiatr.*, 5:226 (1966).
27. C. Wenar, "The Reliability of Developmental Histories," *Psychosomat. Med.*, 25:505 (1963).

3

Temperament and

its delineation

In this chapter we will summarize briefly our sample populations, methods of data collection and analysis, the definitions of the nine categories of temperament, and the delineation of functionally significant temperamental constellations. These issues are discussed at length in our previous volumes (1, 2).

STUDY POPULATIONS

The New York Longitudinal Study (NYLS) is our first and most intensively studied group, comprising 141 children. Sample collection was begun in 1956 and completed six years later; to date, only five subjects have been lost to the study, and the remainder are still being followed. The families are of middle- or upper-middle-class background. Almost all parents were born in the United States. Forty percent of the mothers and 60 percent of the fathers had both college education and postgraduate degrees, and less than 10 percent had no college at all. The study parents are predominently Jewish (78 percent), while the remainder are Catholic (seven percent) and Protestant (15 percent). There are 85 families involved: Forty-five have one child, 31 have two, seven have three, and two families have four children enrolled in the study.

To obtain a population of contrasting socioeconomic background, we initiated a second longitudinal study in 1961 of 95 children of working-class Puerto Rican parents. These families were mostly intact and stable; 86 percent live in low-income public housing projects (3). This group has also been followed longitudinally since early infancy, with the same approach to data collection and analysis as in the NYLS. A small sample of children on an Israeli kibbutz has also been evaluated for temperamental characteristics (4).

In addition, two longitudinal samples of deviant children were also gathered and followed. One comprised 68 children born prematurely, with birth weights ranging from 1000 to 1750 grams. Fifty-five percent of the boys (16 out of 29 cases) and 36 percent of the girls (14 out of 39 cases) have clinical evidence of neurological impairment at five years of age (5). The other comprised 52 children with mildly retarded intellectual levels but without gross evidence of motor dysfunction or body stigmata (6). The first group has been followed from birth, the second from age 5-11 years, with similar protocols for data collection and analysis of behavioral characteristics as in the NYLS.

A special population of 243 children with congenital rubella resulting from the rubella epidemic of 1964 has also been evaluated behaviorally with similar methods (7). This group was studied cross-sectionally when they were two to four years of age, and during a follow-up done four years later. This group has been of special interest because of the large numbers with physical, neurological and intellectual handicaps, including many with multiple handicaps.

The previous chapter indicated the rationale of our data collection methods. The parents were utilized as the primary source of information on the child's behavior in infancy. As the child grew older, behavioral data were obtained through teacher interviews in nursery and elementary school, direct observations in the school setting and during psychometric testing at ages three, six, and nine, and direct interview with each youngster and parent separately at age 16-17 years. Academic achievement scores were gathered from school records. Whenever anyone in contact with the child suspected that there was behavioral disturbance, a complete clinical evaluation was made. Special tests such as perceptual evaluations were carried out as indicated.

Originally we explored the possibility of obtaining data from the neonatal period onward. A pilot study, confirmed by a search of the literature, showed that the newborn infant's behavior varied significantly from day to day, even from hour to hour, and that data collection and analysis would be an exceedingly demanding and complex process. Further exploration indicated that in general the infant's behavioral characteristics usually began to show definiteness and consistency of patterning between the fourth and eighth weeks of life. Therefore, the initial interview with the parents was scheduled when the child was two to three months of age. Initially, some children were accepted into the study at a slightly older age to accelerate the development of the project.

All data, whether obtained from parent or teacher or by direct observation of the child, were described in factual, descriptive terms with a concern not only for what the child did but how he did it. Statements about the presumed meaning of the child's behavior were considered unsatisfactory for primary data, though they often provided useful insights into special attitudes or judgments of the teacher of parent. When such interpretative statements were made, the interviewer always asked for a description of the actual behavior. Special emphasis was placed on the child's first response to a new stimulus (e.g., first bath) and his subsequent reactions to the same stimulus until a consistent long-term response was established. The sequence of responses to new stimuli, situations, and demands, whether simple or complex, provided especially rich information on a child's individual temperamental pattern .

In order to avoid bias of the data by "halo effects," different staff members were used for different phases of the data collection for any individual child. Interview protocol forms were revised as necessary to make them appropriate for succeeding age periods. Each revised protocol was pretested on samples of children not included in the longitudinal study.

DATA ANALYSIS

Nine categories of temperament were established by an inductive content analysis of the parent interview protocols for the infancy periods in the first 22 children studied. Item scoring was used, a three-point scale was established for each category, and the item scores transformed into a weighted score for each category on each record. To avoid contamination by "halo effects," no successive interviews of a given child were scored contiguously. High intra- and interscorer reliability, at the 90 percent level of agreement, was achieved.

The nine categories of temperament and their definitions are:

1) *Activity Level:* the motor component present in a given child's functioning and the diurnal proportion of active and inactive periods. Protocol data on motility during bathing, eating, playing, dressing and handling, as well as information concerning the sleep-wake cycle, reaching, crawling and walking, are used in scoring this category.

2) *Rhythmicity (Regularity):* the predictability and/or unpredictability in time of any function. It can be analyzed in relation to the sleep-wake cycle, hunger, feeding pattern and elimination schedule.

3) *Approach or Withdrawal:* the nature of the initial response to a new stimulus, be it a new food, new toy or new person. Approach responses are positive, whether displayed by mood expression (smiling, verbalizations, etc.) or motor activity (swallowing a new food, reaching for a new toy, active play, etc.). Withdrawal reactions are negative, whether displayed by mood expression (crying, fussing, grimacing, verbalizations, etc.) or motor activity (moving away, spitting new food out, pushing new toy away, etc.).

4) *Adaptability:* responses to new or altered situations. One is not concerned with the nature of the initial responses, but with the ease with which they are modified in desired directions.

5) *Threshold of Responsiveness:* the intensity level of stimulation that is necessary to evoke a discernible response, irrespective of the specific form that the response may take, or the sensory modality affected. The behaviors utilized are those concerning reactions to sensory stimuli, environmental objects, and social contacts.

6) *Intensity of Reaction:* the energy level of response, irrespective of its quality or direction.

7) *Quality of Mood:* the amount of pleasant, joyful and friendly behavior, as contrasted with unpleasant, crying and unfriendly behavior.

8) *Distractibility:* the effectiveness of extraneous environmental stimuli in interfering with or in altering the direction of the ongoing behavior.

9) *Attention Span and Persistence:* two categories which are related. Attention span concerns the length of time a particular activity is pursued by the child. Persistence refers to the continuation of an activity in the face of obstacles to the maintenance of the activity direction.

Each category is scored on a three-point scale, as follows:

1) Activity Level—High, Medium, Low

2) Rhythmicity—Regular, Variable, Irregular

3) Approach-Withdrawal—Approach, Variable, Withdrawal

4) Adaptability—Adaptive, Variable, Non-adaptive

5) Threshold of Responsiveness—High, Medium, Low

6) Intensity of Reaction—Positive, Variable, Negative

7) Quality of Mood—Positive, Variable, Negative

8) Distractibility—Yes (Distractible), Variable, No (Non-distractible)

9) Attention Span and Persistence—Yes (Persistent), Variable, No (Non-persistent)

Three temperamental constellations of functional significance have been defined by qualitative analysis of the data and factor analysis. The first group is characterized by regularity, positive approach responses to new stimuli, high adaptability to change and mild or moderately intense mood which is preponderantly positive. These children quickly develop regular sleep and feeding schedules, take to most new foods easily, smile at strangers, adapt easily to a new school, accept most frustration with little fuss, and accept the rules of new games with no trouble. Such a youngster is aptly called the Easy Child, and is usually a joy to his parents, pediatricians, and teachers. This group comprises about 40 percent of our NYLS sample.

At the opposite end of the temperamental spectrum is the group with irregularity in biological functions, negative withdrawal responses to new stimuli, non-adaptability or slow adaptability to change, and intense mood expressions which are frequently negative. These children show irregular sleep and feeding schedules, slow acceptance of new foods, prolonged adjustment periods to new routines, people, or situations, and relatively frequent and loud periods of crying. Laughter, also, is characteristically loud. Frustration typically produces a violent tantrum. This is the Difficult Child, and mothers and pediatricians find such youngsters difficult indeed. This group comprises about 10 percent of our NYLS sample.

The third noteworthy temperamental constellation is marked by a combination of negative responses of mild intensity to new stimuli with slow adaptability after repeated contact. In contrast to the difficult children, these youngsters are characterized by mild intensity of reactions, whether positive or negative, and by less tendency to show irregularity of biological functions. The negative mild responses to new stimuli can be seen in the first encounter with the bath, a new food, a stranger, a new place or a new school situation. If given the opportunity to re-experience such new situations over time and without pressure, such a child gradually comes to show quiet and positive interest and involvement. A youngster with this characteristic sequence of response is referred to as the Slow-To-Warm-Up Child, an apt if inelegant designation. About 15 percent of our NYLS sample falls into this category.

As can be seen from the above percentages, not all children fit into one of these three temperamental groups. This results from the varying and different combinations of temperamental traits which are manifested by individual children. Also, among those children who do fit one of these three patterns, there is a wide range in degree of manifestation. Some are extremely easy children in practically all situations; others are relatively easy and not always so. A few children are extremely difficult with all new situations and demands;

others show only some of these characteristics and relatively mildly. For some children it is highly predictable that they will warm up slowly in any new situation; others warm up slowly with certain types of new stimuli or demands, but warm up quickly in others.

It should be emphasized that the various temperamental constellations all represent variations within normal limits. Any child may be easy, difficult or slow to warm up temperamentally, have a high or low activity level, distractibility and low persistence or the opposite, or any other relatively extreme rating score in a sample of children for a specific temperamental attribute. However, such an amodal rating is not a criterion of psychopathology, but rather an indication of the wide range of behavioral styles exhibited by normal children.

The body of the NYLS quantitative scores of the nine temperamental categories for each of the first five years of life was subject to factor analyses to determine whether meaningful groupings of the categories could be derived statistically. The Varimax solutions proved to be most useful and three factors were developed. One of these, Factor A, met the criterion of relative consistency over the five-year period. This factor included approach/withdrawal, adaptability, mood and intensity. The scores for Factor A were normally distributed for each of the five years.

It is significant that the cluster of characteristics comprising Factor A corresponds closely to the cluster developed by qualitative analysis which identifies the Easy Child and the Difficult Child. In this qualitative categorization, which was completed *before* the factor analysis was done, the Easy Child corresponds to high Factor A plus regularity, and the Difficult Child to low Factor A plus irregularity.

It has been possible to identify each of the nine categories of temperament in each child at different age-periods in the preschool and early school years in all of the study populations enumerated above: The New York Longitudinal Study, the Puerto Rican working-class children, the mentally retarded group, the premature sample with high incidence of neurological damage, the children with congenital rubella, and the Israeli kibbutz group. In addition, these temperamental characteristics have been identified in a number of populations studied by investigators at other centers in this country and abroad (these other studies are reported in subsequent chapters). It is clear, therefore, that these behavioral traits occur ubiquitously in children and can be categorized systematically.

Detailed scorable behavioral data have been collected on infant, preschool and early school-age children, and a few aged 10-11 years in the mentally retarded study. Data on older children, adolescents and adults have been collected and analyzed clinically and less systematically. This does not reflect any judgment that temperament is less significant in the organism-environment interactional process at these older age-periods. Quite the contrary, we have been impressed in individual cases we have studied by the important roles that temperament continues to play at later stages of development. Methodologically, however, systematic data collection and analysis for temperament become more complex and time-consuming as the individual develops from childhood through adolescence into adult life. Limitations of research resources have therefore dictated a concentration on the early years of life. The special issues involved in the delineation of temperament at older age-periods and the directions taken thus far to explore these questions are discussed in later chapters.

Having identified specific temperamental traits and constellations, and outlined methods for scoring temperament from behavioral data, we will now discuss the functional significance of temperament for psychological development. This issue will be considered in subsequent chapters.

REFERENCES

1. A. Thomas, S. Chess, H. G. Birch, M. E. Hertzig and S. Korn, *Behavioral Individuality in Early Childhood* (New York: New York University Press, 1963).
2. A. Thomas, S. Chess and H. G. Birch, *Temperament and Behavior Disorders in Children* (New York: New York University Press, 1968).
3. M. E. Hertzig, H. G. Birch, A. Thomas, and O. A. Mendez, "Class and Ethnic Differences in the Responsiveness of Preschool Children to Cognitive Demands," *Monographs of the Society for Research in Child Development*, 33:1-69 (1968).
4. J. Marcus, A. Thomas and S. Chess, "Behavioral Individuality in Kibbutz Children," *The Israel Annals of Psychiatry and Related Disciplines*, 7:1:43-54 (1969).

5. **M.** E. Hertzig, "Neurologic Findings in Prematurely Born Children at School Age," *Life History Research in Psychopathology, Vol. III,* eds., D. Ricks, A. Thomas and M. Roff (Minneapolis: University of Minnesota Press, 1974), pp. 42-52.
6. **S.** Chess and M. Hassibi, "Behavior Deviations in Mentally Retarded Children," *J. Am. Acad. Child Psychiatr.,* 9:282-297 (1970).
7. **S.** Chess, S. Korn and P. Fernandez, *Psychiatric Disorders of Children with Congenital Rubella* (New York: Brunner/Mazel, 1971).

4

Temperament and

behavior disorder

All students of psychological development are interested in the phenomenon of individuality in the growing child. Any one investigator may concentrate on a specific aspect of individual differences —biochemical, neurophysiological, psychophysiological, behavioral, cognitive or psychodynamic. Such studies may be of theoretical interest and many shed light on the nature of specific organismic functions and characteristics. But there is one clear imperative for all such investigators: What is the relevance of a phenomenon of individuality to the developmental process and what are the dynamic mechanisms whereby such pertinence is implemented? It is not sufficient to assume that the characteristic under study is relevant to the course of psychological development because it fits into some *a priori* theoretical scheme. Such an assumption may be valid or invalid; it must be buttressed by objective evidence.

These considerations have at all times shaped the framework of the methodology and goals of our studies. Our research plans and protocols have been designed to collect and analyze data on temperamental individuality at sequential age levels in infancy and childhood. At the same time data have been gathered on functionally significant phenomena: parental attitudes and practices, special environmental stresses and demands, peer relationships, coping mechanisms, school functioning, academic achievement, behavioral deviations, psychiatric disorders. With these data, it has been possible to study the correlations between temperament and functionally significant aspects of psychological functioning, the dynamic interplay between them, and the mechanisms whereby temperament and personality structure exert an influence on each other.

In this and succeeding chapters we will present summaries of the data gathered by both ourselves and other investigators on the functional significance of temperament for psychological development. The kind of data, whether statistical or clinical, will be identified for each study which is cited. Results of our longitudinal studies which do not bear directly on temperament will not be reported here.

A comment is also in order at this point on the issue of consistency of a specific temperamental characteristic over time. Originally, as we began to take notice of individual differences in temperament, we were struck by the many instances in which a child expressed the same temperamental pattern at different ages, at each succeeding stage of development, in qualitatively different situations and experiences. It was indeed remarkable to see the same trait manifested in feeding behavior at three months, the initial adaptation to nursery school at four years, the play behavior with a peer group at six years, or the approach to a new school and new academic subjects at 12 years of age. Our own initial theoretical formulations of the significance of temperament tended, as a result, to emphasize the importance of consistency of temperament over time for the dynamics of psychological development. Further experience and the findings in our longitudinal studies, however, have made it evident that the issue of consistency or inconsistency of temperament over time is a complex one, both methodologically and conceptually. This issue is discussed at length in Chapter 12. For the purposes of this chapter we will simply emphasize that the functional significance of temperamental traits is not determined by whether they are consistent over time or not. One temperamental characteristic may be enormously influential in the child-environment interactional process at one age period and in certain life situations but not particularly important at a later period. A temperamental trait may assume an importance at the older age-period which it did not have earlier. Or the same characteristic may play an important role in development at sequential age-stages. The issue for the parent or child-care professional is the child's individual pattern at a specific age and the degree to which environmental demands are consonant or dissonant with that temperament in fostering optimum development at that particular time.

TEMPERAMENT AND BEHAVIOR DISORDER

From the beginning, our research design has emphasized the identification of cases of behavior disorders in our study populations and the analysis of the relationship of these disturbances in development to temperamental characteristics. This decision was motivated by several considerations. We were impressed over and over again in our clinical case material by the inadequacy of the dominant concepts of the etiology of behavior disorders, which focused almost exclusively on the role of environmental determinants. We speculated that temperament was a significant variable and that healthy development depended to a major degree on a "goodness of fit" between temperament and environment. If this were the case, then the identification of temperament and its influence on the course of psychological development could extend our ability to advise parents in child management more effectively—in other words, add a new dimension to prevention in the mental health field. Furthermore, this concern with the etiology and dynamics of deviant development was in line with a long tradition in medicine. Repeatedly, knowledge of the nature and importance of many factors for the normal physiological functioning of the body—hormones, vitamins, etc.—began largely with the study of pathological deviations. Finally, the presence or absence of behavior disorder in a child at one age-period or another provided an objective, functionally significant variable which could be correlated quantitatively and qualitatively with temperamental individuality at preceding and concurrent age-periods.

Therefore, all our research staff interviewers and observers were trained to identify any reports or manifestations of behavior which could indicate the presence of a behavior disorder in the child. The parents were also encouraged to contact the staff interviewer at any time between regularly scheduled interviews if the child's behavior became a source of concern. As soon as the first evidence of any deviant behavior came to attention in this way, the research staff member reported it in detail to one of us (S. C.), who then decided whether it warranted an immediate clinical evaluation or only required advice or reassurance to the parent. The clinical evaluation technique, criteria for diagnostic judgment, and follow-up procedure with the parents are described in a previous volume, together with the symptoms, age of onset and diagnoses of the NYLS children with behavior disorders (1). Our judgment that these cases of behavior disorder represented a vital source of data for our studies impelled us to pay special attention at all times to their systematic evaluation and long-term follow-up. Our earlier report also describes methods of quantitative and qualitative analyses, and the findings resulting from these analyses. The findings are summarized below.

QUANTITATIVE ANALYSIS

In the quantitative analyses, 108 children were included, because the other 22 children were either under five years of age at the time the analyses were done in June 1966, or had gaps in the temperamental data at one age-period or another. Of these, 42 clinical cases (39 percent of the total sample of 136) were identified; this figure approximates the rate found in other prevalence studies (2, 3). This number is cumulative; the actual prevalence of behavior problems at any one time in our study sample was lower than this total figure. Nine additional clinical cases have been identified since June 1966, but they are not included in this analysis.

The clinical cases were divided into those with "active" versus "passive" symptoms. The passive children were largely nonparticipators. Typically, they stood on the sidelines of a group, taking no part in the group's ongoing activity. If this nonparticipation included overt evidences of anxiety or defenses of anxiety, or was accompanied by active tension symptoms such as crying, nausea, stomachache, dizziness or active complaints that nobody liked him, the child was included in the group with the active rather than the passive symptoms. The active symptoms included these or other overt expressions of anxiety: sleep problems, tantrums, aggressive behavior, stuttering, etc.

TABLE 1

Significant t Tests—Total Active (N = 34)
Versus Nonclinical (N = 66)

Activity	Year 4	t = 2.60	p < .01
Rhythmicity	Year 4	t = 2.09	p < .05
Adaptability	Year 4	t = 2.67	p < .01
	Year 5	t = 2.53	p < .05
Approach/withdrawal		None	
Threshold	Year 4	t = 3.19	p < .01
	Year 5	t = 2.26	p < .05
Intensity	Year 3	t = 2.08	p < .05
	Year 4	t = 3.82	p < .01
	Year 5	t = 3.72	p < .01
Mood		None	
Distractibility	Year 4	t = 3.02	p < .01
Persistence	Year 4	t = 3.08	p < .01

The 42 clinical cases were separated into three groups: 1) 14 children with active symptoms who were identified before five years of age; 2) 34 children comprising the entire group with active symptoms, regardless of the age at which they came to notice; and 3) eight children with passive symptoms. The control group of nonclinical cases comprised 66 children, all over five years of age. The three clinical groups were analyzed statistically either separately or in combination, in accordance with the specific question under consideration.

A number of quantitative analyses were done. The patterns of temperament for each of the nine categories for the first five years of life were compared for the total active symptom group, the passive symptom group, and the nonclinical group. The weighted scores for each of the temperamental characteristics for each year were used for these comparisons. The years at which differences in weighted scores between the active clinical and nonclinical groups were sufficiently large to reach acceptable levels of significance are summarized in Table 1.

When the cases with passive symptoms were similarly considered, they differed significantly in the magnitude of their weighted scores from the nonclinical group only in the fourth and fifth years of life. These findings are summarized in Table 2.

TABLE 2

Significant t Tests—Passive (N = 8)
Versus Nonclinical (N = 66)

Activity	Year 5	t = 1.97	p < .05
Rhythmicity		None	
Adaptability		None	
Approach/withdrawal	Year 5	t = 3.27	p < .01
Threshold		None	
Intensity		None	
Mood	Year 4	t = 2.55	p < .05
	Year 5	t = 2.12	p < .05
Distractibility		None	
Persistence	Year 5	t = 2.47	p < .05

TABLE 3

Summary of Analysis of Variance

Variable	Groups Main Effect 2/92 Degrees of Freedom Difference between Groups Across Years 1-5		Groups by Years Interaction 8/368 Degrees of Freedom Difference in Group Trends or Profiles Over Years 1-5	
	F	P	F	P
Activity	4.22	<.05	1.12	N.S.
Rhythmicity	<1.00	N.S.	1.01	N.S.
Adaptability	1.88	N.S.	1.69	N.S.
Approach/withdrawal	1.45	N.S.	1.60	N.S.
Threshold	1.04	N.S.	2.71	<.01
Intensity	5.50	<.01	2.24	<.01
Mood	3.10	<.05	1.01	N.S.
Distractibility	1.74	N.S.	1.05	N.S.
Persistence	3.26	<.05	1.52	N.S.

An analysis of variances was done on all the temperamental variables for the total active and passive clinical groups and the nonclinical group across the first five years of life. The findings are summarized in Table 3.

Parametric analyses of mean values for Factor A in the clinical groups with active and passive symptoms in the nonclinical group over the first five-year period were also compared, and the findings are tabulated in Table 4.

The subsample of children who developed active symptoms before the fifth year of life was also compared separately with the non-

TABLE 4

Significant t Tests—Factor A

a) Total active (N = 34) versus nonclinical (N = 66)

Year 3	t = 1.96	p < .05
Year 4	t = 3.10	p < .01
Year 5	t = 2.63	p < .01

b) Passive (N = 8) versus nonclinical (N = 66)

Year 4	t = 2.43	p < .05
Year 5	t = 2.62	p < .01

TABLE 5

Significant t Tests—Active Before
5 Years (N = 14) Versus Nonclinical (N = 66)

Activity		None	
Rhythmicity	Year 2	t = 3.35	p < .01
	Year 4	t = 2.52	p < .05
Adaptability	Year 3	t = 2.74	p < .01
	Year 4	t = 5.48	p < .01
	Year 5	t = 2.92	p < .01
Approach/withdrawal	Year 5	t = 2.18	p < .05
Threshold	Year 4	t = 2.05	p < .05
	Year 5	t = 2.23	p < .05
Intensity	Year 4	t = 3.42	p < .01
	Year 5	t = 5.03	p < .01
Mood		None	
Distractibility	Year 4	t = 3.08	p < .01
Persistence	Year 5	t = 2.84	p < .01
Factor A	Year 4	t = 3.56	p < .01
	Year 5	t = 3.54	p < .01

clinical group. This comparison was based on the reports in the literature which suggest that disorders of early onset are more clearly linked with organismic variables than are those which emerge at later age-periods (4, 5). For this reason it was anticipated that any relation of temperament to the development of behavior disturbance would be more dramatically evident in these children with early onset of behavior disorders. This analysis is tabulated in Table 5.

The results of these quantitative analyses can be summarized briefly. Both before and after the development of symptoms of behavior disorder, the total active clinical group differed from the nonclinical group in their temperamental characteristics. The former were characterized by an excessive frequency of high activity, irregularity, low threshold, nonadaptability, intensity, persistence, and distractibility. The clinical cases with passive symptoms differed significantly in their temperamental scores from the nonclinical group only in the fourth and fifth years of life. Mood was different in years four and five, and activity level, approach/withdrawal and persistence only in the fifth year. This small number of statistically significant differences may be due to the small size of the sample with passive symptoms. The small N made it possible for significant values to be achieved only with great differences in quantitative scores.

The comparison of Factor A values for the total clinical group with active symptoms and the nonclinical group showed significant differences at years three, four, and five. For the clinical group with passive symptoms and the nonclinical group the comparison showed differences at years four and five. In both clinical groups the differences were in the direction of the Difficult Child constellations and became larger as the children grew older.

The data for the children who developed active symptoms of disturbance before the fifth year of life did indeed show that their differences from the nonclinical group were magnified as compared with the total clinical sample. This was true for all nine categories except activity and mood, and also for Factor A. The findings in the early onset group closely resembled (though were not identical with) those found for the total group with active symptoms, but were expressed more sharply.

QUALITATIVE ANALYSIS

The above quantitative analyses indicate group trends which are sufficiently marked so that statistically significant findings can be identified, even with the relatively small size of the samples involved. It was clear, however, from a review of the longitudinal data, that in a number of the clinical cases specific characteristics or constellations appeared crucially influential in the onset and course of a behavior disorder, even though they did not correspond to those identified in the group quantitative analyses. On the other hand, many children had temperamental traits similar to those which characterized the clinical disturbance. These findings are not surprising in view of our basic view that neither temperament nor environment alone determines the course of psychological development. Both normal and pathological development is determined by the dynamic interaction between the child's individual temperament and the environmental experiences, expectations and demands which the child encounters.

In each clinical case this interactive process was studied by a qualitative analysis of the data. Following the clinical interview all the longitudinal records and other information were selectively culled in detail. The items selected for culling included the child's temperamental characteristics, symptoms, patterns of behavioral deviation, parental attitudes and functioning, and any special or unusual life experiences or trauma. The decision as to which temperamental and parental items should be culled was made by the senior research psychiatrist (S.C.) on the basis of her initial evaluation of the clinical findings. The actual culling was done by a research staff member who had no previous contact with the child or family and no knowledge of the psychiatrist's preliminary judgment of the case. Special psychometric, perceptual or neurological tests were carried out where indicated.

The psychiatrist (S.C.) then received the culled data, clinical findings, and other pertinent available information, such as I.Q. scores, medical history and physical findings. On the basis of this review, a dynamic formulation of the onset and course of the behavior disorder was made. Four examples with case summaries, the selective culling from the longitudinal records, and the dynamic formulations are provided in Appendix B of an earlier volume (6).

Recommendations were then made to the parents for alterations in their child-care attitudes and practices and/or for other specific environmental changes, such as school placement, which could ameliorate dissonances between environmental demands and the child's capacities or characteristics. Where indicated, direct treatment of the child or special remedial instruction was recommended. Systematic long-term follow-up of each clinical case was carried out, including repeat clinical evaluations of the child when judged advisable by the psychiatrist. In those cases where the child underwent direct treatment, reports were obtained from the therapists.

A similar, though less intense, qualitative analysis was carried out in the case of many children without behavior disorder, but with a developmental course which was of some special interest.

This technique involved methodological problems, such as judgmental bias, halo effects and difficulties in determining reliability levels that were absent or minimized in the quantitative scoring and analytic procedures. However, the qualitative analysis made possible the utilization of the richness and variety of the longitudinal data which the quantitative analysis alone did not permit. The complexities of factors influencing an individual child's developmental course, the subtleties of interaction among these factors, the identification of specific organismic or environmental features which appeared of special significance, could all be studied in depth through the qualitative approach to the longitudinal data.

Thus, for example, one child scored high on the temperamental trait of persistence. But the quantitative score alone did not identify the extraordinary level of this characteristic and its functional significance. The parental interviews, however, did dramatize this finding. When he was 18 months of age he spent hours each day practicing tying shoelaces until he finally mastered this activity. Further, when his mother forcibly interrupted this activity one evening, he responded with a prolonged tantrum. Other examples of this extreme persistence and frustration when interrupted were scattered through the parental reports. Problems developed in nursery and elementary school when ongoing activities in which he was absorbed were abruptly interrupted by his teachers and he again responded with explosive tantrums. In another case, a father's hypercritical and destructive attitude toward his son was expressed primarily in his intolerance of the boy's distractible, non-persistent traits. No routine interview or questionnaire scoring could have captured the extreme vehemence and rigidity with which the father, himself a hard-working and highly persistent professional, labeled his son as "weak-willed" and "without character." Or, as another illustration, a mother's difficulty in exercising firmness and consistency in her child-care practices might not have had important consequences except for her infant's bowel difficulties due to a tight anal sphincter. The mother's shifting approaches and inconsistency in following the pediatrician's advice intensified the symptoms, created a hostile mother-child interaction, and were the beginning of a number of psychological problems for the youngster. Here, any scoring of the mother's functioning required a simultaneous consideration of the child's very special physiological problem.

The dynamic formulations made in each clinical case were not restricted solely to an explication of the ontogenesis and evolution of behavior disorder, despite the importance of these issues. The wide range of information available on each child, both longitudinally and cross-sectionally, also made it possible to study a number of phenomena and concepts pertinent to the process of psychological development in general. The anterospective data on behavioral functioning from infancy on included cognitive characteristics, school functioning and academic achievement, parental practices and attitudes, other significant events and experiences, the findings of clinical psychiatric examination, and special physical deviations or medical problems. These records provided a veritable mine of factual information with which to test existing theories of the developmental process and to formulate alternative concepts. In this regard, the study of the development of the children without behavior disorders served to deepen and expand the insights developed in the analysis of the clinical cases. These theoretical issues will be considered briefly in a later chapter. However, a fuller consideration of the general concepts of development generated by our longitudinal studies will have to be taken up in a subsequent volume.

The results of both qualitative and quantitative analyses confirmed the finding that features of temperament played significant roles in development of childhood behavior disorders. The hypothesis that children with certain temperamental attributes and constellations were more at risk for behavioral disturbances was confirmed. Beyond this, it became clear that any temperamental trait or pattern in any individual child could significantly enter into the development of a behavior disorder, if the environmental demands and expectations were sufficiently dissonant with the child's behavioral style. Thus, for example, children with the Difficult Child temperamental constellation were especially prone to symptom development if their parents were inconsistent, impatient or pressuring in their approach. At the same time, those at the other end of the temperamental spectrum, the Easy Children, while able to adapt much more easily to a wide range of parental practices and attitudes, could also at times experience excessively stressful temperament-environment interactions and develop behavior disorders.

In no case did a given pattern of temperament, as such, result in behavioral disturbance. Deviant development was always the result of the *interaction* between a child's individual makeup and significant features of the environment. Temperament, representing one aspect of a child's characteristics, also reacted with abilities and motives, the other two facets of individuality, in determining the specific behavior patterns that evolved in the course of development.

Broad generalizations can be made as to the possible impact of a certain temperamental attribute, I.Q. level, goal-orientation or family or social environment. However, it must be emphasized that the permutations and combinations of the interactional process among these and other variables are so numerous as to defy any precise *a priori* assumptions about an individual child. Temperament, for example, may or may not be a consistent variable over time, as we shall discuss in a later chapter.

Systematic analysis of the role of specific temperamental traits in the ontogenesis and evolution of behavior disorders requires that these attributes be dissected and isolated from other characteristics of the child and his environment, including other aspects of his temperament. Thus, we speak of a "low activity child," a "persistent child," a "highly intense child," and so on, when the particular trait is prominent in the child's behavioral style and exerts a significant effect on his developmental course. In reality, of course, no individual characteristic exists or manifests itself in isolation from other attributes. Also, any one specific temperamental trait may occur in many different combinations with other characteristics. A distractible child may have high or low activity level, be quickly or slowly adaptive, intense or mild in mood expression, of superior or dull normal I.Q. level, highly dextrous or clumsy in fine motor movements, and so on. Furthermore, a temperamental trait (or other attribute of child or parent, for that matter) is rarely, if ever, global in its manifestations. To call a child persistent indicates that his responses are *predominantly* but not *universally* of this type. Different children with the same temperamental pattern may show different admixtures both of degree and kind in the behavioral manifestations of the trait.

Our previous volume details a number of specific types of temperament-environment interaction for different temperamental traits and constellations, and the issues involved in determining the kinds and degrees of consonance or dissonance between the child's behavioral style and environmental demands and expectations. Since publication of this volume, our subsequent data from the NYLS and our other long-term studies have confirmed and extended these formulations.

Some generalizations can be made as to the situations and demands which are more likely to create excessive stress for a child with a specific temperamental pattern. For the Difficult Children the stressful demands were typically those of socialization, namely, the demands for alteration of spontaneous responses and patterns to conform to the rules of living of the family, the school, the peer group, etc. It is also characteristic of these children that once they did learn the rules they functioned easily, consistently and energetically.

The Easy Children, by contrast, usually adapted to the demands for socialization with little or no stress and confronted their parents with few, if any, problems in routine handling. As might be expected, these children, as a group, developed fewer behavior problems in proportion to their representation in the total study sample. However, under certain circumstances, their easy adaptability to parental standards and expectations at home led to the development of a behavior disorder. This occurred when the demands of the extrafamilial environment, such as in a peer group or school, conflicted sharply with the behavior patterns learned at home. In some cases, when such conflict was especially severe, the child was unable to make an adaptation which reconciled this double standard. Thus, Hal, one of the markedly Easy Children in the NYLS, came to clinical attention at age four years because he had become the scapegoat and butt of jokes of his peer groups. When other children took his toys, he did not defend himself and came home crying. Hal had been brought up by parents who set great store by formalistic manners and stereotyped rituals of politeness. The boy, with his easy adaptability, quickly imitated and learned this behavior pattern, which set him apart from other middle-class suburban children. These other children saw Hal as a strange creature because of his formal manners and his habit of asking with meticulous politeness to share their toys. Hal quickly became the target of ridicule and harassment against which he could not defend himself.

For the Slow-To-Warm-Up Child, the excessively stressful situation was typically one in which rigid demands were made for quickness of adaptation to a new situation. For the high activity child difficulties occurred when there was insufficient space or flexibility of schedules and rules in home or school to allow him sufficient constructive motor activity. The persistent child had no special difficulty with new situations but developed frustration responses if his involvement in an ongoing activity was prematurely and abruptly interrupted. The distractible and non-persistent child was put under excessive stress if expected to concentrate and work without interruption for periods of time beyond his capacities.

Any of the other temperamental characteristics or special constellations can also, in individual children, enter as a significant variation in the genesis of a behavior disorder. William Carey's studies, for example, point out the relationship of low sensory threshold to night awakening in infants (7). It can be expected that as studies on temperament continue to develop at various centers, additional significant correlations with specific types of behavioral deviations will be identified.

It should be emphasized that the generalizations as to the kind of environmental situation and demand which can be typically dissonant with specific temperamental patterns have many exceptions. The generalizations have heuristic value in planning research strategies and are useful clinically as leads to the analysis of a behavior problem case. However, all kinds of permutations and combinations occur in real life and the research worker, parent, teacher or clinician must expect that in any individual child the dynamics of the child-environmental interactional process may or may not conform to broad generalizations and group trends.

Finally, our findings and those of others on the importance of temperament in the developmental process do not imply that temperament is *always* a significant variable in the ontogenesis and course of *every* behavior disorder. In some instances, temperament may play a crucial role, in other cases it may be somewhat influential, and in still other instances it may play a minor or even insignificant role. In this regard temperament is no different from any other single organismic or environmental factor. Whether it be the level or style of cognitive functioning, the goals and aims of the child, the characteristics of the mother, the nature of the school situation, the significance of these factors for the developmental process in any individual child cannot be decided *a priori*, but must be determined on the basis of all the concrete information available in the specific case.

SYMPTOM FORMATION

Tabulation of the symptoms in the clinical sample suggested that relative frequency in different functional areas was, in the main, the result of environmental influences. The standards and expectations of parents, peer group or teachers determined the areas in which persistent and insistent demands were most likely to be made on the child. Where such demands were excessive for an individual child the resulting behavioral disturbance usually was expressed in that general functional area. Thus, symptoms in the NYLS sample occurred more frequently in sleep, discipline, mood disturbance, speech, peer relationships and learning—all areas of parental concern and demand. Complaints of problems with feeding, elimination and masturbation, by contrast, were much less frequent, and corresponded to the current value judgments of this middle-class group to tolerate even substantial individual differences in these areas.

Comparisons of the NYLS sample with our Puerto Rican working-class sample affirmed the importance of environmental influences in determining not only the areas in which symptoms were most frequent, but also the age-periods at which they were most likely to occur (8). Thus, 31 percent of the middle-class NYLS sample were diagnosed as having behavior problems by the age of nine years, as compared to 10 percent of the Puerto Rican children. The middle-class parents were child-problem oriented, and even slight behavioral disturbances in their children were reported promptly to the interviewers for review by the staff psychiatrists. As a group, these parents were well aware of currently influential theories of child psychiatry and psychology, which place great stress on the child's development in the first five years of life as being crucial to later psychological functioning. Therefore, these parents were especially worried if evidence of a behavior problem appeared in their children at an early age.

The Puerto Rican working-class parents (PRWC) were also concerned about the well-being of their offspring, but they were not preoccupied with the psychological significance of a behavioral deviation in their young children unless it was severe. Rather than viewing mild disturbances with alarm as a portent of future difficulties, as did the middle-class parents, these parents expressed their attitude typically by the remark, "He's a baby—he'll outgrow it."

The earlier development of symptoms in the middle-class group also may have stemmed from the greater demands for task performance made upon them at home. Their parents emphasized the early accomplishment of self-care activities, particularly feeding and dressing. They also encouraged and even pressured their children to master the use of toys and stressed the educational value of play. In contrast, the demands on the PRWC children in the first five years of life and their extrafamilial experiences with new people and new situations were much more limited. They were not expected to feed or dress themselves early ("If I do it for him I get done faster") and there was little insistence that the children follow through on verbal task instructions. Most of the PRWC parents regarded toys as amusements; educational toys were not purchased, and the children usually amused themselves with household objects in a self-determined manner.

After the age of nine years, the incidence of new behavior problems in the NYLS dropped sharply. We do not have comparable detailed data on the PRWC group because of incomplete follow-up. Our strong impression, however, is that the incidence of behavior problems increased as the children were more and more confronted by demands for task performance both at home and in school.

In comparing the type of symptomatology presented by the two groups of children before the age of nine years, striking differences were also evident. Thus, complaints about sleep problems in the NYLS sample were most numerous in the preschool years. As a group, these parents were not tolerant of deviant behavior in this area and demanded that their children establish regular sleeping habits early. By contrast, the PRWC parents tolerated late bedtimes and night awakening in their preschool children and few sleep problems developed. When these children approached school age, however, the situation changed dramatically. As they began school at age six years, they had to go to sleep and get up promptly at regular hours, eat without dawdling, dress quickly, and arrive at school on time—all functions they had not previously been required to perform. This sequence correlated with the finding that almost half of the PRWC sample that came to notice between the ages of five and nine presented sleep problems, whereas only one child under five had a sleep difficulty. These problems included temper tantrums at bedtime, nightmares, frightening dreams, sleepwalking and inability to sleep without a light.

The development of sleep problems at the time of school entry may also be related to the new stresses and demands posed by the school situation. For the NYLS children, school entry typically occurred at ages three to four with nursery school; for the PRWC children it occurred most frequently at age six years.

Marked differences between the two groups also occurred in the incidence of certain other symptoms. Only one middle-class child out of 42 presented excessive and uncontrollable motor activity, whereas eight of the 15 PRWC children did. Our judgment is that some, if not most, of the "hyperactivity" displayed by the latter group was due to the circumstances of their environment. The families lived in small apartments and the children were likely to be cooped up at home for realistic fear of accidents in the street. For the temperamentally high activity children this represented severely excessive stress. The children in the NYLS with similar temperament, by contrast, usually lived in spacious apartments or suburban homes, with adequate safe play space at home and in the neighborhood.

Discipline problems were significantly more frequent in the PRWC children, whose parents were concerned about the risk of delinquency in the East Harlem community. Learning problems, on the other hand, were more common in the middle-class parents, who frequently had overriding concern with scholastic success and exerted considerable pressure on their children for superior cognitive performance.

These findings emphasize the need for understanding the social and cultural background if one is to evaluate what constitutes excessive stress for any individual child. The incidence at any age-period and the types of presenting symptoms may reflect parental expectations as much as they do problems of functioning intrinsic to the child.

By contrast, the behavioral form taken by a symptom, irrespective of its functional area, appeared to be significantly related to the child's temperamental characteristics. This relationship was evident in the analysis of the individual clinical cases. Excessive pressure on the Slow-To-Warm-Up Child for immediate involvement with a new situation typically resulted in withdrawal behavior of mild intensity such as clinging to parent, quietly refusing to move, or retreat to a corner of the room. The Difficult Child protested loudly and sometimes became oppositional and actively negativistic. The Easy Child did not usually exhibit withdrawal or tantrums in his deviant behavior, but rather continued to exhibit the behavior he had learned in one situation even when inappropriate in another. The active child responded to pressure by increased nonproductive motor activity. The low intensity child whined and fussed.

Once symptoms developed, their future course was, of course, influenced by additional factors, such as psychodynamic defenses, the reaction of others to the symptom, secondary gain phenomena, deficient self-image development, etc.

OTHER STUDIES

Reports from other workers have extended our own findings on the relationship of temperament to behavior disorder. Ross has identified a syndrome of behavioral disturbance which he designates "the unorganized child" (9). According to Ross, this syndrome results from a combination of high distractibility, short attention span and low persistence in the child in interaction with disorganized functioning or overpermissiveness in the parent. If the unorganized child also has high activity level, Ross suggests that he may show restlessness and a tendency to chatter disruptively. If he is less active he may daydream, and if he is intense in his reaction he is likely to show tantrum behavior.

Graham, Rutter and George, three British investigators, studied 60 children, three to seven years old, each of whom had at least one mentally ill parent. The researchers did a quantitative assessment of both temperamental differences and behavior disorder (10). Certain temperamental characteristics, especially low regularity and low fastidiousness (an additional temperamental trait identified by these workers), and to a lesser degree, negative mood, low adaptability and high intensity, were predictive of the development of later psychiatric disorder. The authors conclude that their study "does support the validity of the theoretical framework provided by the New York workers. It has been possible to replicate the earlier findings that certain so-called temperamental characteristics can be reliably identified and that some of these are predictive of the later development of psychiatric disorder." These authors emphasize (as we would also) that the results of their study "suggest that there is a link between adverse temperament and adverse family attitudes and, possibly, relationships. . . . The clinician should now be aware that a growing body of evidence supports the notion that a child, by virtue of his personality structure, requires handling geared to his individuality if he is to stand the best chance of avoiding the development of psychiatric disorder."

Carey has developed a short parent questionnaire form for the infancy period and utilized it to study the relationship of temperament to certain behavioral symptoms in infancy. In an unselected sample of 60 infants six months of age, he found a significant correlation ($p < 0.02$) between night waking and low sensory threshold (11). He suggests two possibilities to explain this correlation: "1) that greater responses to stimuli in the day make the infant continue to be more arousable at night and 2) that the infant is more responsive to internal and external stimuli at night as well." Carey suggests approaches to the management of this problem based on these possible causes and cautions that "maternal anxiety, anger, or feelings of helplessness" may be the result rather than the cause of the baby's waking.

In another study of 13 babies with colic (12), Carey reports a similar correlation between this syndrome and low sensory threshold ($p < 0.02$). A significantly higher incidence of colic was also found in the infants with difficult temperament than in the Easy Child group ($p < 0.05$).

The findings of our longitudinal studies and the reports of other workers, summarized in this chapter, indicate that temperamental characteristics play significant roles in the genesis and evolution of behavior disorders in children. It is clearly necessary for the clinician to give as much attention to temperamental factors as to environmental and psychodynamic influences in diagnosis and treatment. The implications for programs and prevention are also evident. If goodness of fit and consonance between the child's individual characteristics and environmental demands and expectations are decisive for healthy psychological development, then counseling and guidance for parents and other child caretakers must reflect appropriate judgments for the achievement of this goodness of fit.

REFERENCES

1. A. Thomas, S. Chess and H. G. Birch, *Temperament and Behavior Disorders in Children* (New York: New York University Press, 1968).
2. R. Lapouse and M. A. Monk, "An Epidemiologic Study of Behavior Characteristics in Children," *Amer. J. Public Health*, 48:1134 (1958).
3. J. C. Glidewell, H. R. Domke and M. B. Kantor, "Screening in Schools for Behavior Disorders: Use of Mother's Report of Symptoms," *J. Educ. Research*, LVI (1963).
4. I. Belmont, D. F. Klein and M. Pollack, "Perceptual Evidence of Central Nervous System Dysfunction in Schizophrenia," *Archives of Gen. Psychiatr.*, 10:395 (1964).
5. H. G. Birch, ed., *Brain Damage in Children: Biological and Social Aspects* (Baltimore: Williams and Wilkins Co., 1964).
6. A. Thomas *et al.*, *op. cit.*, pp. 207-299.
7. Wm. B. Carey, "Night Waking and Temperament in Infancy," *J. Pediatrics*, 84:756-758 (1974).
8. A. Thomas, S. Chess, J. Sillen and O. Mendez, "Cross-cultural Study of Behavior in Children with Special Vulnerabilities to Stress," *Life History Research in Psychopathology, Volume III*, eds., D. F. Ricks, A. Thomas and M. Roff (Minneapolis: University of Minnesota Press, 1974), pp. 53-67.

9. D. C. Ross, "Poor School Adjustment: A Psychiatric Study and Classification," *Clinical Pediatrics*, 5:109 (1966).
10. P. Graham, M. Rutter and S. George, "Temperamental Characteristics as Predictors of Behavior Disorders in Children," *Am. J. Orthopsychiatr.*, 43:3:328-339 (1973).
11. Wm. B. Carey, *op. cit.*
12. Wm. B. Carey, "Clinical Applications of Infant Temperament Measurements," *J. Pediatrics*, 81:823-828 (1972).

5

Temperament and developmental deviations

This chapter will review the findings from our own studies and those of other workers on the role of temperamental individuality in the functioning of children with various developmental deviations. The deviations considered include mental retardation, perinatal brain damage, and the multiple physical handicaps caused by congenital rubella.

MENTAL RETARDATION

Our own long-term study comprised 52 mildly retarded children from middle-class families (1). At the onset of the study they ranged from five to 11 years of age, had I.Q. scores between 50 and 75, and were all living at home. Cases with gross motor or sensory handicaps or very evident physical stigmata were ruled out. Data collection on each child included parent and teacher interviews, direct observations at home and in school, neurological examination, psychometric testing, and psychiatric examination. Thirty-one of the 52 children were evaluated as having a behavior disorder on the basis of the psychiatric examination and other data. Details on this group have been previously reported (2).

TABLE 1

Number of Signs of Difficult Child and Presence of Behavior Disorder (N = 52)

No. of Signs of Difficult Child	No. of Children Without Behavior Disorder (N = 21)	No. of Children With Behavior Disorder (N = 31)
5	0	5
4	2	8
3	1	6
0-2	18	12

Temperament scores were obtained by item scoring of the parent interview data as in the NYLS. The correlation between the temperamental constellation of the Difficult Child and the frequency of behavior disorders in these 52 retarded children was then calculated. For this comparison, each child was designated as having zero to five signs of the Difficult Child, depending on whether he was above or below the median of the group in the five temperamental categories of irregularity, slow adaptability, withdrawal reactions to new situations, high intensity and negative mood. This comparison is tabulated in Table 1.

As can be seen from Table 1, 31 of the 52 children were identified as having a behavior disorder of one or another diagnostic type. In this group of 31 cases, 19, or 61 percent, had three or more signs of the Difficult Child. Of the 21 children without behavior disorder, only three, or 14 percent, had these three or more signs. Furthermore all five of the children in the total sample of 52 who had all five signs of the Difficult Child had a behavior disorder, as did eight of the 10 with four signs, and six of the seven with three signs. By contrast, of the 30 children with few signs of the Difficult Child—two or less—only 12 had behavior disorders, while 18 did not.

These findings indicate that retarded children with even mild manifestations of the Difficult Child temperamental constellation are especially vulnerable to the development of a behavior disorder. The demands for socialization for the Difficult Child appeared to intensify the stresses to which the retarded child is especially subject in his interaction with the environment, thus multiplying the risk of behavior disorder development. But, as with the intellectually normal child, this risk did not constitute inevitability. It is true that all five retarded children at the polar extreme of the Difficult Child constellation developed behavioral disturbances, but several with three or four signs did not. On the other hand, five children with only one sign of the Difficult Child, i.e., those in the Easy Child category, did develop behavior problems.

Qualitative scrutiny of the individual records confirmed these quantitative findings of the significance of temperament for the psychological development of the retarded child. It also made clear, as with the NYLS sample, that the course of the child's psychological development was at all times the consequence of the *interaction* between the child with his individual attributes and parental management and other environmental influences.

At the six-year clinical follow-up of 44 of this mentally retarded sample, there was still a predictive aspect to features of temperamental individuality, as had been the case in the initial evaluation. At the follow-up, of the 12 children in whom four or five signs of the Difficult Child had been identified initially, eight (67 percent) presented behavior disorder. By contrast, of the 15 children with zero or one sign, only two (13 percent) showed behavioral disturbance at the time of the six-year follow-up. Of the 17 children with two or three signs, eight had a behavior disorder.

These correlations at the six-year follow-up, while significant, were not quite as marked as in the initial evaluation. It is probable that the contribution to behavior disorder of neurologic damage, and the cumulative effect of stressful intra- and extrafamilial relationships and activities became more influential in determining the developmental course of these retarded youngsters as the years went on.

A study of the temperamental characteristics of 18 infants with Down's Syndrome, ranging in age from six to 18 months (mean age 11.3 months) and all living at home, was done by Baron at the Developmental Clinic of the Department of Pediatrics of the University of Pittsburgh School of Medicine (3). The Carey parent questionnaire was used to assess temperament. The ratings obtained were compared with Carey's group of normal infants and the temperamental scores in the first year of the NYLS group. The author concludes that the comparisons show no significant difference between the infants with Down's Syndrome and the normal infants. "In early life a child with Down's Syndrome is not stereotyped in behavior as he is physically handicapped. . . . Some may be easy to raise and others may be difficult." Baron speculates on the reasons for the general impression that children with Down's Syndrome are especially easy to raise. He suggests two possibilities. Since the developmental deviation is usually recognized at an early age, there may then be lower parental expectations with fewer demands than would be placed on a normal child. Also, the typical hypotonia may make dressing, changing, and other infant child-care procedures easier. Baron's other suggestion is that because the child does not function at his chronological age level, it is possible that age-related problems do not occur when expected.

Gregg, the director of the same Developmental Clinic in Pittsburgh, in commenting on Baron's findings estimates that "From our clinical experience with many Down's Syndrome babies, we would speculate that this is a valid result rather than questionnaire insensitivity to subtle temperamental differences" (4).

PERINATAL BRAIN DAMAGE

Three children with perinatal brain damage in the NYLS have been identified.* This has provided the opportunity for at least a limited longitudinal study of the influences of the child's temperament and the characteristics of the environment as sources for individual differences in behavioral development and symptom formation exhibited by brain-damaged children. Our data do not permit us to consider the influence of physiological factors, namely the type, size, and locus of the brain lesion, the time of life at which the nervous system was damaged, and the character of the neuropathologic process.

The findings and conclusions in these three cases have been re-

---

* Portions of this section are reprinted from "A Longitudinal Study of Three Brain Damaged Children," A. Thomas and S. Chess, *Arch. Gen. Psychiatry*, 32:457-465 (1975). Copyright 1975, American Medical Association.

TABLE 2

Case	Early Medical History	Developmental Course	Early Neurological Findings	Later Medical-Neurological Findings	IQ	Temperament	Parental Handling	Behavior Disorder
1 Bert	Premature birth; severe respiratory neonatal distress	Sat without support at 11 mo; walked at 22 mo; marked delay in expressive speech	Grossly uncoordinated adaptive motor functioning; grossly awkward	Letter & number reversals; left-right confusion	112 at 6 yr.	Regular adaptive, positive responses to new situations; mild to moderate intensity; positive mood; persistent	Generally permissive; demands for high intellectual achievement with peremptory & insistent demands by father	Mild; avoidance of school work; social problems with peer group
2 Kevin	Mother had more than 10 yr. infertility & spontaneous abortions; neonatal gastroin-	Delay in motor & language development	Gait disturbance; very brisk tendon reflexes, unsustained bilateral clonus	Tendency to hyperactivity, distractibility, perseveration	72 at 5 yr.; 76 at 6 yr.; 59 at 14 yr.	Moderately active & irregular positive responses to new situations; moderately nonadap-	Patient & consistent; minimized extent of intellectual retardation	No significant behavior disorder; evidence of defensive reactions to new de-

3
Barbara

Essentially
negative

testinal
upsets,
excessive
sweating,
pylora-
spasm, &
repeated
respira-
tory infec-
tions in
early
infancy

Essentially
normal

Gross motor
incoordina-
tion;
tendency to
echolalia &
echopraxia

106 at
age
6 yr.

Alternat-
ing hyper-
phoria;
chorei-
form
move-
ments;
clumsy
gait; di-
minished
muscular
tone;
brisk
tendon
reflexes

Highly active;
irregular,
nonadaptive,
negative
reactions to
new situ-
ations; pre-
dominantly
negative
mood; intense
reactions,
low threshold

tive; positive
mood; low
intensity;
persistent

Permissive
at first,
then in-
consistent;
father
highly
punitive
at times

Very
severe;
hyper-
kinesis;
persev-
eration;
marked
distract-
ibility;
language
deviation;
ritualistic
behavior;
tantrums;
impulsive-
ness;
destruc-
tiveness

mands
& new
situations
& limited
peer rela-
tions; not
severe
enough for
diagnosis
of be-
havior
disorder

ported previously (5, 6). Table 2 summarizes the pertinent longitudinal data for each youngster.

The first youngster, Bert, with the Easy Child pattern of adaptability, positive approach response to most new situations, and predominantly mild to moderate positive mood, coped successfully with the demands of the preschool years, in spite of his lags in motor and speech development. In the school years, however, he was subject to stress in school because of his reading and arithmetic problems, increased difficulty in peer social relationships because of his speech deviations, and the strain of competing with his normal younger sister. Perhaps most important of all, his father became increasingly intolerant and impatient, as the boy could not meet the parent's standards for academic and social functioning. Even with these multiple and intense stresses and excessive demands on him, the neurotic defense mechanisms Bert developed were not extreme and he responded successfully and relatively quickly to psychotherapy.

At our last follow-up, Bert was doing adequate work in his junior year in a demanding private high school. He had learned to respond to his father's pressures by gestures of acquiescence. For example, his father is an expert sailor and Bert pretended to greater enthusiasm for sailing than he, in fact, had, explaining, "It makes him happy and I don't mind." He had two friends, but continued to have difficulty making casual social relationships. He single-mindedly concentrated on areas of his own interests and tended to be oblivious to the shifting relationships and attitudes of others. This reflected a not unusual difficulty of brain-damaged children in changing mental set quickly. Nonetheless, Bert is persistent and hardworking, and is a very friendly youngster in circumstances in which his role is well-defined and he has something to contribute. It is believed that Bert's future friendships will be based on mutual involvement in an engrossing occupation. As an adult, he will be likely to succeed when he can choose his area of functioning and apply his superior intellect and persistence effectively.

The second youngster, Kevin, was also not a difficult child to manage, despite his mildly subnormal intelligence, occasional hyperactivity, and prominent motor and speech disorder. Although he was moderately active and irregular as an infant, he tended to approach new situations and express a positive mood. His thresholds of arousal were fairly high and he was moderately nonadaptive. An early easy distractibility coupled with a high level of persistence in the first year was replaced after the second year by moderate distractibility but continued high level of persistence. Perhaps most importantly, from the early months of life onward, he was a child whose responses were characterized by a low level of intensity. Thus, even abnormal behaviors were mildly expressed.

Kevin's parents accepted from the beginning the fact that his difficulties in learning and his developmental delays derived from primary neurologic damage. On the other hand, they were reluctant to accept the possibility that his intellectual retardation might be permanent and tried to explain away his subnormal I.Q. scores and low academic achievement. Within this framework, however, they were highly accepting and very fond of the boy. Their demands were appropriate to the level of his intellectual and physical capacities, and their efforts at training him were consistent and patient.

With this combination of a relatively Easy Child temperamental pattern and consistent, supportive and protective parental attitudes, Kevin pursued a smooth, benign behavioral course from earliest infancy into adolescence. He has attended a special school for brain-injured children, in which his placement has been at age level. His learning progress has been slow, even with intense tutoring, though reports from the school personnel have not indicated any major behavioral problems.

Our last follow-up and psychiatric evaluation of Kevin to date occurred when he was 14 years of age. His I.Q. score on the WISC was 59. Projective tests did not show sufficient psychopathology to warrant a diagnosis of behavior disorder. In the clinical interview his attention wandered constantly, he repeatedly squirmed in his chair, played with any object within reach, and wandered about the room. His mother stated that this behavior was typical of his reaction to new people in new situations. The testing psychologist also reported similar reactions of distractibility, high activity and avoidance in the test situation.

Kevin's behavioral response to the clinical examination and to psychological testing at this age suggests that he may be developing a defensive reactive pattern to stress and demand. As yet, the data are insufficient for a diagnosis of behavior disorder. The hyperactivity and distractibility are also still mild and there is no evidence that they are producing substantial problems in functioning. However, the stresses and new demands of adolescence may lead to intensification of his defensive reactions and the development of a behavior disorder.

The third youngster, Barbara, showed a combination of the Difficult Child temperamental pattern, brain damage, and inconsistent and contradictory parental attitudes and practices. This made for an increasingly pathological behavioral course, culminating in the need for residential care at age six for almost four years, and prolonged psychiatric treatment thereafter.

Barbara was hospitalized at one of the leading treatment and training child psychiatry centers of the area in which the family lived. One of us (S.C.) visited the center after Barbara's admission to review her case with the staff. The psychiatrists there had made a diagnosis of childhood schizophrenia, based on Barbara's behavior and the extreme concreteness manifest in her thinking. On a phenomenological level, the diagnosis appeared fully warranted.

Through her middle elementary and high school years Barbara attended academic residential schools for youngsters with special behavior problems. She made progress academically and behaviorally and by age 16 was able to handle a summer job as a clerk typist successfully. Visits home, however, were always stormy, with violent altercations developing on the most minimal criticism by her father, ending in violent verbal attacks by Barbara against both parents.

Our latest follow-up and clinical evaluation of Barbara were at age 17. Her affect and visual regard were appropriate, her use of language was clear, connected, relevant and age-appropriate. Her description of her own functioning was realistic and she expressed pride in her work at school and in her summer job. It was clear that Barbara had learned social graces and had acquired important educational and work skills. She continued to be perseverative, however, and to be socially isolated outside the protected environment of the residential school. Her behavior reflected a residual chronic brain dysfunction and a continued hostile interaction with her father; nevertheless, her improvement was substantial. A diagnosis of schizophrenia at this time would have been entirely inappropriate.

These three case studies show that the behavioral sequelae of brain damage can be most diverse, and may range from no apparent behavioral disturbance to neurotic behavior disorders of varying degrees of severity to serious disorganizations of social, intellectual, and interpersonal functioning. The last may even be phenomenologically indistinguishable from the major psychoses of childhood. Because of the continued emphasis in the literature on the syndrome of the hyperkinetic child as the outcome of brain damage (7), it is pertinent to emphasize that only one of our three cases showed this hyperkinetic behavioral pattern.

In each of these three youngsters the analyses of the anterospective longitudinal data indicate that the cause of behavioral development in brain-damaged children, as in other individuals, is the complex product of a child with a given set of capacities, potentialities and temperamental traits in combination with parental attitudes and practices and more general features of environmental demand.

A final point of theoretical interest is raised by the history of the third subject, Barbara. Was the diagnosis of childhood schizophrenia, made when her pathological behavior had reached psychotic proportions, an error? Or is the behavioral syndrome we designate as schizophrenia a final common behavioral pathway that may have many different causes? Of interest, with regard to the latter possibility, is the finding of a strikingly high incidence of the syndrome of autism in populations of children with congenital rubella (8). This is not to suggest that childhood psychosis is a direct reflection of neurologic dysfunction alone. As in the case of Barbara, the psychotic syndrome may be the result of the interaction of a number of pathogenic factors, which may very well be different in different children.

CONGENITAL RUBELLA

Prenatal infection with the rubella virus can result in a wide variety of serious handicaps, either singly or in combination. These include visual, hearing, neurologic and cardiac defects. The opportunity to study the behavioral consequences of such physical handicaps arose after the 1964 rubella epidemic, when the Rubella Birth Defect Evaluation Project (RBDEP) was established in the Pediatric Department of New York University Medical Center. The sample consisted of 243 children in whom the diagnosis of congenital rubella had been confirmed by either virus isolation or serologic procedures. In 1967 one of us (S.C.) undertook a behavioral study to determine the psychological and psychiatric consequences of this disease.

This behavioral study considered a number of issues. The methods of data collection, as well as analysis and findings, have been reported in a previous volume (9). Only those findings relevant to the significance of temperament for physically handicapped children will be discussed here.

These children infected with the rubella virus in prenatal life suffered a wide variety of physical handicaps. These included:

1) *Visual:* cataracts, glaucoma, myopia, microphthalmia, esotropia, nystagmus, ptosis, and strabismus. Visual defects were further broken down according to degrees of severity. Thus, unilateral or bilateral microphthalmia, esotropia, nystagmus, and ptosis were grouped as mild defects—1; unilateral cataract, glaucoma, and strabismus as moderate—2; and bilateral cataract, glaucoma, and strabismus as severe—3. Rubella retinopathy, although found in many of the children, was not included as a handicap, since it is a non-interfering defect.

2) *Hearing:* losses of unspecified—1, moderate—2, or severe or profound—3—degree.

3) *Neurologic:* hard signs, as spasticity, cerebral palsy, seizures, paresis, or encephalitis; and soft signs, as myotonia, clumsiness of gait, and falling. (We did not include neuromotor retardation in our classification of neurological defect because it is identical with the psychiatric diagnosis of mental retardation.)

4) *Cardiac:* unspecified congenital heart disease, patent ductus arteriosis, pulmonic stenosis, aortic stenosis, atrial septal defect, and ventricular defect.

The children in our sample ranged from two and a half to four years at the time of the behavioral study. Their physical status and physical defects were categorized as shown in Tables 3 and 4.

TABLE 3

Physical Status of Rubella Children

Number of Defects	N	%
Well (no defect)	50	20.6
One area of defect	72	29.6
Two areas of defect	47	19.3
Three areas of defect	47	19.3
Four areas of defect	27	11.1
Total	243	99.9

TABLE 4

Physical Defect Combinations

Single Defect:	Number of Children
Hearing	65
Visual	4
Cardiac	2
Neurologic	1
Total Single	72

Double Defect:	
Hearing and Neurologic	18
Hearing and Visual	14
Hearing and Cardiac	10
Visual and Neurological	1
Neurological and Cardiac	2
Visual and Cardiac	2
Total Double	47

Triple Defect:	
Hearing, Visual and Cardiac	17
Hearing, Cardiac and Neurologic	15
Hearing, Visual and Neurologic	11
Visual, Cardiac and Neurologic	4
Total Triple	47

Total Quadruple:	
Hearing, Visual, Cardiac and Neurologic	27

TABLE 5

Frequency of Concurrent Signs of the "Difficult Child" in the
Rubella, NYLS (At Age Five), and Mentally Retarded Children

No. of Signs	Rubella (N = 227)		NYLS (N = 105)		Mentally Retarded (N = 52)	
	N	%	N	%	N	%
5	19	(8.4)	6	(5.7)	5	(9.6)
4	43	(19.0)	19	(18.1)	10	(19.2)
3	37	(16.4)	30	(28.6)	7	(13.3)
2	55	(24.3)	26	(24.8)	12	(22.9)
1 or 0	73	(31.9)	24	(22.9)	18	(35.0)

Behavioral information scorable for temperament was obtained by
a semi-structured interview with the mother or other person responsible for the youngster's daily care. The data were scored and rated
for each of the nine temperamental categories as in the NYLS.

Since we were particularly interested in the cluster of traits describing the Difficult Child, because of their relationship to the development of behavior disorders, we focused on their distribution
among the rubella children. We used the median scores of the NYLS
children on each of the five crucial temperamental traits (rhythmicity, adaptability, approach/withdrawal, intensity, and mood) as criteria for scoring. Any rubella child whose score for one of these
traits fell between this criterion point and the vulnerable extreme
was considered to have a "sign" of the Difficult Child. For example,
any child whose score in rhythmicity was between the NYLS median
and the polar extreme "irregularity" was considered to have this temperamental sign of the Difficult Child.

Using this technique, we then compared the frequency with which
the five temperamental characteristics comprising the Difficult Child
syndrome appeared in the rubella children, the mentally retarded
study children, and the NYLS children at age five (Table 5).

Although the five signs of the Difficult Child are found somewhat
more often in the rubella children than in the NYLS youngsters and
somewhat less often than in the retarded sample, these variations are
not statistically significant. Similarly, the distribution of four, two,
one or zero signs among the three populations is no more than would
be expected on the basis of chance alone. Only in the case of three

TABLE 6

Number of Signs of Difficult Child in Rubella Children with and
without Behavior Disorder (N = 227)

No. of Signs of Difficult Child	No Behavior Disorder (N = 117)		Behavior Disorder (N = 110)	
	N	%	N	%
5	6	(5.1)	13	(11.8)
4	11	(9.4)	32	(29.1)
3	17	(14.5)	21	(19.1)
2	27	(23.1)	27	(24.5)
1	35	(29.9)	12	(10.9)
0	21	(18.0)	5	(4.5)

TABLE 7

Initial Signs of Difficult Child in Rubella Children and
Behavior Disorder Four Years Later (N= 189)

No. of Signs of Difficult Child	No Behavior Disorder (N = 97)		Behavior Disorder (N = 92)	
	N	%	N	%
4 or 5	14	(14.4)	42	(45.7)
2 or 3	41	(42.4)	33	(35.9)
0 or 1	42	(43.3)	17	(18.5)

concurrent signs is there a significant difference across the groups, with the NYLS children having a much greater frequency and the retarded and rubella children a lower frequency of their occurrence.

In general, therefore, the presence or absence of the signs of the Difficult Child did not appear to be a meaningful distinction among these three groups.

The frequency with which the number of signs of the Difficult Child are found becomes more significant when it is related to the incidence of behavior disorder in the rubella children. Table 6 shows striking and significant differences with respect to children with or without behavior disorder. Almost half (40.9 percent) of the behavior disorder group had four or five signs of the Difficult Child, as contrasted to only 14.5 percent of the group without behavior disorder. On the other hand, only 15.4 percent of the children with behavior disorder showed zero or one sign of the Difficult Child, as contrasted to 47.9 percent of the children without behavior disorder. There were no significant differences between the two groups with regard to two or three Difficult Child signs.

A four-year follow-up of this rubella sample was done (10). This permitted a comparison between temperament in the initial study period and behavior disorder at the time of follow-up four years later. (Temperament measures were not obtained in the follow-up study.)

As can be seen from Table 7, the differences found between the two groups initially (Table 6) are duplicated in the comparison of number of signs of the Difficult Child and the presence or absence of behavior disorder four years later. The differences are all in the same direction and of the same order of magnitude as in the initial study.

The findings in this congenital rubella sample parallel those for the mentally retarded sample detailed earlier in this chapter. Both groups show a high incidence of behavior disorder, and in both there is a significant correlation between the temperamental signs of the Difficult Child and the occurrence of behavioral disturbance. The Difficult Child is more vulnerable to behavior disorder development even without intellectual or physical handicap, as seen in the NYLS findings, but the presence of handicap increases this vulnerability.

Qualitative analysis of the data in the congenital rubella study indicates that a number of temperamental traits may significantly affect the ability of a physically handicapped child to master environmental demands. The importance of understanding the temperamental traits of a physically handicapped child was also repeatedly affirmed in discussions with those parents who came for advice and guidance as to practical management of the child at home. The same issue came up consistently in similar discussions with teachers responsible for these children and in more general professional conferences with teachers dealing with other groups of handicapped children. This was over and above the pertinence of temperament in general for the child-environment interaction process, which was as evident in the handicapped child as in the normal one.

The influence of temperamental traits on the psychological development of the rubella children with physical defects was especially evident in those suffering from deafness. Communication with a parent, teacher or peer has special difficulties for a deaf child. He usually cannot express his desires, confusions, or reasons for negative mood effectively through words. He cannot apprehend the vast majority of messages from the other person except through visual cues —lip reading, sign language or gestures. This demands that the deaf child fix his attention without distraction and for long periods on the other person.

Thus, numerous problems of management, training and teaching arose for the deaf children in our rubella sample at home and in school. The distractible and short attention span child, or the highly active one, frequently missed important cues and messages from parents and sibs because his gaze was diverted. His learning capacity in school was similarly impaired. In the case of a child who is visually distracted, the parent or teacher can usually regain his attention by auditory communication. This is not possible for the deaf child.

The deaf youngster with frequent negative mood expressions was unable to communicate the reasons for this displeasure to parents, teacher or peer, especially if sign language or lip reading was not available to both. Parental effort to identify the reason for the negative mood tended to become a fatiguing and futile exercise. The effort was often given up, leaving the child frustrated. Or the parental goal was diverted to attempts to mollify and pacify the child, who then easily became the tyrant of the household.

New situations can be stressful and demanding for any handicapped child. For the deaf child with the temperamental tendency of initial withdrawal from new situations, unfamiliar places, people or academic demands were especially difficult to master, and required great understanding, patience and empathy on the part of parent or teacher for the child to cope successfully.

The deaf child who approached new situations easily and quickly could also sometimes present management problems. Warnings of danger were often hard to give without spoken language, and parents sometimes limited the youngsters' new experiences for fear of this problem. Counseling was often needed in such instances on the need for rehearsing the child ahead of time before exposure to the new, rather than restricting him to familiar routines and places.

Similar issues arose with blind children, though generally not as severely as with the deaf child. It was easier to maintain or reestablish communication with the blind child than with the deaf child by spoken language when his attention was diverted or he wandered away. For the children with other handicaps, the combination of certain temperamental traits with specific physical handicaps made for severe problems of adaptation and stress. In each instance, what was required was a detailed evaluation of temperament, the special demands imposed by the handicap, other pertinent attributes of the child, the nature of the environmental demands and expectations, and an analysis of the interaction among these factors. To take a simple example, a child with a high activity level and athetosis required special planning and programming of motor activities and demands and careful attention to the surroundings of home and school to ensure his physical safety.

It is clear that goodness of fit between child and environment is especially crucial if a developmental deviation exists, whether it be mental retardation, brain damage, physical handicap, or other perceptual or physiological problems. The deviant youngster at best finds the mastery of normal developmental sequences more stressful than does the normal child. If, simultaneously, there is a significant degree of dissonance between the child's temperamental characteristics and environmental demands and expectations, the occurrence of excessive stress and suboptimal and psychopathological development becomes very likely. To put it another way, healthy development for the deviant child requires special concern for consonance between his individual capacities and attributes and the environment. Furthermore, each type of cognitive, physical or other handicap may modify or change the type of management which is optimal for a specific temperamental constellation, as compared to that of the nonhandicapped child. For these reasons it is important that those responsible for the care and education of the deviant child identify his temperamental traits. Once this is done, the approach which will be optimal for that child with his specific temperament and developmental deviation can be formulated and implemented.

REFERENCES

1. S. Chess and S. Korn, "Temperament and Behavior Disorders in Mentally Retarded Children," *Archives of Gen. Psychiatr.*, 23:122 (1970).
2. S. Chess and M. Hassibi, "Behavior Deviations in Mentally Retarded Children," *J. Am. Acad. Child Psychiatr.*, 9:282-297 (1970).
3. J. Baron, "Temperament Profile of Children with Down's Syndrome," *Develop. Med. and Child Neurol.*, 14:640-643 (1972).
4. G. Gregg, "Clinical Experience with Efforts to Define Individual Differences in Temperament," *Individual Differences in Children*, ed., J. Westman (New York: John Wiley and Sons, 1973), pp. 306-322.
5. H. G. Birch, A. Thomas and S. Chess, "Behavioral Development in Brain-Damaged Children," *Archives of Gen. Psychiatr.*, 11:596 (1964).
6. A. Thomas and S. Chess, "A Longitudinal Study of Three Brain Damaged Children," *Archives of Gen. Psychiatr.*, 32:457-465 (1975).
7. P. H. Wender, *Minimal Brain Dysfunction in Children* (New York: John Wiley and Sons, 1971).
8. S. Chess, S. Korn and P. Fernandez, *Psychiatric Disorders of Children with Congenital Rubella* (New York: Brunner/Mazel, 1971).
9. *Ibid.*
10. S. Chess, "Behavior and Learning of School-Age Rubella Children." Final Report to Department of Health, Education and Welfare, December, 1974.

6

Temperament and

parent-child

interaction

All psychological theories, no matter how they differ from each other, agree in emphasizing the crucial significance of the parents or parent surrogates for the child's development in the early years of life. This is the period in which the young child masters the initial demands for socialization within the family. The establishment of regular sleep and feeding patterns, toilet-training, mastery of self-feeding and dressing, acceptance of family rules and prohibitions, response to masturbatory experiences, the emergence and growth of interpersonal relations with parents, sibs and other significant members of the family group—these are the areas in which consonance or dissonance between infant and environment is elaborated.

In all these areas it is primarily the parents or parent substitutes who make the demands and communicate environmental expectations, establish and implement routines, mediate the infant's relationships with the outside world. The parents may or may not get guidance and assistance from others—grandparents, baby nurses, pediatricians, or child-care professionals. In any event they are generally held responsible for the kind of patterns of socialization developed by the infant and preschool child.

In the preschool years the development of peer group relations becomes an increasingly important issue. Here, too, it is the parents who are usually most directly influential in helping or hindering the course of the youngster's mastery, whether or not the child is involved in nursery school or day care center experiences. As the youngster grows older, new and increasingly more complex developmental issues emerge, such as formal learning, incorporation of socio-cultural values and standards, and adolescent group adaptations. The role of the parent becomes progressively less dominant, and the parents' influence is more and more shared with and modified by teachers, other important adults in the child's life, peer groups, and community organizations.

A similar evolution over time is evident in the contribution made by the child's own characteristics to the developmental process. The infant's behavior patterns are relatively simple, and variations in cognitive and perceptual levels and expression of special skills are uncomplicated in most normal infants. Motivations are only beginning to develop, and psychodynamic mechanisms are not structured as yet. In this infancy period, temperamental traits and their contribution to the child's development are relatively easy to identify.

As the child grows older, environmental demands, expectations and opportunities become increasingly more complex, elaborate and varied; at the same time the child's own attributes increase in complexity, as perception, cognition, motivations, psychodynamic mechanisms, special skills and talents are developed and crystallized. The role of temperament remains important, sometimes even decisive, but increasingly more complicated to isolate for analysis, as the child's behavior patterns become more and more complex in their determination and expression.

GENERAL ASPECTS OF PARENT-CHILD INTERACTION

Central to the consideration of the parent-child relationship is that each influences the other from the beginning in a constantly evolving process of interaction. The infant is not a *homunculus*, as previous centuries had it, in which his final adult psychological structure was present within him at birth, and in which development consisted of the maturation and unfolding of these fixed inherent characteristics.

In this simplistic constitutional view, the parents and other child caretakers could enforce specific modifications of behavior and ideas by discipline and persuasion but were not the primary shapers of the child's personality.

Neither is the infant a *tabula rasa,* as recent theories might indicate, a clean slate on which the family and society can inscribe any pattern and outcome at will. It seems amusing to think of John Watson's behaviorist assertion of 50 years ago, "Give me a dozen healthy infants, well-formed, and my own specified world to bring them up in, and I'll guarantee to take any one at random and train him to become any type of specialist I might select—doctor, lawyer, artist, merchant-chief, and yes, even beggarman and thief, regardless of his talents, penchants, abilities, vocations, and race of his ancestors" (1). In actual practice, this view dominated the thinking of most mental health professionals until very recently, dressed up though it may have been in the professional and sophisticated language of one theory or another.

In truth, of course, the infant is neither a *homunculus* nor a *tabula rasa,* either in his psychological or biological development (2). The influence of the infant's biochemical and physiological characteristics, temperamental traits and cognitive and perceptual attributes is determined by the opportunities, constraints and demands of the family and society. Conversely and simultaneously, the influence of the family and society is shaped by the quality and degree of its consonance or dissonance with the infant's capacities and style of functioning. Furthermore, this reciprocal interaction is not a static process. It is a constantly evolving dynamic, as the child and family and society change over time.

Recent research on the infancy period has documented dramatically the active participation of the infant, even in the newborn state, in this interactive process. The young baby's perceptual, behavioral and cognitive capacities are developed to an extent not imagined by students of development even 10 years ago (3, 4, 5). The newborn infant not only responds actively to stimulation from the mother but initiates communication with vocalizations, facial expressions and body movements. Rutter summarizes this research in three generalizations.

First, it is evident that, although limited in many ways, the young infant has a surprisingly sophisticated response to his environment and quite substantial learning skills. Second, these skills and capacities have a marked influence on the process of parent-child interaction. In many instances it is the baby who shows initiative and the parent who responds by following. Third, even in the early months of life there are striking temperamental differences between infants which influence both their response to the environment and also how other people react to them (6).

As indicated above, in the infancy period temperament and parental attitudes and practices play a major role in the child-environment interaction. The effect of the child's specific temperament on the parent can take many directions, depending on the latter's personality structure, goals and expectations for the child, and on socioeconomic opportunities and constraints. The effect of the parent's attitudes and practices on the child can also be varied, depending on the latter's specific style of response and adaptation.

In the remainder of this chapter, these generalizations will be documented by a number of specific examples and contingencies. While numerous, these illustrations will in no way exhaust the myriad ways in which this mutual influence can take place. The relationship between parent and young child is so fundamental and so complex that it is impossible in any single discussion to exhaust all its possible manifestations, even in this one area of the child's temperament and its role in parent-child interaction. Our hope is that the specific examples cited are sufficient in their variety and quantity to document adequately the fundamental thesis of a constantly active and evolving reciprocal process between parent and the child's temperament.

EFFECT OF CHILD'S TEMPERAMENT ON PARENT

It is a static mechanical concept to assume that a parent's attitudes and behavior toward the child are fixed and determined by pre-existing fully formed parental personality patterns and psychodynamic defenses and conflicts. Any adult or child, unless suffering from serious mental illness, has the capacity and flexibility to respond differentially and selectively to the wide range of external situations and people which make up his life. In each specific instance the response is shaped by some aspect of the individual's personality structure, but, in the absence of serious mental illness, this structure is not homogeneous, global or insensitive to the nature of external reality.

A child's specific temperamental traits can affect the parent's attitudes and behavior in many ways, and this has been clearly evident in many families in our various longitudinal studies. The anterospective nature of the data has made it possible to identify temporal relationships between the child's temperament and parental functioning, and the differential responses of parents to their children with different temperamental patterns. This was usually most dramatically evident in those instances where the parent's reaction was antagonistic or anxious, but was also obvious and important in the many instances where the parent responded favorably to the child's individual characteristics.

In the infancy period, parental responses are most frequently and strongly influenced by whether the infant has the temperamental constellation of the Easy or Difficult Child. This determines whether management routines proceed smoothly or with turmoil, and whether the landmarks of early socialization (regular sleep and feeding schedules, toilet-training, adaptation to family living patterns, etc.) are achieved quickly with initial efforts or after prolonged trial and error. If the mother believes the middle-class conventional wisdom that the course of the infant's development is determined primarily by her maternal attitudes, motivations and needs, an Easy Child will reassure her that she is an adequate, healthy and loving mother. She will be delighted with her child who has given her this opportunity to prove herself and may even feel superior to those other mothers who are struggling painfully with their Difficult Children. If the father has the same standards he will reinforce his wife's judgments and perhaps even gain an unrealistic estimate of her psychological assets. Unfortunately, this outcome is not always an unmixed blessing to the mother. As in any case where self-esteem is built on the evidence of one specific achievement, the mother can become vulnerable and easily threatened by any failure of her Easy Child to adapt quickly and smoothly to every new situation and demand.

The parents of an Easy Child may be pleased and even grateful that they have to exert relatively little effort, time and attention to the child's care. This may have a positive effect on the parent-child relationship, stimulating the expansion and growth of parental love and affection, and in turn enhancing the child's sense of being wanted and loved. In other instances, however, the needs of the Easy Child may be ignored because he adapts so quickly and fusses so little. The parents may concentrate their efforts and attention on another child with special needs or problems, such as physical handicaps or cognitive lags. In such cases, the Easy Child may very well react with feelings of rejection, with all the deleterious psychological consequences that such a reaction may bring. It may also happen, even if infrequently, that a parent, with his or her special value system, may be displeased if the youngster has the Easy Child characteristics of quick adaptability or mild mood expressiveness. Thus, one father was highly critical of his daughter's easy adaptability because in his eyes she was "a pushover," someone who wouldn't fight for what she wanted.

By contrast, the parents can hardly ignore a Difficult Child. The special child-care demands made by such an infant can in general create three types of parental responses, depending on the parents' personality structures and the socio-cultural pressures of their group. The parents may feel threatened and anxious because they feel that the turmoil and difficulties of care expose their inadequacy as parents. They may believe they are unconsciously rejecting their child, or unloving, or just plain inept as caretakers. Or the parents may blame the infant and resent the extra burdens and demands he puts on them. Finally, the parents may be intimidated by the infant's frequent loud screaming and "resistance" to training procedures.

In all these cases, whether the parents are threatened, resentful or intimidated, they can hardly provide the patient, gradual and repeated exposures to new situations and demands that such a child requires to make a positive adaptation. They are more likely to pressure, appease, punish, or vacillate, all the time communicating a host of negative feelings to the infant, such as hostility, impatience or bewilderment. This only leads to intensification of the infant's negative mood expressions and difficulties in adaptation. A vicious cycle is created, leading to behavior disorder development. It is then all too easy for the mental health professional or pediatrician to incorrectly identify the parents' unhealthy attitudes and behavior as the sole cause of the disorder.

Occasionally, a parent may respond positively to the temperament of the Difficult Child. One parent, the father of a child with one of the most extreme Difficult Child patterns in the NYLS, took pride and pleasure in his infant's vigor and "lustiness." He was also aware that after the initial storm and turmoil that accompanied the exposure to any new situation, his son gradually adapted positively and energetically. Because of his positive attitude and patience, he was able to be very supportive to his wife, who felt anxious and guilty over the child's behavior pattern. As a consequence, this youngster did not develop a behavior disorder.

In fact, most parents of Difficult Children with behavior disorders responded positively once they understood that their child's temperament existed independently of their own attitudes and functioning, and that a specific management approach was required. Basically, this resulted from the reassurance that their patient efforts would finally be rewarded by a change in adaptation by the child, who would then function on a level congenial to their own value system. Because of this, parent guidance in the cases of Difficult Children with behavior problems was as successful as in the Easy Child clinical sample.

Gregg, in her Infant Accident Study, postulated that some mothers with difficult infants might perceive these children as "evil" or "mean" and be more likely to subject them to abuse. Also, child-abusing mothers might perceive their children as more difficult than they actually were (7). Her clinical study, in which mothers' temperamental ratings were compared with those obtained by the pediatrician's direct observation, suggested that both possibilities might be true. In addition, she found that babies who showed neglect, chronic illness or failure to thrive were, as a group, less active, less intense and bland in mood. She could not decide, from her data, whether she was tapping poor physical and mental status or temperamental characteristics.

Other temperamental traits can, of course, initiate inappropriate parental reactions to their infants. For example, Carey has found that sleep disturbance in infants with night waking is significantly correlated with low sensory threshold (8). He points out that if the mother is automatically held responsible for this sleep problem she may develop "anxiety, anger or feelings of helplessness" which may be, in reality, "the result rather than the cause of the baby's waking."

In the preschool years the temperamental constellation of the Easy or Difficult Child can continue to affect the parents' responses as new demands for adaptation and self-mastery arise. In addition, these new demands and expectations, combined with the child's ever expanding range of activities and capabilities, enhance the significance of other temperamental attributes in the developmental process. Here, too, as in the earlier period, temperament can affect the parents' attitudes and behavior toward the child.

For example, the highly active young child, once he is walking and running, can present special problems of management, especially in an urban environment. He is more apt to get burned and bruised, to break things, to dart out into the street in front of an oncoming car and to interfere unintentionally with the activities and comforts of others than is the child with a moderate or low activity level. Some parents can enjoy the liveliness of a highly active child. Others become resentful, overwhelmed or anxious at the more vigilant attention such a youngster demands. They may also interpret lack of compliance with demands for unrealistic restraint of motor activity as deliberate disobedience, especially if their other children respond easily to similar requests. If this leads the parents to scold or punish the highly active child for each infraction of the rules, the youngster may decide there is no point in trying to please his parents and that he might just as well ignore or resist their wishes altogether. He may then, in fact, become disobedient.

By contrast, the low activity child may be a convenient member of the household. He does not require special vigilance and his slow movements will interfere very little with the activities of other family members. Parental impatience and displeasure may develop, however, when the child's slowness in finishing meals or getting dressed interferes with the family's schedule. The parents may also compare him unfavorably to their other more active children, and even interpret the slow motor activity as evidence of inferior intellectual ability.

A highly distractible child may facilitate management during infancy. Such a child's resistance to being held still while being dressed or diapered can easily be countered by offering him a toy or other distraction. The crawling infant's attention can be quickly diverted from a potentially dangerous activity, such as poking at an electrical socket. As the child grows older, however, this quality of easy distractibility becomes less convenient, especially if combined with low persistence and attention span. These characteristics interfere with the goal of quick and complete task completion, a demand which is made increasingly on the growing child, especially in middle-class families. The parental response to these traits is frequently crucial for the child's developmental course. If the parents understand that the distractibility is not motivated by a desire to avoid the completion of a task and that the child is not deficient in "a sense of responsibility," they can avoid a derogatory or punitive attitude. They can then accept with good humor and patience the frequent "forgetting" to finish a task and appreciate the high level of general alertness and awareness of the nuances of other people's behavior and feelings such distractible children frequently show. Other parents, to the contrary, interpret the typical behavior of the distractible child as reflecting conscious disobedience, laziness or lack of willpower and responsibility. These derogatory judgments lead to excessive pressure on the child, hypercritical and punitive attitudes, and foster a pathological child-parent interaction which may produce increasing malfunction and symptomatology in the child.

Parental response to high persistence in the preschool child can be influenced greatly by the selectivity of his interests and activities and by coexisting temperamental traits. If the youngster's persistence is focused on areas which the parents value highly, this will gain parental approval and more than counterbalance the inconvenience and annoyance that result when the child's attention cannot be turned easily. The child who resists coming for meals, getting dressed or going to bed because he is absorbed in putting a puzzle together, trying to learn to read, or practicing an athletic skill will meet parental tolerance and even encouragement if the parents approve of these activities and goals. If, however, the child focuses on activities

which may be unsafe, or interests which appear unimportant or un-
productive, then his persistence may be interpreted as nagging, stub-
bornness or inconsiderateness.

The persistent preschool youngster is likely to suffer many frustration reactions as he struggles intently to master difficult new activities and tasks, and attempts are made to call him away to meals or
bedtime. If his mood expression is mild, these frustrations will typically be expressed in a way which is likely to be acceptable to the
family. If, however, his mood expression is intense, there may be
storms, loud protests, and even tantrums which may tax or overwhelm the parents. Patience and tolerance with the persistent child
are also easier if he has a low activity level and sits quietly or moves
slowly as he is absorbed in his pursuits. If, however, he has a high
activity level which annoys or interferes with other people, this trait
in combination with his persistence may easily create serious dissonances with parental expectations and demands.

Finally, the typical behavior of the Slow-To-Warm-Up Child
usually creates few if any issues in infancy, but may begin to do so
in the preschool period. As an infant he may react negatively to the
bath, to new foods, to strangers, as does the Difficult Child. But
inasmuch as the Slow-To-Warm-Up Child expresses his withdrawal
reactions mildly and quietly, it is usually easy for the parents to
tolerate them and wait patiently until the infant finally makes a
positive adaptation. But this tolerance and patience are harder for
the parents to maintain when the withdrawal reactions begin to occur
in an area which has high priority in their value system. Thus, the
middle-class parents in the NYLS were uniformly unconcerned if
time was required to persuade the infant to accept various foods.
But many of them became deeply concerned when this same child,
two or three years later, showed similar negative reactions to a new
nursery school or preschool play group. For these parents, the development of a varied and regular diet ranked low in the scale of their
hierarchies of goals and standards for the child. By contrast, the
ability to make quick and positive interpersonal relations ranked
very high.

For the parents who understood the initial social withdrawal reactions of their Slow-To-Warm-Up Child as part of his normal be-

havioral style of functioning, a willingness to wait and give the youngster time to make a final positive adaptation was exhibited. For the parents who saw the initial negative reaction as "timidity or anxiety," such patience was much more difficult to achieve. Some of them pressured the child to adapt quickly and actively to the new group, which usually resulted in an intensification of the child's withdrawal response, increased parental pressure and the initiation of a snowballing pathogenic parent-child interaction. Other parents were similarly threatened by the slow-to-warm-up social behavior but responded with overprotectiveness, trying to shield the youngster from these demanding new situations. As a result, the child was denied the opportunity for frequent exposure to new situations that he needed in order to achieve a positive adaptation, and tended to develop only a constricted range of activities and interests.

In the school years, each child's developmental course was increasingly affected by the school setting and peer groups. Parental influences, though not as dominant as in the infancy and preschool periods, continued to be important. Patterns of parent-child interaction established in these earlier years were sometimes reinforced by the child's school functioning. This occurred especially when the child's temperament made the adaptation to formal learning demands slow or stressful, as we will discuss in a later chapter on school functioning. In many other families the increasingly complex and varied aspects of the older child's psychological functioning made for significant shifts in parental attitudes and behavior. In these instances the child's temperament was only one of a number of interacting factors in influencing the course of the parent-child relationship.

As a final comment on the effect of the child's temperament on the parent, it is our impression that this was not determined in any uniform way by congruence or lack of congruence of parent and child characteristics. In some instances it was difficult for parents to understand a child with temperamental traits different from their own. Thus, in one family the parents were both lively, expressive and predominantly cheerful individuals. Their oldest child, Dorothy, had a low activity level and frequent negative mood reactions of low intensity. The parents grew to feel that their daughter was disinterested in most activities because of her slow movements and negative mood and that they did not know what she wanted because her needs were expressed with such mild intensity. They became increasingly impatient with Dorothy, failed to recognize the cues she gave as to her desires, and labeled her as "fussy" and "whiney."

Another mother, by contrast, was concerned over her daughter Kaye's pattern of quiet easy adaptability. The mother felt she herself had been this type of child and had been pressured by her parents into patterns of adaptation which were not in her own best interests. She was therefore determined that her own daughter would not suffer a similar fate. The mother's child-care practices were consequently guided by the determination to keep demands on Kaye to a minimum and allow her to develop "spontaneously." As a result the youngster had difficulties with any situation demanding specific task performances. This was evident by age three years in her response to psychometric testing and became a serious impediment to academic achievement.

As a general rule, the nature of the parents' response to the child's temperament was determined not so much by the degree of congruence with their own personality characteristics as by consonance with their goals, standards and values. In discussing parent-child interactions, this is indicated throughout this volume. It is sharply demonstrated by our analysis of the outcome of parent guidance in the NYLS clinical cases. As reported in our previous volume, the need for the parents to know and respect their child's temperament was a major element in our approach to parent guidance. To implement this respect for the child's temperament, specific advice was given to eliminate inappropriate and harmful attitudes and practices and to substitute practices which were consonant with the child's behavioral style. Where indicated, and where possible, parents were advised to change other excessively stressful demands in the environment, whether at home, in the school setting, or elsewhere.

In the majority of the 42 clinical cases tabulated (9), parent guidance was successful in varying degrees in each temperamental pattern group, with the exception of the distractible, non-persistent group where parent guidance was a failure in four out of four cases. In other children, whether easy, difficult, slow-to-warm-up, persistent, or with high or low activity level, most parents responded positively to the assurance that appropriate behavior on their part would lead to final adaptive patterns on the child's part which would be consonant with the family's standards and goals. For the distractible and non-persistent children, however, the parents had to accept the judgment that the child might never pursue a difficult task doggedly, might always lack persistence, and might always have problems in carrying through a responsibility from beginning to end in one sustained effort. For these middle-class and largely professional parents, this judgment appeared to run counter to their own deep commitments to disciplined work and persistence in the face of obstacles which had shaped their lives and careers. To them, a youngster without these virtues "lacked character," was "irresponsible" or "lazy." Repeated discussions with the parents uniformly failed to change these judgments. It is of interest that all four clinical cases with distractible characteristics were boys. The parents of both sexes considered these traits to be especially objectionable in boys, reflecting the sexist values of our society for male achievement.

EFFECT OF PARENT ON CHILD

In contrast to the importance of the child's temperament in influencing the parent, especially in the early childhood years, the parent's influence on the child at all ages is compounded of many factors. The discussion above has emphasized the significant role played by the parent's values, standards and goals. The professional literature over a number of decades has considered this issue as well as a number of others. Psychological and psychodynamic characteristics have been emphasized. The contrast for the course of the child's development between favorable parental attitudes such as love, tenderness, acceptance and empathy, and noxious attitudes such as rejection, overprotection, and ambivalence or anxiety in the parental role have been documented. As indicated in Chapter 2, our quarrel with the formulations arises when they assume an all or nothing character, when they are credited with exclusive significance in determining the child's psychological development. Similarly, these concepts can be criticized when the parental attributes are reified and given a global dimension. It is insufficient and inaccurate to characterize a parent in an overall, diffuse way as "rejecting," "over-protective," "insecure," etc. A parent may be unsympathetic and antagonistic to certain of the child's characteristics and accepting and approving of others; overprotective and restrictive of some of the child's activities but not of others; insecure and unsure in specific areas of child-care responsibilities and self-confident and assured in others.

An interesting question concerns the possibility that the effective communication of the parents' attitudes to the child may be influenced by their own temperamental characteristics. For example, is it possible that a parent may have tender, empathetic feelings toward the child, and yet communicate these attitudes inadequately because of his or her own traits of low intensity of mood expression and frequent or predominant reactions of negative mood? Or may a parent's own characteristics of high persistence and low distractibility result in frequent oblivion to important cues from the child? Unfortunately, we have no data on which to base even impressions as to the significance, if any, of this issue. It remains a fruitful, if complex, project for future investigation.

Recent years have also witnessed an increasing emphasis on socio-cultural influences on the child's development, either as mediated through the family or directly through the child's life and experiences outside the family group. We ourselves consider these influences as significant, and even decisive in many cases. We have explored the issues by mounting a longitudinal study of a cohort with major sociocultural differences from the NYLS sample. This is the study of children coming from Puerto Rican working-class families. Thus far, cross-cultural analyses of our data have revealed significant differences between the two samples in the age of incidence and types of symptoms in those with behavior disorders (10), in their response to the demand for task performance in cognitive evaluation (11), and in their response to the examiner in a psychometric test situation (12). These findings have been clearly related to sociocultural differences between the two populations.

Thus, parental attitudes and practices may affect the child's developmental course, depending on the child's temperament and other attributes and the degree of consonance or dissonance between parental demands and expectations and the child's temperament and capacities. This is clearly seen in the early years in the child's ability to respond positively to the specific child-care practices of the parents. An approach to the child as a *tabula rasa* results in the assumption "that each child will react in the same way to any specific approach by the parent, whether in feeding, toilet-training, discipline or any other area of functioning. A child-care practice which has a favorable effect on some children is assumed to be desirable for all; a practice which has unfavorable effects on some children is considered undesirable for all. Where a particular child-care practice appears to have varying effects on different children, explanations for these deviations tend to be given in terms of the presence of counteracting influences in the mother, father, or sibling relationship" (13).

This approach, criticized by us 20 years ago, unfortunately still is believed by many parents and professionals. Such an approach has several unfortunate consequences. The child who cannot respond to a currently favored categorical rule becomes at risk for the development of behavior disorder. The mother whose child does not respond favorably and smoothly to the prescribed rule is held culpable because of postulated ineptitude, disinterest or hostility to the child (14). The inevitable finding that all children do not respond positively to the prescribed child-care regime initiates a swing of the pendulum and a search for a new, universally applicable set of rules. It indeed appears difficult for many mental health professionals, though easier for parents, baby nurses and pediatricians, to accept the fact that babies respond differently and that no single set of prescriptions can be desirable for all infants.

It is clear that the exhortations "treat your child as an individual," and "respect the uniqueness of your child" become clichés and slogans unless given content and substance. And this content demands that the child-care expert and adviser be fully aware of the phenomenon of temperamental individuality, the different types of temperamental characteristics, and the manner in which such temperamental individuality shapes the infant's responses to specific child-care practices.

REFERENCES

1. J. B. Watson, *Behaviorism* (New York: W. W. Norton, 1924).
2. T. Dobzhansky, *Mankind Evolving* (New Haven: Yale University Press, 1962).
3. R. Lewin, ed., *Child Alive* (London: Temple Smith, 1975).
4. H. Papousek and M. Papousek, "Cognitive Aspects of Preverbal Social Interaction Between Human Infants and Adults," *Parent-Infant Interaction*, Ciba Foundation Symposium 33 (Amsterdam: Excerpta Medica, 1975), pp. 241-260.
5. N. Calder, *The Human Conspiracy* (London: British Broadcasting Corporation, 1976).
6. M. Rutter, "A Child's Life," *Child Alive, op. cit.,* p. 208.
7. G. Gregg, "Clinical Experience with Efforts to Define Individual Differences in Temperament," *Individual Differences in Children*, ed., J. Westman (New York: John Wiley and Sons, 1973), pp. 306-322.
8. W. B. Carey, "Night Waking and Temperament in Infancy," *J. Pediatrics*, 84:756-758 (1974).
9. A. Thomas, S. Chess and H. G. Birch, *Temperament and Behavior Disorders in Children* (New York: New York University Press, 1968), pp. 198-201.
10. A. Thomas, S. Chess, J. Sillen and O. Mendez, "Cross-cultural Study of Behavior in Children with Special Vulnerabilities to Stress," *Life History Research in Psychopathology, Vol. III*, eds., D. F. Ricks, A. Thomas and M. Roff (Minneapolis: University of Minnesota Press, 1974), pp. 53-67.
11. M. Hertzig, H. G. Birch, A. Thomas and O. A. Mendez, "Class and Ethnic Differences in the Responsiveness of Preschool Children to Cognitive Demands," *Monographs of the Society for Research in Child Development*, 33:1-69 (1968).
12. A. Thomas, M. E. Hertzig, I. Dryman and P. Fernandez, "Examiner Effect in I.Q. Testing of Puerto Rican Working-Class Children," *Am. J. Orthopsychiatr.*, 41:5 (1971).
13. S. Chess and A. Thomas, "Characteristics of the Individual Child's Behavioral Responses to the Environment," *Am. J. Orthopsychiatr.*, 24:791-802 (1959).
14. S. Chess, "Mal de Mère," *Am. J. Orthopsychiatr.*, 34:613-614 (1964).

7

Temperament and other interpersonal relations

In the infancy and preschool years the child's response to other individuals, as well as their response to him, is mediated to a large extent through the parents. It is they who have a major role in structuring the environment with which the young child must cope, and in protecting, supporting or pressuring the youngster as he struggles to master difficult interpersonal situations. The previous chapter has indicated some of the specifics of parental influence in such interpersonal situations. The present chapter will consider these issues more broadly—though always with concrete examples—with a major, though not exclusive, emphasis on the role of temperament.

TEMPERAMENT AND OTHER FAMILY MEMBERS

In the early years of life, the child's interpersonal relationships are usually developed primarily within the family circle. First and foremost come the parents or parent surrogates, then the sibs and finally other members of the extended family group with whom the infant or preschool child may have active and regular contact.

For any adult who consistently and continuously assumes a parent surrogate nurturing role, the interaction with the young child will in general parallel that of a parent, as detailed in the previous chapter.

For any family member who lives elsewhere and visits, the relationship with the infant will be determined by a number of factors—the frequency of visits, the adult's personality and the child's temperament. A relative who visits infrequently may encounter a negative initial response each time from the child with a tendency to withdrawal reactions to new experiences and persons. If the adult pushes the contact aggressively and insists on eliciting a positive response too quickly, the child's initial negative reaction will only be prolonged and intensified. If the infant is given time to adapt, then the relative may establish a cheerful interchange before the visit is over. Where the visits are more frequent, the positive response may carry over to the next occasion, which is then close enough in time so that it does not represent another new situation to the infant.

For the young child with quick approach responses and fast adaptability, the reactions to visits by adults or children will be different. A cheerful friendly greeting may come quickly or even immediately each time, and the visitor may often interpret this as an expression of special fondness for him.

The young child's reaction to a visitor may also be influenced by other specific temperamental traits. Thus, an infant with a low sensory threshold may fuss or cry in response to an adult or child who has an unusually loud voice or who handles him relatively roughly, while this may not bother another child with a high sensory threshold. A baby with a high activity level may squirm and struggle to get away from an adult who holds him tightly, while another infant with a low activity threshold may accept this peacefully.

The psychoanalytic literature has made much of Spitz's concept of "eight-month anxiety" in the reaction to strangers (1). A recent influential text describes this phenomenon: "Instead of responding to a stranger's smile with a smile, the baby shows evidence of apprehension, tends to turn away and may start crying. . . . It is as if the infant were upset at the dissonance from the familiar." This is considered an essential element in the developmental process, and "may appear any time after six months" (2).

We have reviewed the anterospective data of the NYLS, in which parents were asked to describe specifically their infants' reactions to strangers, in an attempt to verify this concept of "eight-month anxiety." Our data indicate that the development of a negative reaction to strangers at or after six months of age is a highly variable phenomenon in its occurrence and extent. Some infants showed this reaction markedly and for a prolonged period of time, others showed in mildly and for a short period, and others did not show it at all. The only overall correlation that appeared related to the occurrence and extent of the phenomenon was with the child's temperament. The Easy Child, with initial positive responses and quick adaptability, most usually showed little or none of this negative reaction to strangers. The Difficult or Slow-To-Warm-Up Child, with predominantly negative responses to the new and slow adaptability, tended to show more marked and prolonged negative responses. In some instances, other factors, such as extremely low sensory threshold in the infant, or unusually unfavorable experiences with visiting adults, also appeared to influence the infant's response.

It does appear true that many infants develop negative reactions to strangers in the second half of the first year, when this had not been present previously. One can speculate that it may indicate the beginning of the infant's ability to clearly differentiate other adults from the parents. Hard data, however, are absent as to a verification of this or other speculations. In any case, we question, from our own data, the validity of characterizing this phenomenon of "eight-month anxiety" as a constant and ubiquitous feature of infant development. Its manifestations are just too variable in occurrence, time sequence, intensity and duration, to justify such a characterization. Furthermore, we question the validity of labeling this negative reaction to strangers, when it occurs, as anxiety. The term "anxiety" connotes an intrapsychic state of fear or apprehension, a subjective judgment of being threatened. Whether a six-month-old infant has as yet attained the level of central nervous system maturation required for the conceptualization of such a subjective judgment is open to serious question. Furthermore, the assumption is being made that the infant's expression of distress by fussing, crying and movements of avoidance are to be automatically equated with anxiety. This ignores the possibility that a state of discomfort or distress can exist without anxiety. The issue of separate identification of negative mood reactions and anxiety has important theoretical and practical implications and is discussed further in later chapters.

The importance of the young child's sib relationships in influencing his developmental course has been emphasized in many professional reports. An extensive literature has developed on this subject, following Levy's monograph (3). Much of the discussion, especially in psychoanalytic writings, has focused on the concept of sibling rivalry and its presumed ramifications and pathogenic potentiality. Relatively little attention has been given to other aspects of sib interaction, especially the positive and constructive possibilities. As summarized by Lidz, "Indeed, the whole question of the influence of sibling relationships upon a child's development beyond the relatively simple problems of sibling rivalry and twin relationships has received insufficient attention" (4).

In the NYLS, detailed descriptive data were obtained on the child's reactions to his sibs throughout infancy and the preschool years. A striking finding was the great frequency with which conspicuous positive reactions to an older sib were reported by the parent. The usual, though not universal description was that the infant's attention was quickly and selectively turned to his brother or sister when the latter entered the room. The older sib could also usually make the infant smile and laugh more easily and more strongly than any other family member, though this response varied from infant to infant in accordance with the temperamental traits of quality and intensity of mood expression.

The older brother or sister also frequently served as a model and motivational source for the young child. In a number of instances, successful toilet-training ensued when the child began to imitate his older brother's or sister's toilet pattern. In the preschool years, it was also not unusual for the child to attempt reading and writing in direct imitation of his older sib's activity.

The issue of sibling rivalry was studied in the NYLS by analyzing the child's response to the birth of a younger sibling. The data were reviewed in the first 18 families in the sample in which a younger sibling was born after the start of the study, and the character and intensity of the older child's response to the introduction of an infant into the family were tabulated (5).

Over half of the 18 children showed disturbances at this event. The two main types of disturbance noted were: 1) reversion to more infantile patterns of functioning in socialization, sleeping, feeding and toileting; and 2) aggressive behavior toward the new baby. In six cases the reactions were mild and transient, in one moderate, and in three prolonged and severe. Three children showed no discernible disturbance in functioning and five actually showed an improvement in their social responses. Thus, children reacted with various degrees of positive and negative behavior to a new sibling.

Both environmental factors and the temperamental characteristics of the individual child appear to contribute to variability of response to new siblings. The entry of a younger infant into the family group necessarily affects the amount of time and attention given to the older child by the mother and by other members of the household. Where this change in circumstances leads to disturbance in the child, the mother is objectively unable to appreciably modify the situation as she can for weaning or toilet-training. It is of interest, therefore, that the intensity and duration of negative responses were greater in those who were themselves first children than in those who already had older sibs. For the only child, the entry of a new baby into the family group seemed to constitute a much greater environmental change. Age at the time of new births also influenced reactions. There was less disturbance in those children who were under 18 months of age when the new sibling was born. A third influential factor was the degree of prior paternal involvement. In several children whose fathers had been especially active in caring for them and whose fathers continued to be so even after the arrival of the new baby, the turning of the mother's attention to the younger sibling was not an especially disturbing event. In one family where both parents were very much involved with the first child, there was no reaction when the mother took care of the new baby, but the child, a boy in his third year, developed stuttering as soon as the father began to handle the baby. When the father stopped this and devoted himself again to the older child, the stuttering disappeared.

Qualitative analysis of the data indicated a definite relationship between temperamental characteristics and the type of response to the birth of a sibling. Those children who from early infancy on showed mild, positive regular responses with quick adaptability to new stimuli, such as the bath, change in sleep schedule and the introduction of new foods, manifested a similar pattern with the new baby. In this group, disturbances were minimal or non-existent. On the other hand, those children characterized by intense, negative responses to the new with slow adaptability tended to show greater and more prolonged disturbances after the birth of a sibling. In other words, the initial response appeared specifically influenced by the Easy Child or Difficult Child temperamental pattern.

While the character of the child's initial reaction to the birth of a younger sibling was an important influence, it did not by itself determine the subsequent course of the sibling relationship. Here, as in any other aspect of the child's development, the multiple influences operating in the constantly evolving child-environment interaction could reinforce, modify or alter the quality of the initial reaction.

We have as yet made no systematic analysis of the influence of temperament on the later course of the child's relationship with his sibs. Our impression, from the scrutiny of the longitudinal records of some of the families, is that no simple, linear correlations exist. As with other aspects of development, the outcome appears multi-determined and variable.

TEMPERAMENT AND PEER RELATIONS

The development of peer relationships usually represents the first major social demand on the young child after the mastery of the processes of early socialization within the nuclear family unit. Whether these peer relationships occur primarily in informal settings with relatives or neighbors or in more structured nursery schools or child-care centers, they represent for most preschool children a qualitatively new situation and experience to master. As such, temperamental patterns play a significant role in the dynamics of adaptation.

In contrast to the earlier infancy period, however, the preschool child brings to the new issue of peer relationship not only his temperamental traits but also the more complex behavioral patterns he has already begun to develop. In addition, parental expectations and goals for the child may be different for peer group adaptation than for the development of regular feeding and sleep schedules, toilet-training and the other issues of infancy. Furthermore, the preschool child may find that individual members of his peer group may vary greatly in their behavior from his nuclear family unit and from each other. The peer group may also show and expect standards of behavior at variance from those of his parents. Finally, the child for the first time now has to cope with a new and demanding life situation without the continuous presence and assistance usually provided by the parents in the earlier adaptational issues within the family.

For these reasons, even the initial interactions of the preschool child with peers are already elaborate and multidetermined as compared with the earlier processes of socialization and adaptation in the infancy period. With increasing age the factors influencing the course of peer relationships become increasingly complex and interwoven, culminating in the highly demanding and complicated issues we see in adolescence. The present discussion will concentrate on the preschool and early school years, where the factors are still relatively easy to define and where our data are most detailed.

Dissonance between the child's temperament and the demands for adaptive peer relationships may in some children represent a continuation, in a new area, of an already established pattern of stressful child-environment interaction. This is especially true for the youngsters with the Difficult Child temperamental pattern. Such children typically responded with loud, prolonged negative reactions to the new situations and demands experienced at home in infancy, starting with the first exposures to the bath and new foods. When a similar reaction occurs with the first contacts with peers, whether it is in an informal play group, children's parties, or nursery school, the parents can usually recognize the consistency in the child's reaction. The parental attitude and handling of the youngster's initial difficulties with the peer group will generally also be consistent with their response to the child's earlier expressions of behavioral style. If in the past they were patient, understanding and not threatened by the child's intense negative withdrawal reactions, they were likely to maintain the same approach with the youngster's initial difficulties in peer adaptation. As an example, in one such family the parents enrolled the child in nursery school. After a few weeks the teacher advised the parents to withdraw him because his behavior indicated he was "not ready for nursery school." The parents responded that he was "never ready" and to be patient. By the end of the school year the teacher was enthusiastically rating the child as her best pupil.

In other instances where the parents had previously responded to the Difficult Child with hostility, guilt, anxiety or intimidation, these attitudes were reinforced and intensified by the child's initial intense negative reaction to peer contacts. These antagonistic parental attitudes were usually easily communicated to the parents of other children in the nursery school, and to the children themselves, with an unfortunate increase in the number of individuals from whom the Difficult Child experienced impatience, annoyance, criticism or appeasement.

By contrast, the Easy Child's temperament typically made for a benign and smooth child-environment interaction in the family in infancy. The development of peer relations in the preschool period frequently took the same positive, uneventful course. In some instances, however, the Easy Child experienced difficulties and excessive stress in adapting to peer group expectations. This resulted, characteristically, from sharp contradictions and conflicts between the family standards and values and those of outside peer groups. The Easy Child had quickly and firmly adapted to the rules, regulations and manners of the parents. If the peer group then demanded different standards and patterns of behavior, the Easy Child was faced with a situation of conflict and dissonance. If the contradiction between parental and peer expectations was not too severe, the Easy Child could usually develop flexible adaptive responses so that his functioning in different environments and with different individuals was appropriate to each. When, however, the contradiction between parental and peer group standards and demands was extreme, and when the parents insisted that the child conform to their expectations in all settings, it became impossible for even the Easy Child to adapt his behavior differentially within and without the family. When the child attempted to maintain family behavior patterns outside the home, this led typically to problems of peer relationship.

One example from the NYLS can be cited to illustrate this sequence. Isobel had parents who placed high value on self-expression and the right of all persons to their own individuality and uniqueness. This approach had many positive features, but it also resulted in the young girl's disregard for rules in play with peer groups. As a result, Isobel became progressively alienated from her peers in recreational situations. The same pattern made her ignore the teacher's instructions in the classroom situation, insisting on listening and responding only in a one-to-one relationship. Isobel quickly fell behind in reading and the parents, who also valued academic achievement highly, were then willing to listen to the recommendation for a clarification of their approach to their daughter.

The Slow-To-Warm-Up Child's temperament generally, as with the Easy Child, did not create sharp conflicts with our middle-class parents' values and judgments in the infancy period. This contrasted with the Difficult Child's case, in whom the loud crying and struggling which accompanied initial withdrawal reactions from the new were interpreted by many of the parents as expressions of disturbance and anxiety, which then triggered off pathogenic responses on their part. In the Slow-To-Warm-Up infant, on the other hand, the parents could be tolerant and patient with this first negative response and slow adaptability because it was expressed quietly and occurred in bathing, feeding and toilet-training, areas in which they as a group were not concerned whether positive adaptation occurred quickly or slowly. These parents, however, did place value on quick social adaptability. When the Slow-To-Warm-Up infant reacted negatively to a strange child or adult visiting the home, parents were frequently embarrassed or worried. But inasmuch as these visits were usually brief and relatively infrequent, parental conflict with the infant was not a significant issue.

The issue, however, became different in the preschool years, when positive peer relations became an important goal for the parents. The Slow-To-Warm-Up Child who held back when taken to a children's party and clung to his mother, and was reported by the nursery school teacher to have emotional problems because he stayed on the fringe of the group, now frequently provoked concern, anxiety and impatience in his parents. Their judgment usually coincided with the nursery school teacher's opinion and that of other parents, that the youngster must have an emotional problem with social relationships. All too often, this led to pressure on the child to adapt at a pace too rapid for him, or to overprotective maneuvers to shield him from such disturbing social experiences. In either case, the Slow-To-Warm-Up Child was not given the opportunity to master new social situations effectively and integrate such experiences constructively into his developing personality structure.

The weight of social group judgments was dramatically illustrated by the anecdote of one of the mothers in the NYLS. Fortunately she knew that her slow-to-warm-up daughter, Karen, was psychologically healthy and that with time and patience the girl always made a positive and active adaptation to individuals and groups. (This is still true, now that the girl is an adolescent.) On one occasion, Karen's nursery class put on an evening performance for their parents. This child, who had been doing well socially with her group, came into the room, saw all the strange adults, immediately climbed on to her mother's lap and stayed there for the entire evening. The mother reported with amusement that she could see the other parents directing critical glances at her all evening and knew they were questioning her child's emotional stability and her own functioning as a mother. As she put it, if she had not understood her child and had been vulnerable to these judgments, she would have been anxious or angry at her daughter, or both, and tried to insist that Karen go up front and perform with her group.

Thus, the Slow-To-Warm-Up Child typically found the adaptation to peer groups more demanding and stressful than the mastery of early socialization and routines of daily living within the home. For the high activity or distractible child, the reverse was most often the case. In the home, as indicated in the previous chapter, the high activity child often met with demands and pressure for control and limitation of his motor activity. The distractible child often met increasing parental annoyance as he "forgot" to come to meals when called, neglected to put his clothes or playthings away, or took excessive time to get dressed while everyone waited impatiently for him. While some of these or similar issues arose in peer group activities, the positive aspects of these temperamental traits were often more in evidence here than in the home situation. The high activity child often became a favored choice for the group because of his lively and spirited motor energy. The distractible youngster with his quick and expressive awareness of new stimuli often became a welcome member or even a leader in a social group because of his sensitive responsiveness to the feelings and desires of others.

The discussion in this chapter has attempted to indicate the increasing differentiation in the patterns of temperament-environment interaction as the developing child moves from simpler to more complex life situations and experiences. The different interactive permutations and combinations detailed in this and subsequent chapters can really only hint at the richness and complexity of outcomes that result from the interplay of so many influences—organismic, family, peer group, school, sociocultural, accidental events, etc.—each with its own wide range of variability. This phenomenon bears significantly on a number of important theoretical questions which will be considered at the end of this volume.

REFERENCES

1. R. A. Spitz, *The First Year of Life* (New York: International Universities Press, 1965), pp. 150-162.
2. T. Lidz, *The Person* (New York: Basic Books, 1968), p. 139.
3. D. Levy, *Maternal Overprotection* (New York: Columbia University Press, 1943).
4. T. Lidz, *op. cit.*, p. 223.
5. A. Thomas, H. G. Birch, S. Chess and L. C. Robbins, "Individuality in Responses of Children to Similar Environmental Situations," *Am. J. Psychiatr.*, 117:434-441 (1961).

8

Temperament and school functioning

With the onset of formal schooling, a new and more complex hierarchy of stimuli, demands and expectations begins to influence the developmental process. The elementary school setting becomes a new center of struggle, adaptation and mastery, rivaling and even surpassing the significance of the home and playground for the child's psychological development.

The school makes a number of new demands on the child, separately and in combination. These include the mastery of increasingly complex cognitive tasks, and the simultaneous requirements to adapt to a new geographic setting, to strange adults in unfamiliar roles, and to a host of new rules and regulations. Peer group activities become more elaborate and challenging, even to the child with previous nursery school experience.

Temperament plays an important role in shaping the course of a child's school functioning, as it did in earlier socialization demands. Other workers besides ourselves have indicated the importance of temperamental issues in the adaptation to school (1, 2, 3). In the school setting, however, the influence of temperament, as of all other significant factors, is part of a much more elaborate and varied interactional process, when compared to the simple dynamic interplay in

93

sleep and feeding regularization, toilet-training, etc., in infancy, or even the more complex issues in the preschool period. Temperamental characteristics will help determine the individual child's response to a new and demanding cognitive school task, but so will his intellectual and perceptual capacities, level of motivation, psychodynamic patterns, teacher characteristics, curriculum structure and nature of peer social relations. The same is true of the child's struggle to master the new and more complicated social issues he meets in the school setting.

The complexities of the child-school interaction have been evident in the qualitative analysis of our NYLS data. Quantitative analysis has been useful, but the richness of the school data on the individual children has required qualitative study for their full exploitation.

QUANTITATIVE STUDIES

A quantitative analysis of the correlation between children's temperamental characteristics at five years of age and their academic achievement scores in reading and arithmetic at various points in their schooling was done by Sam Korn of the NYLS (4). The academic achievement data were obtained by gathering, from each school the youngsters had attended, their scores in all standard tests that had been administered. Because of the wide array of tests and test ages in these data, it was not possible to generate large enough subgroups of children for statistical analysis of those who had taken the same test at the same age or grade level. To deal with this problem, the results of all achievement tests administered to each child were combined for school grades 1-3 and 4-6 and separately for reading and arithmetic. This gave each child four academic achievement scores: reading and arithmetic, for grades 1-3 and grades 4-6. Adequate achievement score data were available on 116 children, 57 boys and 59 girls. In all cases the percentile scores were based on national norms, not on the distribution of scores within the NYLS sample. The Wide Range Achievement Test (WRAT) had also been administered by our research staff psychologist to 79 of the children between the ages of 10-14 years; it was scored separately for reading, spelling and arithmetic. This made a total of seven achievement scores available for each child.

The temperamental scores at age five years, the last year for which they were available, were compared with the academic achievement scores. This showed a substantial relationship between low academic achievement scores and the temperamental characteristics of non-adaptability (four out of seven statistically significant correlations) and withdrawal (five out of seven significant correlations). There were scattered significant correlations beyond the .05 level of confidence for activity level, sensory threshold, intensity of reaction, persistence and attention span. No significant correlations were found for rhythmicity, distractibility or quality of mood.

In addition, no significant correlations were found between temperament and I.Q. score.

This analysis suffered from a number of methodological problems which may have attenuated the significance of the findings. The achievement test scores were obtained from a number of different tests. The schools and ages of the children varied. Furthermore, the temperament measures were employed predictively and temporally concurrent relationships could not be obtained.

It is, nevertheless, of interest that statistically significant correlations were found between low academic achievement scores and the temperamental traits of non-adaptability and withdrawal, but not for high intensity, negative mood, or arhythmicity. The significant relationship, therefore, appears to be with the constellation of the Slow-To-Warm-Up Child and not that of the Difficult Child.

This finding is supported by a study of another sample of 93 children in a suburban middle-class kindergarten (5). Two teachers, each highly experienced in this age group, were asked to rate each child on a Quality of Participation Scale. This rating referred to the child's typical style of reaction to new situations and activities in the classroom and corresponded to a characterization of a quick versus slow-to-warm-up child. Four types of children were defined:

1) The child who plunges into new activities and situations quickly, positively and unhesitantly (plungers).

2) The child who goes along in a positive manner but does not plunge right in (go-alongers).

3) The child who stands on the sidelines waiting, then slowly and gradually gets involved in the new activity (sideliners).

4) The child who remains a non-participator in a new situation for weeks or months (non-participators).

The teachers were also asked to estimate each child's general intellectual level on a seven-point scale ranging from very inferior to very superior. The children had not as yet been given psychometric tests so that neither the teachers nor the investigators had any knowledge of the measured intellectual level. Group I.Q. tests (Kuhlmann-Anderson) were done the following September when the children were in the first grade.

Discrepancies between the teachers' estimates of the children's intellectual levels and the I.Q. scores obtained six months later were compared with the teachers' ratings on the Quality of Participation Scale. The intelligence of six children was overestimated by the teachers. Five of these six were rated as *plungers*, the sixth as a *sideliner*. The intelligence of 50 children was underestimated by the teachers. Eleven of these 50 were rated as *plungers*, 28 as *go-alongers*, and 11 as *sideliners*. Furthermore, the underestimation was greater for the *sideliners* than for the *plungers*. (The teachers rated only one child in the total sample as a non-participator, and this child moved out of the school district before the I.Q. test was administered.)

These findings are summarized in Tables 1-7.

It would appear from the study that teachers may tend to underestimate the intelligence of a Slow-To-Warm-Up Child. This is consistent with similar misjudgments by teachers of several such children in the NYLS. Such incorrect estimates may lead teachers to expect a lower level of academic achievement from such a youngster which may then affect the child's actual learning (6).

Seegars has developed a behavior checklist to rate five characteristics of the elementary school child (7). Three of the categories are identified as the Easy Child, the Difficult Child, and the Slow-To-Warm-Up Child. The criteria for these three constellations are derived from the NYLS, though there are a few specific differences in the criteria. Seegars labels his other two categories as the Environmentalist Child and the Emotionally Fragile Child. The checklist

TABLE 1

Teacher Categorizations of Quality of Participation[a]

Category	N
Plungers	25
Go-alongers	47
Sideliners	20
Non-participators	1
Total	93

[a]One teacher categorized almost twice as many of her children *plungers* as *sideliners*, while the other had one and a half times as many *sideliners* as *plungers*. When their categorizations are pooled, however, they are approximately symmetrically distributed over the first three "points" of the participation scale.

TABLE 2

Teacher Estimates of Intelligence

Estimates	N
Superior	3
Above Average	26
Average	55
Below Average	8
Total	92[a]

[a]One teacher failed to estimate the intelligence of one of her children.

TABLE 3

Kuhlmann-Anderson I.Q.'s

Score	N
Very Superior (130+)	9
Superior (120-129)	25
High Average (110-119)	23
Average (90-119)	28
Low Average (80-89)	4
Total	89[a]

[a]Four children moved from the school district during the summer between kindergarten and 1st grade.

TABLE 4

Relationship Between Teachers' Estimates of Intelligence and
Kuhlmann-Anderson I.Q.'s

I.Q.'s	Estimates of Intelligence			
	Below Average	Average	Above Average	Superior
Very Superior		3	5	1
Superior		14	8	2
High Average	1	15	7	
Average	4	19	5	
Low Average	3	1		
Total	8	52	25	3

TABLE 5

Relationship Between Teachers' Categorizations of Quality of
Participation and Kuhlmann-Anderson I.Q.'s

I.Q.'s	Quality of Participation			
	Non-participator	Sideliner	Go-alonger	Plunger
Very Superior		1	3	5
Superior		3	18	4
High Average		4	12	7
Average		7	13	8
Low Average		4		
Total		19	46	24

TABLE 6

Relationship Between Teachers' Estimates of Intelligence and
Categorizations of Quality of Participation

Quality of Participation	Estimates of Intelligence			
	Below Average	Average	Above Average	Superior
Plunger		8	15	2
Go-alonger	2	32	11	1
Sideliner	6	14		
Non-participator		1		
Total	8	55	26	3

TABLE 7

Correlations Among Teachers' Estimates of Intelligence,
Kuhlmann-Anderson I.Q.'s, and Teachers' Categorizations
of Quality of Participation

	Estimated Intelligence	Measured Intelligence
Quality of Participation	.54**	.24*
Estimated Intelligence		.49**

*p < .05
**p < .01

was filled out by the teachers of 508 children in grades 3 through 6 and the findings compared with academic achievement as measured by school grades and with I.Q. level as measured by the California Mental Maturity Scale. In the three temperament categories, the Easy Children were the highest achievers, the Difficult Children lowest, and the Slow-To-Warm-Up Children were intermediate. There was no correlation with I.Q. level.

QUALITATIVE STUDIES

The parents in the NYLS uniformly gave great importance to the children's school functioning and academic achievement. Any evidence of a school problem was usually brought quickly to the research staff for consultation and advice. The types of difficulty varied greatly as would be expected and in a number of instances involved issues such as delayed reading readiness in which the child's temperament was not a significant factor. The present discussion, however, will be limited to the school problems in which the child's temperament played an important role.

Empirically, five general patterns of difficulty involving temperament could be defined as the child moved into the formal school learning situation: school problems which essentially duplicated those in the infancy and preschool periods; minor issues at home which became major ones in school; no issue at home, but issue in school; behavior pattern encouraged at home, but source of problem in school; behavior pattern disapproved at home but approved in school. These different sequences of child-environment interaction can each be illustrated by specific examples.

The Difficult Child with his slow adaptability and intense negative reaction to new situations presented the teacher with the same need for understanding and quiet firm patience as was required of his parents at home. In those instances where the parents had appreciated the temperamental issues and had handled them adequately, they were often helpful in orienting the first teacher to the significance of the child's initial reaction to school. Where the parents, on the contrary, had become entangled in an unhealthy interaction with the child at home, the same sequence was more likely to occur in school. In general, the adaptive course of the Difficult Children tended to be smoother at school than in the earlier years at home. Their biological irregularity which had contributed to the difficulties in establishing regular feeding and sleep routines and bladder and bowel control did not present any significant problem in the school schedule. Experienced and competent teachers and principals could often pragmatically identify these children accurately and expect them to eventually make a positive and even enthusiastic adaptation to school. These teachers were also not likely to feel guilty or intimidated by the initial behavior of a Difficult Child, as was so often the case with the parents.

These considerations may help explain the lack of significant correlation found in the quantitative comparison of the Difficult Child temperament and academic achievement reported above. One can speculate that the story might be different in inner-city poverty area schools. With teachers harassed and burdened by the frequently inadequate resources and working conditions in these schools, the Difficult Child may not find the sympathetic and patient approach the youngsters in the NYLS generally found in their schools. We do not have the data, however, to attempt to verify this speculation.

The highly active or distractible child may also have similar problems adapting to the demands of school as he did in the home setting. Children with difficulties in sitting quietly or following directions without distraction can create annoyance and impatience in teachers as in parents. In several instances these children did poorly in very permissive unstructured school settings. The highly active child was allowed to roam at will and the distractible youngster was permitted to turn his attention to whatever caught his eye or ear. The children did not "settle down" spontaneously, and learned little until structured, consistent, though flexible, demands were finally made on them.

The temperamental trait of low or high persistence and attention span usually presented minor problems in the preschool years at home, but sometimes made for greater difficulties in school. The needs and expectations of the family in the child's early years were generally not significantly affected by whether his attention span was short or long or whether he stuck to a difficult task or gave up quickly. Whichever his response, the child did learn to toilet, and dress and feed himself without great stress. For the persistent preschool child, there were also few occasions in which his absorption in an activity inconvenienced the family greatly.

In school, however, prolonged concentration was usually expected in academic tasks, and this demand became excessively stressful for the child with low persistence and short attention span, especially if combined with high distractibility. A similar problem developed at home for such a child if the parents insisted that he sit down with his homework and finish it without interruption. Sustained pressure by teacher and parent for a level of persistence which was impossible for the non-persistent child to attain led inevitably to anxiety, self-derogation and defensive techniques to avoid any difficult task performance. By contrast, where the teacher and parent understood and accepted the child's limits, task assignments were structured so they did not exceed the child's concentration span, and learning proceeded successfully.

The highly persistent child with a long attention span, on the other hand, often seemed to be made for learning. Parents and teachers only had to guide the child gently to maintain his steady and persistent effort to learn whatever was put before him. Problems did develop, however, if such a child insisted on continuing an activity and the teacher demanded that he shift to the next scheduled activity with the rest of the class. Such forcible interruption of his absorbed attention and effort, whether at home or in school, is typically a source of intense frustration for a very persistent child. The expression of this frustration in tantrums or other explosive reactions sometimes led to the child being labeled by the school as anxious or a disciplinary problem.

For the Slow-To-Warm-Up Child, as indicated in the previous chapter, excessive stress typically developed with the onset of active peer relations if there was a demand for quick adaptability. This issue sometimes arose with play or nursery groups in the preschool years, but in other instances not until the child entered first grade. There he was also confronted with the need to adapt to all the unfamiliar routines and expectations involved in formal learning. As we have indicated earlier, the slow-to-warm-up pattern was easily misjudged by teachers as evidence of inferior intelligence. One such girl in the NYLS, Jane, was accelerated to the third grade at the end of the first grade because of her superior intelligence and quick learning. In the first months of the third grade her work was unsatisfactory and she appeared apathetic and disinterested in learning. The teacher judged that the acceleration had been a mistake and recommended to the mother that Jane be put back to the second grade. The mother, who knew and appreciated her daughter's temperament, told the teacher that this slow beginning was typical of her child, that the acceleration had confronted Jane with new classmates and new academic subjects, and that if the teacher were patient, her daughter would soon begin to improve. As the teacher reported this story several months later to our research staff interviewer, "I thought this mother was just making excuses for her daughter, but I decided to wait. And you know, the mother was right. Jane has now caught up to the rest of the class, is alert, interested and involved with the other pupils."

Low activity level was a temperamental trait which usually created no special stresses in positive adaptation at home or with peer groups in the preschool years, but sometimes became a problem in the school setting. Parents might wish that such a youngster were more lively at times, but on many other occasions in the early years this motor slowness could even be very convenient in caring for the child. Problems did develop at home for a few such children as they grew older if the family grew impatient and highly critical of the child's slowness in dressing, finishing dinner, or getting ready for a family expedition.

Even if the family accepted and tolerated the low activity level, such a child was sometimes confronted with a very different situation in school. If his slowness was conspicuous and the school program rigidly and tightly scheduled, he easily became the butt of the teacher's impatience and his classmates' ridicule as the class "slowpoke." In the case of one girl in the NYLS, Kate, this slowness of movement was especially prominent and combined with the slow-to-warm-up pattern. Kate was labeled "sluggish" by the kindergarten teacher and the slow movements and adaptability misjudged as intellectual slowness. The teacher reluctantly promoted her to first grade where the new teacher felt at first that this had been a mistake because Kate was so "slow and plodding." By the end of the year, however, it was clear that the girl was intellectually competent and learned well. This positive judgment was passed on to succeeding teachers and Kate had no further problems with teacher attitudes.

Most of the youngsters with the Easy Child temperamental pattern adapted quickly and smoothly to the demands of formal learning as they had to those of early socialization and peer group activity in the preschool years.

In some instances, these children adapted to special idiosyncratic goals and standards of their parents all too easily. Their behavior patterns met unqualified approval at home, but caused conflict and dissonance with the different standards of the outside world. In the previous chapter we described how this had negatively affected the child's relationship to his peer group. In one of the cases cited, Isobel, school functioning was especially affected. This was the girl whose parents set special store by self-expression and spontaneity and the right of all persons to their own individuality and uniqueness. The youngster, a very Easy Child temperamentally, took her cues decisively from these parental attitudes. She became a delightfully expressive and charming young person, with many interests and activities. However, Isobel's disregard of externally imposed rules and the demand for conformity to group modes of functioning alienated her from organized play activities and seriously interfered with formal learning in the first school grade. She ignored the teacher's schedule

and participated indifferently or not at all in the basic group classroom learning activities. She was spontaneously responsive only to
an individualized relationship to the teacher, in effect looking for a
private tutor. When Isobel fell far behind in reading achievement,
in spite of superior intelligence, her parents, who also prized academic achievement, were responsive to our counseling that they
modify their approach to their daughter. The girl, being the Easy
Child that she was, quickly learned appropriate patterns of group
functioning, and her peer group and academic functioning changed
dramatically for the better.

Another Easy Child with difficulties in formal learning, was the
girl mentioned in Chapter 6, Kaye, whose mother was determined that her daughter should not be subjected to the rigid and
arbitrary parental authority she herself had experienced as a child.
For the mother, this meant avoiding, and even openly rejecting,
training Kaye in task performance. The girl became a charming and
socially vivacious individual who used these attributes to sidestep
demands on her. Her response to requests to clean up or help with a
simple household task was to smile, engage her parents in conversa-
tion, or turn the request into a game. The parents were pleased to
respond, forgot or shrugged off their original request and the interchange became pleasant and frictionless.

In the preschool years, these social techniques served Kaye well
with her playmates and especially older children and adults. Unfortunately, as she grew older, her ineptness with task performance
crystallized progressively into immaturity of functioning, made
worse by social diversionary techniques. This difficulty with task
mastery interfered more and more with her peer relations. It was
especially disastrous in the school setting. Her problem in following
instructions and focusing on academic achievement resulted in increasingly poor academic functioning. Unfortunately, Kaye's parents,
in contrast to Isobel's, were unresponsive to counseling and guidance. As a result, Kaye's development through the elementary school
years was characterized by marginal academic achievement, a self-
evaluation as "stupid," and increasing social difficulties and loneli-
ness.

These two Easy Child vignettes may make it appear as if we are emphasizing "conformity" and "adjustment" as necessary goals—a charge often made against psychiatrists. To the contrary, the prime thesis of our research and the major thrust of this volume is that a child's deviation from a single stereotyped concept of normality may be the healthy expression of his temperamental individuality and should be recognized and respected as such. However, individuality of personality does not develop in a vacuum. Every society sets goals and standards for its children. Some are desirable and foster healthy and creative psychological growth and fulfillment. Others may be restrictive, even corrupting in their effects, and in conflict with those that are positive and desirable. Parents, teachers, pediatricians and mental health professionals have the responsibility—often difficult and complex—of helping the children in their care to distinguish between constructive and destructive standards and goals. But just as it is pernicious to demand that every individual conform strictly to his social group demands, no matter what they may be, so it is unrealistic and self-defeating to encourage generalized *a priori* goals of "spontaneity" and "self-fulfillment" abstracted from meaningful social contexts. Thus, Isobel became more self-expressive, more spontaneous, more able to pursue her own interests effectively *after* she learned the necessity of accepting certain group rules and routines. Kaye, who did not learn this, progressively lost her ability at constructive self-fulfillment.

The final pattern of school difficulty versus home functioning considered here concerns those temperamental patterns disapproved within the home but approved at school. This was perhaps most evident in the persistent child with long attention span. It is true, as cited above in this chapter, that school problems could develop if such a child was severely frustrated by the teacher's frequent forcible interruption of his absorbed attention and effort. Otherwise, these temperamental traits, when combined with high motivation for learning, are usually significant assets in the school setting. Such a child gives high priority to the teacher's instructions and assignments, concentrates his efforts on carrying them through to completion, and does not get distracted by other classroom diversions. At home this behavior may also meet with approval and encouragement. In some instances, however, critical or anxious judgments may be made by parents, depending on their own standards and priorities. The youngster may become the victim of repeated scolding and pressure because he insists on sticking with his chosen activity when it is time for a family excursion, dinner or bedtime. The parents may set high store by social peer group activity and worry that their persistent child gets so absorbed in a solitary academic activity that he refuses to join his friends in play or socializing. Or the parents may have heard of the dangers of "overachievement" and conclude that their child's top standing in his class, surpassing that of "brighter" classmates, is an ominous omen of psychological disturbance. We have over the years seen these adverse judgments in parents who come for consultation over their children's "problems." Some accepted the evaluation that the child was normal with a promising future even if he plugged away in school and sometimes chose a solitary activity over peer group play. Other parents were themselves so much the victims of the conventional wisdom that "overachievement" is pathological and that the All-American boy or girl is always gregarious that they could not reorient their attitudes and judgments.

In several children in the NYLS with the temperamental pattern of the Difficult Child, discrepancy between parental and teacher attitudes has also been evident. In one striking instance the father and, to a lesser degree, the mother were highly critical and excessively and rigidly demanding of the daughter because of her irregular biological patterns, her intense negative reactions to the new, and her slow adaptability. The youngster developed severe neurotic symptoms and psychotherapy was instituted with modest improvement. In school she met with more flexible and understanding teacher attitudes and also developed musical and dramatic talent. As the teachers encouraged these interests, her intense emotional expressiveness now became an asset. Fortunately, the parents also gave high value to these artistic talents and responded favorably to the teachers' enthusiastic reports of their daughter's activities and accomplishments. Their criticisms and inappropriate expectations were replaced by acceptance and praise, and the girl's neurotic symptoms improved dramatically.

The above discussion emphasizes some of the many reasons for the disparity, or even contradiction, that is so often evident between a child's behavior at home or in a social peer group and in the school setting. Our longitudinal data emphasize the complexity and variability of the interaction between child and school, even in the early school grades. These complexities in coping with school experiences increase enormously, of course, as the child goes from elementary school, to high school, and to college. This makes any simplistic and unidimensional model, whether it concentrates exclusively on temperament, psychodynamic defenses, neurochemical mechanisms, or sociological influences, entirely inadequate for the understanding of the course of normal or pathological school functioning.

REFERENCES

1. D. C. Ross, "Poor School Achievement: A Psychiatric Study and Classification," *Clinical Pediatrics*, 5:109 (1966).
2. M. Rutter, "Emotional Disorder and Educational Under-Achievement," *Arch. Dis. in Childhood*, 49:249-256 (1974).
3. J. E. Seegars, Jr., "Identification and Intervention in Child Personality Temperament." In preparation.
4. S. Korn, "Temperament and Academic Achievement." Unpublished data.
5. E. M. Gordon and A. Thomas, "Children's Behavioral Style and the Teacher's Appraisal of Their Intelligence," *J. Sch. Psychol.*, 5:292-300 (1967).
6. R. Rosenthal and L. Jacobsen, *Pygmalion in the Classroom* (New York: Holt, Rinehart and Winston, 1969).
7. J. E. Seegars, Jr., *op. cit.*

9

Temperament and

health care

practices

The health care professional—pediatrician, general practitioner, clinic doctor or baby nurse—is usually a most influential adviser to the parents, especially in the child's early years. It is this health care professional, and not the psychiatrist, who is likely to be consulted consistently and frequently on the management of problems in feeding, sleeping, weaning, and toilet-training. It is this doctor or nurse who takes the major responsibility for illnesses or accidents that the child may suffer.

The doctor's and nurse's regular contact with many normal children from birth onward makes the phenomenon of behavioral individuality evident to them, as it does to many parents. This empirical experience impressed many health care professionals with the significance of such individual differences in the young child for his management and care. It is therefore no surprise that we found a positive reception from pediatricians and nurses from the very beginning of our work on temperament. We might add that we found the same understanding and responsiveness in experienced nursery and elementary school teachers who, in many ways, have similar regular contact with and responsibility for normal children.

The increasing involvement of the pediatrician in recent years in the management of psychological problems of children has been well stated by Gregg:

> The role of the pediatrician has undergone drastic change. Today he is less often called on to perform the traditional duties of diagnosing and prescribing for children with life-threatening organic illnesses than in previous times; more of his time is devoted to parents who question the normalcy of their children's growth, intellectual and emotional development, and their personal adequacy in child rearing. This role change has been attributed to the loss of cultural guidelines usually available to young families in more stable societies, and as a consequence they require much professional counseling in regard to parenting. Since the situation will in all likelihood intensify, the pediatrician cannot anticipate relief from the role of family counselor unless he chooses to relegate this responsibility to other professionals, a complicated and questionable solution (1).

The responsibilities and activities of the pediatrician as a family counselor have many aspects and ramifications. This is also true of the family physician, and of those clinic doctors and public health nurses who are able to maintain regular contact with a family. The present discussion, as is true throughout this volume, will focus on their professional activities with families as they are influenced by the phenomenon of the child's temperamental individuality. The issues will be refined in terms of the pediatrician's functioning, though the same considerations apply in general to other child health care professionals.

The pediatrician's role with regard to the child's temperamental individuality can be considered under a number of headings: advice on child-care practices; reassurance to parents; routine examinations and procedures; management of minor problems; evaluation of the acutely ill child; management of the chronically ill or handicapped child; and preventive counseling.

In carrying out these activities it is necessary, of course, for the pediatrician to be able to assess the child's temperamental characteristics with a reasonable expenditure of time. To a large extent this can be accomplished through the information the pediatrician obtains from the parents and from his own observations of the child in the course of his ongoing care and management of the child. In our own contact with a number of pediatricians, as with parents and teachers, we have been impressed at their ability to rate a child's temperamental qualities, once they were familiar with the categories and the behavioral criteria for their rating. Furthermore, as Gregg has pointed out, the pediatric examination, whether in the office, clinic, or at home, provides an opportunity to observe the child's behavior in a number of situations in sequence. This is especially true in the office or clinic, in which the child's reactions can be observed when he is brought into the unfamiliar consulting or examining room by the mother or other familiar adult, meets the pediatrician, sits on the mother's lap while the history is being taken, is undressed and weighed, is placed on the examining seat or table, is given a toy, is subjected to the routine physical examination and procedures, and is redressed. Gregg reports that in this observational setting it was possible to rate activity level, mood, intensity, approach-withdrawal and distractibility. She was unable to differentiate between persistence and distractibility consistently. Threshold to stimuli was too difficult to evaluate in a noisy clinic; it might perhaps be different in a quiet office setting. Adaptability and rhythmicity were not applicable since they depended on behavioral characteristics over time. In some cases a rating of adaptability might be possible if the child's initial reaction to the pediatric setting were negative and the contact were sufficiently long to permit observation of the presence or absence of adaptation.

An important aid to the pediatrician in evaluating temperament now exists in the form of Carey's parent questionnaire for the infancy period (2). This questionnaire is described in detail in the next chapter. It usually requires about 20 minutes of the parent's time, can be scored in 10 minutes, and all nine categories can be rated. The questionnaire has been used successfully by Carey routinely in his pediatric practice, and has also been utilized by a number of other investigators, as reported in various sections of this volume.

In addition to filling out the questionnaires, Carey also asked the mothers of 101 infants to describe briefly their general impression of their infants' temperament and to give an overall rating of their babies in each of the nine categories. He found differences between the mother's global judgments and the questionnaire ratings in about 25 percent of the cases. In most instances, the discrepancy involved babies with a Difficult Child temperament pattern delineated by the mother's responses to the specific questionnaire items versus the mother's general impressions which minimized these behavioral difficulties. A smaller number of cases showed differences in the opposite direction, namely, the mother giving her child's general rating more toward the Difficult Child pattern than indicated by the questionnaire scores. The occurrence of such discrepancies appeared to bear no relationship to the mother's previous experience with babies, her educational level, a history of medical problems during pregnancy, or with the baby, or whether the global judgments were made before or after filling out the questionnaire. The more difficult the baby, as indicated by the questionnaire rating, the more likely was the mother to make such misjudgments in her global evaluation.

It was Carey's evaluation that the questionnaire data were more accurate and he felt that where mothers minimized their children's difficult temperament pattern "an important factor may have been the mothers' wishes to make their babies seem more socially desirable."

In general, our own experience is consonant with Carey's judgments. Data obtained by questions regarding specific concrete and descriptive items of behavior are much more likely to be reliable and valid than data obtained from global opinions and impressions.

The pediatrician's role as a family counselor is usually first manifest in the area of child-care practices. Because he assumes responsibility for well baby care in the infancy period, the parent naturally turns to him for advice and guidance regarding the sequential steps in feeding schedules, the development of regular sleep patterns, and the initiation and carrying through of toilet-training. Problems in other child care areas, such as negative reactions to the bath, resistance to dressing or undressing, or difficulty in training the young child to avoid dangerous objects, are frequently brought to the pediatrician for his advice and judgment. If the parent develops confidence in the availability and helpfulness of the pediatrician for guidance with such issues, more complex behavioral problems such as apparent shyness and timidity with adults and other children, frequent temper tantrums, etc., will also be brought to him for advice and guidance.

All pediatricians are aware that babies are different behaviorally from birth onward. Some pediatricians will tend to ignore these differences and their significance if they have embraced enthusiastically one psychological theory or another which postulates invariant universal causes for all children's behavior, especially if such a formulation includes distorted judgments on the pathogenic influences of the mother. Other pediatricians will be skeptical of such theoretical systems and rely on an empirical pragmatic approach to each child and each issue. While this latter approach can be adequate and satisfactory in most instances, its effectiveness can be buttressed and enhanced by an appropriate and valid theoretical framework. Thus, we have found repeatedly that practicing pediatricians have welcomed the formulations of temperamental individuality, have sensed immediately their applicability to their clinical work, and have in a number of cases explored their significance by studies of their own.

The definition of the infant's temperamental characteristics by the pediatrician and parent can be enormously useful in a jointly developed optimal approach to early child care. The pediatrician, more than any other professional, can offer vitally important reassurance to anxious, insecure mothers. For the inexperienced mother who has been bombarded with all the pat formulations which warn that her every move or expression may affect her baby's future mental health, any difficulty or problem in her infant's management may appear ominous indeed. If her child fusses a lot during the night, does not take to new foods or feeding schedules easily, cries when approached by strangers, resists toilet-training or ignores her safety rules, she may all too frequently interpret such difficulties as proof that she is a "bad mother." It is the pediatrician who can step in, evaluate the issue, identify the aspects of the child's temperament that are relevant, and advise the mother appropriately. Guidance of this kind is the most effective kind of reassurance for an anxious mother. By contrast, simply to brush aside the mother's concern with general assurances, "Don't worry, everything will be all right," or "Be patient, your baby will outgrow this," will most often have limited and temporary value.

An infant's responses to new people and procedures, especially if associated with any discomfort or pain, is strongly influenced by his temperamental characteristics. The infant brought to the pediatrician's office for the first time or at subsequent irregular intervals is confronted with a strange place, a number of unfamiliar persons, perhaps unusual sounds, and is then subjected to physical examination and vaccinations which are restraining, discomforting and sometimes painful. Depending on his temperament, the child may fuss quietly and briefly, squirm a bit and then be immediately cheerful once the procedures are completed. Or he may howl loudly from the moment he enters the pediatrician's office, struggle violently during the physical examination and inoculation, take up to several hours to subside, and start up again even more intensely at the next visit. The child with a low activity level will sit quietly in the waiting room. The high activity youngster, by contrast, will fidget, jump around, try to poke into drawers and closets, and make a nuisance of himself if he has to wait a long time before the doctor sees him.

The pediatrician who evaluates the temperament of his patients and understands its implications will be in a good position to minimize the distress or trauma of each child's office visit. With the Easy Child, no special management approach is necessary. However, even such an adaptable child may be overwhelmed if the busy doctor rushes him too quickly through the office procedures. The Slow-To-Warm-Up Child should be given time to get used to the waiting room, and further time in the examining room before proceeding with the physical examination. The highly active child should be seen quickly. If he has to wait, he should be given toys and space to move around in without disturbing others. The Difficult Child should also be given a warm-up period, but should still be expected to respond to the examination or inoculation with loud and long protests. The painfulness or discomfort of any of the office procedures should certainly be minimized for all patients, but this should be a special concern for the child with a low sensory threshold.

Many of the minor problems of a young child brought to the pediatrician's attention are significantly related to temperamental issues

(3). Frequent night waking, as reported by Carey (4), is more likely to occur in an infant with a low sensory threshold. He suggests two possible explanations of this relationship: The low threshold child's greater responsiveness to daytime stimulation makes him more arousable at night; or the infant is more responsive to internal and external stimuli at night as well. Carey recommends dealing with the problem by reducing environmental stimulation before bedtime and, if necessary, during the night.

The prolonged loud crying spells of the infant with colic present a difficult and disturbing management problem to the parents. In our own experience, this syndrome appeared related to the Difficult Child temperament and not to pathological maternal attitudes, as was so often assumed in the past. Our impression is confirmed by Carey's work which also suggests a relationship to low sensory threshold as well as to the Difficult Child pattern. The pediatrician can provide much needed reassurance and support to the parents in such cases, in addition to any other specific therapeutic measures he utilizes.

We have seen a sleep problem develop in several Easy Children after a minor acute illness. Such children, previously sleeping well through the night, awoke frequently when ill, crying with the discomfort of their acute symptoms. Parental care naturally involved picking the child up each time, soothing him and alleviating the discomfort. Following recovery from the illness, the child continued to awaken crying each night. The parents continued to pick him up and soothe him in the same way, now interpreting the awakening as a sign of anxiety. Evaluation of the problem indicated that there was no other evidence of anxiety and that the night awakening undoubtedly reflected the quick adaptability of the child to the new nighttime behavior established during his acute illness. Because he was an Easy Child, it was also predictable that his night crying would quickly disappear if he were no longer picked up. And indeed this was the outcome when the parents followed this recommendation.

The response of a child to the irritation of a skin rash can be significantly influenced by temperamental traits. The intense reactor may cry loudly and complain vigorously even if treatment is proceeding effectively, and this reaction should not lead doctor or parent into a misjudgment of the treatment procedures. The child with a low sensory threshold may have great difficulty in obeying the injunctions not to rub or scratch the irritated skin, and special measures may be necessary to reduce the sensory stimulation from the rash.

The above instances illustrate, but by no means exhaust, the many ways in which the child's temperament influences the response to physical symptoms and the management of minor ailments. Every pediatrician can document this relationship extensively from his own clinical experience.

A major professional responsibility of the pediatrician is the evaluation of the gravity of the symptoms of an acutely ill child. Is the sudden high fever the first sign of a serious illness or of a minor upper respiratory infection? Is the lethargy an indication of severe toxicity or the reaction to the discomfort and malaise of a more benign condition? Are the acute restlessness and thrashing about an ominous sign or the reaction to acute pain? Certainly these judgments depend primarily on careful diagnostic clinical evaluation. But there are many occasions in which a knowledge of the child's temperamental characteristics can be helpful in making these judgments. All other things being equal (which they often are not!), if the child's behavior when acutely ill is qualitatively different from his usual temperamental style, this is a more serious indication than if his behavior is similar though exaggerated. Mothers are aware of this issue pragmatically when they express their concern to the doctor because the acutely ill child "is not behaving like his usual self."

The high-activity, high-intensity child who is restless, thrashes around vigorously and complains loudly when taken ill is showing a quantitative exaggeration of his usual temperamental traits. The same behavior in a low-activity, low-intensity child represents a qualitative change from his normal temperament. By and large, the qualitative change is more likely to reflect a more severe acute physical change than is the simple quantitative exaggeration of the child's usual temperament. The same considerations apply in reverse, that is, listlessness in a normally high-activity child is a more ominous sign than an increase in activity. In a similar vein, the complaint of intense pain in a high threshold child is likely to have substantial significance, while the same complaint of a low threshold child may be significant or may represent the reaction to a relatively minor irritation.

While these and similar temperamental phenomena are not the decisive issues in the evaluation of the acutely ill child, we have seen many instances in which their consideration has been of significant value to doctors and nurses in making their diagnostic judgments. We have indeed been impressed over the years at the astuteness of doctors and nurses in their utilization of temperamental data as part of their evaluation of a sick child.

Complicating the above considerations is the phenomenon some mothers have reported to us. They have observed, no doubt accurately, that their child's behavioral pattern is different when ill, but also typical for him. This seems to involve one kind of expression of temperament when healthy and another when acutely ill. Thus, the manifestations of intense negative responses when ill may be the expression of extreme discomfort, in contrast to the vigor and liveliness of intense mood expression at other times. Here, too, both doctor and parent must be alert to the significance of the acutely ill youngster's behavior.

In the management of the more chronically ill or physically handicapped child, temperamental issues are not infrequently of major importance. The ease with which a child can follow a regime of restricted physical activity and engage in substitute sedentary occupations or adapt to the stringent demand of a prolonged period of bed rest is strongly influenced by his temperamental characteristics. Low-activity and highly adaptive children will find such regimes much easier to tolerate than high-activity or slowly adaptive youngsters. The child who is persistent and has a long attention span can be content once his interest is engaged in a sedentary activity. On the other hand, if it is necessary to terminate a more physically exhausting activity in which a persistent youngster has become absorbed, this may be difficult and stressful. The distractible child will be much more easily diverted from an undesirable activity, or one which should be time-limited, but it may be difficult to keep him interested in any single sedentary occupation for more than a short period of time. Where hospitalization is necessary, the adaptations to the multiple new people and situations that this requires may be especially stressful to the Difficult or Slow-To-Warm-Up Child.

It is important for the physician, together with the parents and nurses, to formulate schedules and routines for the physically restricted child which will be most consonant with the youngster's temperament. This will insure the maximum cooperation of the child and the best assurance that the necessary management procedures will be carried through. It will also minimize the danger that the stress imposed by the illness or handicap will precipitate a reactive behavior disorder.

Finally, the pediatrician is in a strategically influential position to guide the family on a preventive level for the benefit of the child's physical and mental health. It is the pediatrician who is the professional most likely to counsel and influence the family with regard to their youngster's nutritional, immunological, psychological and related needs. He is in a position to detect the first signs of unhealthy physical or emotional developmental trends and to advise the family as to the most desirable remedial measures.

With regard to psychological issues, especially in the young child, temperamental aspects play an especially significant role in these preventive activities of the pediatrician. Two goals are paramount in this regard: the achievement of a goodness of fit between parental attitudes and practices and the child's temperamental traits; and the alleviation of inappropriate parental guilt and anxiety when the child shows behavioral patterns which deviate from the stereotype of what is normal and optimal for that sociocultural group. Both these issues have been spelled out in this and preceding chapters. It is the physician or baby nurse who can usually be the most effective and influential parent counselor for the benefit of the child's optimal psychological development.

REFERENCES

1. G. A. Gregg, "Clinical Experience with Efforts to Define Individual Differences in Temperament," *Individual Differences in Children*, ed., J. C. Westman (New York: John Wiley & Sons, 1973), pp. 306-322.
2. W. B. Carey, "A Simplified Method for Measuring Infant Temperament," *J. Pediatrics*, 77:188-194 (1970).
3. W. B. Carey, "Clinical Applications of Infant Temperament Measurements," *J. Pediatrics*, 81:823-828 (1972).
4. W. B. Carey, "Night Waking and Temperament in Infancy," *J. Pediatrics*, 84:756-758 (1974).

10

Measurement and

rating of

temperament

Our own original work in developing methods for the identification and rating of temperamental characteristics necessarily involved rather elaborate data collection and data analysis procedures.
No other systematically tested protocols for this purpose existed in
the literature at the time we began to explore the issue of individual
differences in early childhood. Several pretests were carried out before the final methodology for our longitudinal study was elaborated.
Our first volume, *Behavioral Individuality in Early Childhood* (1),
reproduced our final data collection interview protocol for the infancy period, the criteria and methods of item scoring, and the use
of preponderance, ranks model and percent-rank index schemes of
data analysis. The interview protocols and scoring criteria were
modified as necessary for parents and teachers of older children and
a weighted score scheme for data analysis was adopted (2). These
modifications, however, did not alter the painstaking and time-consuming nature of the interview and scoring methods. If anything,
these procedures became even more extensive in order to encompass
the increasingly varied and complex behavioral repertoire of the
older child.

As the findings of the NYLS on the pertinence of temperament for normal and deviant development have become disseminated, there has been an increasing number of requests from researchers, clinicians and educators in this country and abroad for shorter methods of measuring and rating temperament. Such methods, especially if put in the form of short questionnaires, would make the determination of temperament economically feasible for research workers in normal and deviant child development, for child psychiatrists and pediatricians dealing with problems of parental practice and behavior disorders in children, and for educators working with nursery and elementary school children.

Because of this need for short rating scales and other methods for measuring temperament, a great deal of attention has been paid to this issue by a number of workers in the past few years. We ourselves have also turned our efforts in this direction. The present chapter will summarize this work to date. The material to be presented focuses on the early and middle childhood years. Lesser attention thus far has been paid to the elaboration of rating methods for older children and adults.

CAREY QUESTIONNAIRE FOR INFANCY PERIOD

A short questionnaire for rating temperament in infancy has been developed by Dr. William B. Carey, a pediatrician associated with the Children's Hospital of Philadelphia (3, 4, 5). Carey felt the need for such a questionnaire because "the observant pediatrician soon learns that babies are not all alike physiologically or psychologically, even at birth. In helping mothers take care of their infants and children, he should make allowances for their behavioral style. . . . No practical clinical method has yet been made available for obtaining information that is both objective and comprehensive" (6).

In his review of the literature Carey found only the approach of our NYLS to be an appropriate basis for developing a useful clinical instrument. Utilizing the material of our interview protocol, he set up a three-point multiple choice questionnaire for the infancy period, with 70 items, from which the nine temperamental categories could be rated. The total ratings in each category were reduced to a single score between zero and two for that category, corresponding to the

TABLE 1

	Carey Questionnaire	NYLS interview (Period I: mean age 5.9 months)
Activity	0.52 ± 0.32	0.80
Rhythmicity	0.53 ± 0.46	0.56
Adaptability	0.35 ± 0.26	0.50
Approach	0.48 ± 0.35	0.67
Threshold	1.08 ± 0.39	1.20
Intensity	1.05 ± 0.32	1.21
Mood	0.40 ± 0.25	0.83
Distractibility	0.57 ± 0.32	0.59
Persistence	0.69 ± 0.38	0.40

weighted scores used in the NYLS. Appendix A reproduces the Carey questionnaire and scoring key.

Carey used 101 subjects to standardize his questionnaire. These comprised babies between four and eight months of age seen in his private practice in one year. The sample was primarily middle-class; 66 were males and 35 females. The average time for completion of the questionnaire by the mother was slightly over 20 minutes. The scoring took eight to ten minutes.

The means and standard deviations for the ratings on the nine categories in these 101 infants were calculated and compared with those of the NYLS.

Carey has reported an expansion of this original sample to 200 infants with similar age and demographic characteristics (7). The mean values for the nine categories with this expanded group show no significant differences from those in Table 1. The largest change in mean value for any category was 0.03 on the 0 to 2 scale. Carey is also currently working on a modification of his questionnaire which he feels will increase its usefulness.

As can be seen by Table 1, there are significant differences in mean scores between the Carey questionnaire and the NYLS interview but both yield the same modal results. In other words, the average baby at four to eight months of age is active, regular, adaptable, high in initial approach, mild, preponderantly positive in mood, low in threshold, distractible and persistent, as scored by both methods. The direction of the differences in mean scores is consistent, with the questionnaire results showing a more marked shift to the modal position than the ratings of the NYLS. It is possible that this reflected a bias of middle-class mothers to describe their infants as conforming to a preferred cultural norm, and that this bias was circumvented more effectively by the extensive open-ended interview method of the NYLS than by the forced choices imposed by the questionnaire. This explanation is confirmed by Carey's finding when he compared the mothers' brief general impression of the infants' temperament and the ratings from the questionnaire. In about 25 percent of the cases the mothers markedly minimized the more difficult temperamental characteristics in their general statements as compared to the questionnaire responses. Carey's judgment was that these distortions may have been related to "the mothers' wishes to make their babies seem more socially desirable" (8). This judgment is in line with our own position that the accuracy of behavioral data is directly related to the emphasis on objective descriptive reports from a wide variety of life situations and experiences.

Inasmuch as the differences between the Carey questionnaire and NYLS ratings are quantitative and not qualitative, the practical usefulness of this short questionnaire and its comparability to the more elaborate NYLS protocol may not be seriously impaired. This issue was explored by comparing the frequency of signs of the Difficult Child (irregularity, slow adaptability, initial withdrawal, intensity and negative mood) in the two populations. Carey found a close resemblance (9), as indicated in Table 2.

Sameroff and Kelly (10) administered the Carey questionnaire to a Rochester, New York sample of 300 women with four-month-old infants. Their data from 286 white mothers, presented in Table 3, are almost identical with Carey's norms.

Additional confirmation of the reliability of the Carey questionnaire has been reported by Wilhoit (11). She administered the questionnaire and the NYLS interview to the mothers of 24 white middle-class children (10 boys and 14 girls) at ages three and nine months. The comparison of the ratings obtained by the two methods supported the conclusion that the questionnaire is a reliable method of measuring infant temperament as defined by the NYLS interview protocol.

From a practical viewpoint, the questionnaire has already demon-

TABLE 2

Number Signs of Difficult Child	Carey Questionnaire (4-8 mos, N = 101)	NYLS interview (12 mos, N = 108)
5 signs	8%	10%
4 signs	15%	17%
3 signs	23%	20%
2 signs	22%	27%
0-1 sign	32%	26%

TABLE 3

Comparison of Means from Infant Temperament Questionnaire for Carey Norms and Rochester Norms

	Carey Norms	Rochester Norms
Activity	0.52 ± 0.32	.50
Rhythmicity	0.53 ± 0.46	.54
Adaptability	0.35 ± 0.26	.31
Approach	0.48 ± 0.35	.46
Threshold	1.08 ± 0.39	1.27
Intensity	1.05 ± 0.32	1.04
Mood	0.40 ± 0.25	.41
Distractibility	0.57 ± 0.32	.58
Persistence	0.69 ± 0.38	.75
N	101	286

strated its usefulness. Carey has utilized it to study the temperamental characteristics of infants with night awakening and colic (see Chapter 4) and adoptees from psychiatrically disturbed biologic parents (see Chapter 13), with significant findings. Baron's use of the questionnaire in children with Down's Syndrome has also been productive (see Chapter 5). Several other studies by other investigators utilizing the Carey questionnaire are in progress and their findings should contribute to a future definition of the value of this instrument.

QUESTIONNAIRES FOR THREE-TO-SEVEN-YEAR AGE PERIOD

We have ourselves just completed the development of a separate short questionnaire form for parents and teachers for the three-to-seven-year age period. These forms and the scoring keys are reproduced in Appendix B.

The parent questionnaire was developed by first culling a number of specific items of behavior for each of the nine categories of temperament from a group of our parent protocols. Items for each category were selected which from the experience of our interviewers, scorers and senior research staff appeared most typical, ubiquitous and unambiguous and did not overlap with the other eight temperamental categories. The items were then presented to a group of 10 mothers with three-to-five-year-old children and 10 mothers with five-to-seven-year-old children. The same items were used for the two groups. The mothers were asked to comment in detail on each question as to clarity and specificity. Numerous comments were obtained and were utilized to eliminate some questions, refine the wording of the remaining ones, and add a few additional questions. The mothers were also presented with two forms of the questionnaire. In one, three forced choices were offered for each item—such as from very low to very high activity level in ball-playing—and the respondent made the choice of the appropriate description for the child. In the other form, a seven-point rating scale of the relative frequency of occurrence of a specified description of behavior was presented and the mother circled the rating which most closely fitted her child. The consensus of the mothers was that the rating scale was more satisfactory and appropriate than the forced choice method, and the former was adopted for the final testing. The revised questionnaire comprised 132 items, distributed approximately evenly among the nine categories.

For the refinement of the parent questionnaire a sample of 50 mothers with three-to-five-year-old children and 50 mothers with five-to-seven-year-old children was gathered. The socioeconomic characteristics of these families were similar to those in the NYLS. The number of boys and girls was approximately equal.

Each group of 50 mothers was divided in half. In one half the long parent interview of the NYLS was done first and the short questionnaire administered within the next two weeks. In the other half the procedure was reversed. The same questionnaire was used for both groups of 50 mothers. The long interviews were scored according to the procedures established in the NYLS.

The questionnaire was also reviewed by four independent judges,

TABLE 4

Age of Children (N = 148)

Age in Months	%
30-35	0.7
36-41	10.3
42-47	14.4
48-53	17.8
54-59	16.4
60-65	13.0
66-71	9.6
72-77	5.5
78-83	4.8
84-89	1.4
90-95	6.2

who rated each item for the temperamental trait for which it should be scored. Each of the four judges had been a member of the NYLS research team for a number of years and was intimately familiar with the scoring criteria for each category of temperament.

For the final statistical analyses the total sample was increased to 148. The questionnaire was administered to the additional 48 mothers, but the long interview was not conducted. The median age of the children in the enlarged sample was 55 months. All were between 36 and 95 months old except for one child between 30 and 35 months.

For the total sample of 148 mothers, mean scores and standard deviations were calculated for each questionnaire item and for each of the nine categories of temperament obtained from the questionnaire and from the scored long interviews. The scores on the questionnaires were minimally related to the ages of the children. The correlations with age for each of the categories were not significant in seven categories and only significant in mood and distractibility (.26 and .25).

Each questionnaire item was scrutinized by the two authors and Dr. Sam Korn jointly to determine whether it should be included in the final questionnaire, included with modification of language, or eliminated. The following criteria were used:

1) Statistically significant level of correlation of mean score of item with mean category score of questionnaire and of interview.

2) Absence of marked skewing in distribution of mother's responses to the item.

3) Zero or only small percentage of mothers failed to respond to the item.

4) Agreement among the four judges as to which category the item was applicable.

5) The behavior described in the item should define the category unambiguously—i.e., the criterion for the category should be clear from the content of the item.

6) The event cited in the item should be one with a fairly frequent recurrence of a representative daily activity, unless it is a specially exceptional event of functional significance.

7) The item should apply generally and not relate to a special activity found only in a minority or bare majority of the families.

8) Compounded items should be avoided. Thus, in the statement, "When playing with other children my child is generally happy," playing may be equated with being happy, and the item should be changed to "When with other children my child is generally happy."

9) The terminology should be behavioral rather than attitudinal. Thus, "My child prefers" should be changed to an appropriate behavioral term such as "My child selects."

A few items appeared excellent according to the above criteria except for marked skewing in the distribution of scores. In these instances the scale was shifted. Thus, in one such item, most mothers answered "almost always." The wording was then changed from "hour" to "half-hour."

The scrutiny of the items resulted in a final questionnaire of 72 items, with eight for each of the nine categories. In each category half the items were phrased in terms of one extreme (high activity, positive mood, etc.) and the other half for the other extreme (low activity, negative mood, etc.). Inasmuch as there were no significant differences across the ages three to seven years or for boys versus girls, this questionnaire is recommended for the three-to-seven-year age period and for both sexes.

The questionnaire is currently in use by ourselves and other investigators in a number of studies of normal and deviant populations. The results of these studies should be available within the next few years.

TEACHER QUESTIONNAIRE

A teacher questionnaire for the three-to-seven-year age period has now been developed. The 132 items in the parent questionnaire draft were modified or changed in specific content to make them appropriate to the school setting. Some items were dropped as totally inappropriate, leaving 15 items for this teacher questionnaire. Sixty questionnaires were completed by a group of teachers, utilizing two or three children in classes between the ages of three and seven years for each teacher. The long interviews were not conducted with the teachers.

Decisions as to the final items and their wording were determined through the same procedures as used for the parent questionnaire, as detailed above, except that comparisons of the questionnaire and long interview responses could, of course, not be made. Also, the rating of rhythmicity, which required knowledge of a child's functioning over 24-hour periods, could not be done adequately by the teachers. The final teacher questionnaire, therefore, comprises eight questions for each of the other eight categories.

OTHER SHORT FORMS FOR RATING TEMPERAMENT

A number of other investigators have explored short approaches for rating temperament. McDevitt and Carey have developed a questionnaire for measuring the nine categories of temperament in three-to-seven-year-old children (12). Initial item selection was determined by inter-judge agreement of category designation, utilizing eight judges familiar with the NYLS categories. A preliminary questionnaire of 112 items resulted, which was pretested on 53 children. The items were evaluated on the basis of intercorrelations with the designated temperament subscale and the total instrument. A final revision with 108 items on a six-point scale has been termed by the authors the Behavioral Style Questionnaire (BSQ). High test-retest reliability was determined. The questionnaire has been used with the parents of 350 children and the authors are preparing a report analyzing their findings.

In addition, McDevitt and Carey are planning to test the usefulness of their questionnaire with children below three years and above seven years.

Graham, Rutter and George (13) developed an interview protocol in London to categorize temperament in children with a mentally ill parent. The protocol is reproduced in Appendix C. The data were used to rate activity level, regularity, approach-withdrawal, adaptability (designated malleability in their scale), mood, and intensity. An additional category, called fastidiousness, was added. The interview protocol was pretested on the mothers of 26 children, ages four to five years, inter-rater and test-retest reliabilities were established, and the protocol was then applied to the mothers of the study sample of 60 children, ages three to seven years. They found that certain temperamental characteristics, especially irregularity, low malleability and low fastidiousness, were predictive of the development of later psychiatric disorders in these children with at least one mentally ill parent.

Graham, Rutter and George caution that they have reservations about the test-retest reliability of the instrument. They advise that other research workers intending to use this method would need to repeat the methodological studies before proceeding with confidence to further hypothesis testing.

Garside et al. (14), at the University of Newcastle, England, have developed a temperament questionnaire to cover our categories, which they have tested on 209 five-year-old children, equally divided between boys and girls. The questionnaire consists of 98 specific questions, each with a five-point scale. Clear descriptions were provided for every point on some of the scales. For others, this was difficult to achieve and only the two extreme points and the midpoint were defined. The scales were pretested on clinic cases before applying them to the 209 unselected school children. As in our approach, the emphasis was on *how* the child behaved rather than on *what* he did. The interviewers concentrated on the day-to-day activities over the previous fortnight if considered representative, but if the previous fort-

night was not typical, the interviewer could choose a two-week period in the previous month. The ratings were based on examples of
behavior rather than on maternal judgments about child behavior.
Satisfactory inter-rater reliability levels were obtained.

The Newcastle group employed a principal component analysis of
their questionnaire data. The analysis resulted in the delineation of
four components: a) withdrawal, poor adaptation, dependence; b)
high activity, intensity, distractibility; c) moodiness, sulkiness; and
d) irregularity. Tentative norms have been provided for these dimensions.

Seegars has developed a short teacher checklist which has been
applied to several large populations of elementary age children in
South Carolina (15). He has formulated his data in terms of five
categories: Easy Child, Difficult Child, Slow-To-Warm-Up Child,
Environmentalist and Emotionally Fragile Child. The definitions and
criteria for the first three categories are derived from the NYLS.
Seegars defines the Environmentalist as a child highly skilled at
manipulation, insensitive to discipline and free of anxiety. The Emotionally Fragile Child, by contrast, is defined as a fearful perfection-
ist, with difficulty in coping with stress. As reported in Chapter 9,
Seegars has found correlations between these categories and academic
functioning, though not with I.Q. level.

For the neonatal period, Katcher (16) has determined that temperamental individuality could be identified and rated. He obtained
behavioral data on 16 full-term neonates with normal pregnancies
and deliveries, using two periods of direct observation on the second
and fourth days of life, and a semi-structured interview with the
nurse. All nine categories of temperament could be item-scored from
the data except for rhythmicity and approach-withdrawal. For mood,
only negative mood statements could be scored because of the absence of the smiling response in the neonate. Levels of correlation
between the nurse and observer reports and between the second and
fourth days varied greatly for the different categories, with only a
few reaching the .05 level of significance.

Katcher's study indicates that temperamental characteristics can
be identified in the neonatal period. They also appear to vary from
day to day, perhaps even from hour to hour, which undoubtedly re-

flects the rapid fluctuations of behavior and psychophysiological functions in the neonate. This behavioral variability would make for special methodological problems in any attempt to develop short rating forms for temperament in the neonate.

The development of short rating scales and questionnaires for temperament in the older child and adult also presents special methodological problems. They are discussed in Chapter 13, "Temperament in the Older Child and the Adult." The first exploratory effort in this direction has been made by Scholom (17) through the utilization of the Thorndike Dimensions of Temperament Questionnaire. He has also tested a brief questionnaire for adults with a five-point rating scale for each of the nine temperament categories in 264 adults. Further reliability and validity studies of both instruments are still required before their usefulness can be evaluated.

Buss and Plomin (18) have recently reported a rating scale for temperament, utilizing four categories: activity, emotionality, sociability and impulsivity. They have constructed a 20-item questionnaire, five items for each temperament. Most of the items are general in nature, though some relate to specific behaviors. Mothers of 139 pairs of same-sexed twins completed the questionnaire for both their twins, the age range being one to nine years. The intrapair correlations were significantly higher for identical than for non-identical twins, with the exception of impulsivity in girls.

The three temperament categories of emotionality, activity and sociability, as defined by Buss and Plomin, appear to be contained within our categories of intensity and quality of mood, activity level, and approach-withdrawal and adaptability. The category of impulsivity appears unrelated specifically to any of our nine categories. The authors have not provided data as to the validation of their rating scale or its functional significance.

OBTAINING DATA ON TEMPERAMENT IN CLINICAL PRACTICE

The clinician and teacher can also obtain useful data on the child's temperament through flexible semi-structured parent interviews. This information can be used to make qualitative judgments, as is done for the clinical assessment of parental attitudes and practices, family relationships, and sociocultural influences. Retrospective parental reports are, of course, subject to distortions of recall, whether they relate to temperament, previous medical history, special behavior patterns, child care practices, etc. In all cases, the clinician must assess the accuracy, completeness, and pertinence of both retrospective and current information. In our experience, the collection of behavioral data from which evaluations of temperament can be made has proved no more difficult than gathering information on other aspects of the child's characteristics. The protocol for obtaining temperamental data in clinical practice is detailed in Appendix D.

These questions can be modified or focused on several of the categories as appropriate for a specific clinical or school problem or for the interview exigencies with a particular parent. The ratings of temperament from such a clinical interview will necessarily be qualitative and impressionistic, but, as with other similarly obtained data, may be extremely useful in practice. It is also frequently possible to check the impressions obtained from the parent by querying other adults familiar with the child and by the clinician's own observation of the child's behavior.

SUMMARY

A number of investigators, in addition to ourselves, have been increasingly involved in developing short rating scales and questionnaires for temperament which are reliable and valid as well as economical to administer and score. These efforts have already resulted in the development of useful instruments for the infancy, preschool and early school age periods. The neonatal, older child and adult age periods present special methodological problems for this goal, though the studies thus far indicate that temperamental individuality can be identified in each of these age periods.

REFERENCES

1. A. Thomas, S. Chess, H. G. Birch, M. Hertzig and S. Korn, *Behavioral Individuality in Early Childhood* (New York: New York University Press, 1963).
2. A. Thomas, S. Chess and H. G. Birch, *Temperament and Behavior Disorders in Childhood* (New York: New York University Press, 1968).

3. W. B. Carey, "A Simplified Method of Measuring Infant Temperament," *J. Pediatrics*, 77:188-194 (1970).
4. W. B. Carey, "Measuring Infant Temperament," *J. Pediatrics*, 81:414 (1972).
5. W. B. Carey, "Measurement of Infant Temperament in Pediatrics," *Individual Differences in Children*, ed., J. Westman (New York: John Wiley and Sons, 1973), pp. 293-306.
6. *Ibid.*
7. W. B. Carey, *op. cit.*, 1972.
8. W. B. Carey, *op. cit.*, 1970.
9. *Ibid.*
10. A. J. Sameroff and P. Kelly, "Socio-economic Status, Racial and Mental Health Factors in Infant Temperament." Unpublished manuscript.
11. P. D. Wilhoit, "Assessment of Temperament During the First Months of Life." Doctoral dissertation, Florida State University, 1976.
12. S. C. McDevitt and W. B. Carey, "The Measurement of Temperament in 3 to 7 Year Old Children." In preparation.
13. P. Graham, M. Rutter and S. George, "Temperamental Characteristics as Predictors of Behavior Disorders in Children," *Am. J. Orthopsychiat.*, 43:328-339 (1973).
14. R. F. Garside, H. Birch, D. McI. Scott, S. Chambers, I. Kolvin, E. G. Tweddler, & L. M. Barber, "Dimensions of Temperament in Infant School Children," *J. Child Psycho. Psychiat.*, 16:219-231 (1975).
15. J. Seegars, "High Risk Indices in Early Recognition Intervention." Presented at meeting of American Psychological Association, New Orleans, 1974.
16. A. Katcher, unpublished data.
17. A. H. Scholom, "The Relationship of Infant and Parent Temperament to the Prediction of Child Adjustment." Doctoral dissertation, Michigan State University, 1975.
18. A. H. Buss and R. Plomin, *A Temperament Theory of Personality Development* (New York: John Wiley and Sons, 1975).

11

Origins of

temperament

As stated in Chapter 2, temperament is a phenomenologic term and has no implications as to etiology or immutability. The question of the origins of temperament is, however, of great interest. Is there a genetic component to temperament? Are temperamental characteristics, as they become manifest in the first few months of life, constitutional in origin or are they determined by parental influences in the early postnatal period? Is temperament influenced by neurophysiological, neurochemical, psychophysiological or endocrine factors? This chapter will review a number of studies which are relevant to these questions.

GENETIC INFLUENCE

The identification of a possible genetic component for temperamental individuality has been achieved through the classical method of comparing same-sexed homozygotic and heterozygotic twins.

The major twin study has been done by Torgersen in Bergen, Norway (1) under the supervision of Professor Einar Kringlen, an eminent authority in this type of investigation. Torgersen collected a sample of 53 same-sexed twin pairs. On the basis of blood typing,

TABLE 1

Differences as F-Ratio Between Intrapair Variances of Weighted Temperament Scores in MZ and DZ Twins at Two Months and Nine Months

| | 2 months | | 9 months | |
	F-ratio	p-volume	F-ratio	v-value
Regularity	4.98	< 0.001	12.86	< 0.001
Threshold	2.82	< 0.01	9.90	< 0.001
Approach	0.83	insign.	6.77	< 0.001
Intensity	2.55	< 0.25	5.32	< 0.001
Activity	1.52	insign.	5.26	< 0.001
Persistence	—	insign.	4.40	< 0.001
Distractibility	1.40	insign.	3.94	< 0.001
Mood	1.54	insign.	3.31	< 0.01
Adaptability	0.57	insign.	2.28	< 0.05

34 pairs were identified as monozygotic, 16 pairs as dizygotic, and three pairs were of uncertain zygosity. Obstetrical, medical and demographic data were gathered. Behavioral histories on each twin pair were obtained by interviews with the mother in her home setting, once when the twins were two months old and again at age nine months. The protocol of the NYLS for obtaining temperamental data was used as the basis for the interview. The NYLS criteria for item scoring of temperament were utilized, and the reliability confirmed by our NYLS scorer checking Torgersen's results in detail.

If a given temperamental trait has a strong genetic component, the difference between the monozygotic twins for this trait should be less than the difference between the dizygotic twins. Table 1, taken from Torgersen (2), details this comparison. The relationship between the two intrapair variances (monozygotic and dizygotic) were determined by calculating F-ratios.

As can be seen from Table 1, at two months there were statistically significant differences between the monozygotic and dizygotic twin pairs in regularity and threshold and a similar trend for intensity. Persistence could not be adequately scored from the data at that age. The differences for the other five categories were not significant.

At nine months the differences were significant for all nine categories, in seven of them reaching the .001 level. In all categories, as at two months, the monozygotic twin pairs were more similar to each other than were the dizygotic twins.

In comparing the findings at two and nine months, Torgersen found that the monozygotic twins had a weak tendency to decreased intrapair differences between the two ages, and the dizygotic twins had a more marked tendency to increased differences in all categories.

Torgersen also examined the possibility that the mothers of monozygotic twins might treat the infants more similarly and report their behavior as more alike than it really was. However, neither at two months nor at nine months did the great majority of mothers have any definite opinion regarding the zygosity of their twins. At two months, only one mother believed her twins were monozygotic, seven thought they were dizygotic, and 37 had no opinion at all. Data on this issue were not available on the other eight mothers. Similar results were obtained on questioning the mothers when the twins were nine months old. Torgersen's judgment was that the infants' behavior at two months still reflected the influences of pregnancy and the birth process. This had disappeared by nine months, at which time the definitive expression of temperament per se was clearer. (This judgment corresponds to our own experience in the NYLS. We found that the infant's behavior in the first six to eight weeks of life was frequently quite variable from week to week, and even from day to day. This has led us to set the first behavioral interview with the parents at two to three months of age.)

From her findings, Torgersen concluded that "the results of this study show a strong genetic influence on temperament, and that future studies on this topic . . . should not ignore the significance of the genetic influence" (3).

Our own NYLS sample includes nine pairs of twins and a number of families in which two or more sibs were enrolled in the study. Rutter, Korn and Birch analyzed the temperamental data for the first three years of life for eight twin pairs (one pair was still too young at the time of their analysis) and 26 sib pairs (4). Three sets of twins were monozygotic and five dizygotic. This twin study postulated that if a temperamental trait had a significant genetic basis: 1) monozygotic pairs would be more alike in this infancy period than the dizygotic pairs; 2) dizygotic pairs would be no more alike than sibs; 3) intrapair differences for the trait should be small in the monozygotic pairs. The number of scores in some infants in the first year for distractibility and persistence were too few to permit their use, and these two categories were not included in the analysis.

The results suggested that all three methods did not agree in indicating a preponderantly genetic basis for any of the temperamental categories. The strongest evidence for a genetic component was present for activity level, approach-withdrawal and adaptability, and less so for threshold, intensity and mood. No genetic component was evident for rhythmicity in any of the three methods of analysis.

It must be remembered, however, that the size of this sample was small, with only three pairs of monozygotic twins and five dizygotic pairs. This made the delineation of statistically significant findings difficult to achieve, even if functionally meaningful relationships in fact existed. In this regard, the substantially larger size of Torgersen's sample makes her quantitative analyses much more meaningful.

The two infants of one monozygotic twin pair in the NYLS were adopted at birth into separate families who had no contact with each other. The behavioral data on these two girls provided additional evidence for a genetic factor in temperament, even keeping in mind all the caveats regarding single case studies. Both children showed strikingly similar temperamental traits in the preschool years. They were highly irregular in sleep patterns, had marked intensity in negative mood expression, and were moderately active and adaptable, distractible and persistent. The parental handling of night awakening with loud crying in the first two years, which characterized both twins, was markedly different in the two families. In one, the parents were consistent and affectionate and ignored the night crying after it became apparent that this did not reflect physical discomfort. The infant's night awakening gradually diminished and finally disappeared without any behavior problem developing. The other parents commented that they could not bear to hear the infant scream and gave her what she wanted. Picking the child up at night and soothing and feeding her only reinforced the night crying pattern. Clinical evaluation at 28 months judged this second twin to be basically normal with a mild reactive behavior disorder. The parents were counseled to ignore the night crying, as well as tantrum behavior in the daytime. They followed the advice, the sleep problem gradually disappeared, and the child's subsequent behavioral development was without incident.

When the twins were 16 years old they were interviewed separately by one of us (S.C.). Their physical and behavioral similarities were indeed remarkable. Both girls were easily adaptable, quite persistent and showed intense emotional expressiveness. Mood was predominantly positive. They were both doing well in school, and each was gregarious with many friends and an active social life. They both had the same special interests and group activities, namely music and acrobatics. They had both been raised in families with similar sociocultural characteristics and goals for their children. Our judgment, therefore, is that the striking similarity in temperament, behavior and interests in the adolescent period is the result of environmental reinforcement of congruent genetic factors. A detailed report on the development and findings in this pair of separated monozygotic twins is in preparation (5).

Another approach to the investigation of a genetic component of temperament would be the comparison of parent and child temperament. To be methodologically sound, such studies should utilize samples in which the children have been separated from their biological parents at birth. Otherwise, the postnatal parental influence on the child's behavior would make it extremely difficult to separate this environmental factor from any genetic component. No such study of temperament in parents and in children separated at birth has been done. A major obstacle to such a research project has been the problem of developing a satisfactory method of measuring temperament in adults.

The various twin studies cited in this section do appear to warrant the conclusion that there is a significant genetic component to temperament. It is also highly probable that other factors are equally or more influential in shaping temperamental individuality. It should also be clear that a genetic influence in no way implies fixed predetermination and immutability of temperament, any more than it does of any other psychological or physical characteristic of an organism. Phenotypic characteristics, as emphasized by modern geneticists, are always the final product of the continuously evolving interaction between genetic and environmental factors (6). Depending on the nature of this interaction, an infant's separate temperamental characteristics may be reinforced, modified or changed as he grows older.

PRENATAL AND PERINATAL INFLUENCES

A substantial body of data on possible relationships between prenatal and perinatal factors and temperament has been developed by a number of investigators.

Carey, Lipton and Meyers studied a sample of infants separated from their mothers at birth and placed with an adoptive or foster mother (7). Their review of the literature had indicated that "pregnancy anxiety does have short-term effects, that is, observable differences in the fetus and newborn." Their own study tried to determine whether pregnancy anxiety had more enduring effects on the infant's behavioral characteristics. Temperament was determined for each child at six months by the Carey questionnaire. Data were available from the case records of a local child welfare agency on 41 of the biological mothers which permitted a rating score for the amount of anxiety expressed in the third trimester of pregnancy. The score was obtained from five items: 1) reaction to the pregnancy and its outcome; 2) effect of the pregnancy on the mother's life; 3) reactions to baby's father; 4) reactions to other family members; and 5) conflict over surrendering the baby. A comparison was then made of the percentage of infants of the Difficult Child temperamental constellation in this sample with a control sample of 200 infants living with their biological parents. No significant differences were found between the two groups. The Difficult Child pattern was slightly more evident in the control group (14 percent) than in the sample group of adoptive and foster children (11.9 percent). Inasmuch as all the pregnancies in the sample group were unwanted, it can be presumed that they were, as a group, more stressful than wanted pregnancies. This stress did not result in a greater tendency for a difficult temperament in the infant.

Carey's comparison of maternal pregnancy anxiety and the adopted infant's six-month temperament score showed a relationship which almost reached statistical significance. The more anxious mothers had six out of 17 babies, or 35.3 percent, with a tendency toward or marked difficult temperament, as compared to three of the 24 infants from the less anxious mothers (chi square = 1.9, p > 0.05). However, the three babies of the most anxious mothers were all rated as having either an easy temperament or a tendency toward easy temperament.

The effect of maternal emotional health or temperament was given support in Sameroff and Kelly's (8) study of 300 infants. Most of the mothers in this Rochester sample received a psychiatric interview during the last few months of their pregnancies. Based on this interview the women were rated as having either a clinical diagnosis or no mental illness. When the infants of the two groups of women were compared on the Carey questionnaire scores, major differences were found in three of the difficult temperament categories. Infants of mothers who were judged to be emotionally disturbed were less adaptable, more intense, and more negative in mood than infants of mothers rated as having no mental illness. Sameroff and Kelly noted four possible mechanisms by which a mother's emotional health may adversely affect infant temperament: 1) the mother's anxiety during pregnancy might cause biochemical changes which would affect the infant in utero; 2) the mother's anxiety might affect the delivery process itself, influencing complications which might affect the infant; 3) the mother's prenatal anxiety would continue into the postnatal period during which it would adversely affect her ability to relate to the child; 4) lastly, there is always the outside possibility that some third unmeasured factor is affecting both the mother's anxiety and the infant's temperament.

A study of temperament in adoptees from psychiatrically disturbed biologic parents has been reported by Cadoret and co-workers (9). Their sample comprised 114 children separated at birth from their biologic parents. The study was done when the children were adolescents, their mean age being 17 years. Information on a number of aspects of the child's behavior was obtained by interviewing the adoptive parents. Eight questions for rating the Difficult Child temperamental pattern retrospectively for the preschool years were included. Data were available for classifying the biologic parents as normal, antisocial or psychiatrically disturbed from the clinical records of the adoption agencies. The authors found that the male adoptees of psychiatrically disturbed biologic mothers had a greater number of temperamental traits in early childhood characteristic of the Difficult Child, when contrasted to the male adoptees of normal mothers. No such differences were found for female adoptees. Because of the methodological problems of this study, including the retrospective nature of the temperament data, the findings can only be considered suggestive.

In her Norwegian twin study, Torgersen also compared temperamental characteristics at two and nine months with prematurity and pregnancy and birth complications (10). She found only a few statistically significant correlations with low activity level, irregularity, slow adaptability and low threshold. The correlations were scattered, only one or two were found for each of the three variables, and they were less marked at nine than at two months. She also compared the intrapair differences in twin pairs with different degrees of pregnancy and/or birth complications. There were greater intrapair differences with more severe obstetrical complications, but none was statistically significant, and the differences were less marked at nine than at two months.

The longitudinal study of children born prematurely has also provided some data on the relationship of prenatal and perinatal factors to temperament. This sample comprised 68 children of mostly middle-class parents, with birth weights ranging from 1000 to 1750 grams. Fifty-five percent of the boys (16 out of 29 cases) and 35 percent of the girls (14 out of 39 cases) had clinical evidence of neurological impairment at five years of age (11). Behavioral protocols were obtained from the mother starting at two to three months, using the interview form of the NYLS, and the records were item-scored for the nine temperament categories, again according to scoring methods of the NYLS. The distribution curves of the weighted scores in all nine categories for each of the years one to five were virtually superimposable on those of the NYLS. The minor variations were not statistically significant (12).

Infants born prematurely are known to be vulnerable to brain trauma in the birth process. This is especially true in a markedly premature group, such as the above sample. This is borne out in the high prevalence of neurological impairment clinically evident by five years of age. A pathological prenatal environment was also presumptively present for at least some of these children as cause for the markedly premature birth. The absence of any differences in temperament from the NYLS group is therefore especially noteworthy.

This lack of correlation between perinatal brain damage and temperament is pertinent to the contention of Wender that the temperament traits of activity, approach-withdrawal, intensity and distractibility are "relevant to the minimal brain dysfunction syndrome" (13). Clearly, the findings in this longitudinal premature study do not bear out Wender's interpretation of temperament. Along the same lines, two of the three children with perinatal brain damage in the NYLS had the easy temperament pattern, and only one was a Difficult Child.

Finally, some of the data in our own longitudinal studies of children with mild mental retardation and congenital rubella are of interest for this discussion. The first group comprised 52 children followed from age five to 11 years (14). The second 243 children were followed from age two to four years (15). Temperamental data were obtained and scored according to the protocols of the NYLS at the beginning of each study.

In the congenital rubella group, it is clear that the children suffered from prenatal pathology because of infection with the rubella virus during the mother's pregnancy. In the mentally retarded group the presumption for prenatal or perinatal trauma is only inferential for many, if not most, of the children. No history of mental retardation in other close family relatives was obtained, no history or other evidence of any postnatal cause for the retardation was elicited, and close to 50 percent developed clinical signs of neurologic dysfunction (16).

Table 5 in Chapter 5 tabulates the frequency of the temperamental signs of the Difficult Child in these two populations as compared to the NYLS sample in the first five years of life. Although the signs of marked difficult temperament were found somewhat more often in the mentally retarded and the rubella children than in the NYLS youngsters, these differences were not statistically significant. Similarly, the distribution of the easy temperament and less marked difficult temperament groups among the three populations was no more than would be expected on the basis of chance alone. In general, the presence or absence of the temperamental signs of the Difficult Child did not appear to be a meaningful distinction among the three groups.

To sum up the studies cited in this section, there is suggestive but not definitive evidence that if mothers have psychiatric disturbances or marked anxiety in pregnancy their children may be more likely to have the Difficult Child pattern. Other prenatal and perinatal traumata, such as obstetrical and birth difficulties or perinatal brain damage, do not appear to significantly influence temperamental characteristics.

PSYCHOPHYSIOLOGICAL STUDIES

There are a host of other prenatal or perinatal influences which might conceivably influence the patterning of temperament in infancy—biochemical, endocrine, psychophysiological, circulatory, nutritional, psychological etc. Only a few studies in these areas have as yet been undertaken. Two explorations of possible relationships between psychophysiological phenomena in the neonate and temperament in the young infant are of interest.

Birns et al. have found significant correlations between measurements of visual pursuit and arousal responses to a cold stimulus in 15 neonates, and irritability and social responsiveness at three to four months (17). Social responsiveness was rated by the amount and intensity of smiling and vocalization in response to a strange adult in two standardized observation test situations. Irritability was rated on the amount of crying and whimpering observed during specific periods of direct observation. The investigators suggest two possible explanations for these correlations: "On the one hand, the neonatal behavior may evoke specific maternal responses which in turn produce the behaviors evidenced at three and four months. On the other hand, both the neonatal and the later behaviors may reflect a common underlying trait, which is relatively unaffected by environmental interaction."

Bell et al. have reported a study of 75 newborns by direct observation and experimental procedures in which mouth and closed-eye movements, respiration rates and heel tactile threshold during sleep, a righting reflex, sucking pattern and crying with interruption of sucking during the waking period were all rated (18). Correlations for the 27-33 month period were established with intensity of behavior (interest, participation, assertiveness, gregariousness, and communicativeness), but of an inverse character. In other words, high ratings in the neonate were associated with low intensity in the preschool period. The authors comment that "newborn behavior is more like a preface to a book than a table of its contents yet to be unfolded. Further, the preface is itself merely a rough draft undergoing rapid revision. There are some clues to the nature of the book in the preface, but these are in code form and taking them as literally prophetic is likely to lead to disappointment."

TEMPERAMENT AND I.Q. LEVEL

Sameroff (19) obtained Bayley I.Q. scores on 50 infants at four and 30 months of age. Temperament ratings using the Carey questionnaire were also obtained at four months. The correlation between the infant test scores on the Bayley at four and 30 months of age was .18, typical of the low correlations found between age periods. However, the comparison of the Difficult Child temperament score at four months showed a highly significant correlation with the Bayley I.Q. score at 30 months (.49, p < .01). Two other psychometric assessments at 30 months of age, the Peabody and Binet Vocabulary tests, also correlated strongly with the four-month Difficult Child temperament assessment. Sameroff concludes from these data that "if one wants to predict an infant's I.Q. score at 30 months of age from a child's behavior at four months of age, a much more reliable prediction can be made based on his temperament than on his intellectual functioning." Thus far, our own data in the NYLS and the Puerto Rican Study have not been analyzed to determine correlations between temperamental constellation and I.Q. level.

EARLY POSTNATAL INFLUENCES

The professional literature has emphasized the profound influence of the mother on the young infant because of her nurturing role throughout the day and night and the intimacy and intensity of contact. We would expect that this mother-infant interaction would influence the developmental patterns and modes of expression of temperament in the young child. The definition of this correlation, however, is not a simple matter. A change in a neonate's behavioral pattern in the first months of life may be the result of parental influences. Or, it may be the consequence of the gradual postnatal disappearance of pregnancy and birth process effects. A genetically determined characteristic may show itself at birth, or it may not become manifest for months or years. The fact that a behavioral trait only appears some time after birth is, therefore, in itself neither evidence for or against a primarily environmental etiology.

The studies of several investigators have identified a number of temperamental characteristics in the neonatal period. The evidence is also clear that these traits undergo modification in the succeeding months of life. Katcher (20) studied the behavioral characteristics of 50 neonates with uncomplicated pregnancies and deliveries, using two-hour periods of direct observation and interviews with the baby nurse, each on the second and fourth days of life. Categories were derived from the protocols by inductive analysis. For each child the following categories could be identified and item-scored: 1) activity level; 2) adaptability; 3) sensory threshold; 4) response to stimulation other than sensory; 5) intensity of response; 6) mood; 7) distractibility; and 8) persistence. As can be seen, these categories correspond to our nine temperamental traits, except that satisfactory criteria for rhythmicity and approach-withdrawal could not be established and an additional category, "response to stimuli other than sensory," was identified. Mood could only be scored for the number of negative mood expressions, inasmuch as smiling and related responses are absent in the neonate. When each infant reached three months of age, each mother was interviewed, utilizing the NYLS protocol, and the data scored for the nine temperamental categories. Correlations with the neonatal characteristics were not impressive.

Sarett (21) rated the behavior of 31 neonates on the third or fourth day of life through a 90-minute period of direct observation and also obtained assessments of temperamental characteristics from the mother and two nurses. At 14 weeks, the babies were observed for another 90-minute period, and the Carey temperament question-naire was filled out by each mother. The neonatal assessments did not correlate significantly with these measures at 14 weeks.

Korner and her co-workers have described significant behavioral differences in the neonate in spontaneous oral behavior (22) and ease of soothability when crying (23). This latter trait may well be re-lated to our temperamental category of adaptability. They have not, however, reported any follow-up studies of correlations between these neonatal findings and later individual differences in tempera-ment.

Finally, in our own parental interviews in the NYLS when the in-fants were two to three months of age, many of the mothers gave definite descriptive accounts of shifts and changes in the child's be-havioral characteristics during the first four to six weeks of life. In an initial pilot project to assess temperament in the neonatal period it was clear that behavior during this period typically fluctuated from day to day. This finding actually influenced our decision to initiate our data collection at two to three months of age, when a beginning stability in behavioral characteristics was more likely.

It is true, on the other hand, that some parents report striking consistencies between their child's behavior in the neonatal period and later infancy: "The nurse said she cried the loudest of all the newborns, and she still shrieks and yells whenever she's upset or hurt." "After he was born he wiggled so much I could hardly hold him and now he thrashes around so much it is hard to dress or bathe him." "Her sleeping time was very regular even when she was five days old, and a year later this is still true." It would be a valuable study to analyze patterns of continuity and discontinuity of tempera-ment from the neonatal to later infancy periods, and what relation-ship, if any, these patterns bear to parental characteristics identified prenatally. Such research could illuminate the question of parental influence on individuality in temperament as it crystallizes in early' infancy.

Several studies have explored possible relationships between ma-ternal characteristics and difficult temperament in the infant. Sam-eroff (24) worked with four groups of 26 mothers, each having a diagnosis of schizophrenia, neurotic depression, personality disorder, or no disorder. The mothers were matched for age, race, socioeconomic status and mental status. The Carey questionnaire was used to determine each infant's temperament at four months of age, and the children were rated on the basis of how closely they approximated the Difficult Child temperament.

Comparisons were made on the basis of degree of psychopathology, rather than psychiatric diagnosis, and Sameroff found significant differences. Severity of mental illness did appear to be a contributor to difficult temperament. Prenatal scores on maternal anxiety and attitude to pregnancy were also available, as well as ratings for race and social class. All four variables were found significantly correlated with difficult temperament in the four-month-old infant, i.e., prenatal maternal anxiety, poor attitude toward pregnancy, black race, and low socioeconomic status. Also, the more previous children a mother had had, the more her current child tended to have a difficult temperament. Regression analysis showed that, of all the variables, mother's anxiety score measured before the child's birth had the greatest influence on the development of difficult temperament.

Sameroff's finding of a relation between maternal anxiety during pregnancy and difficult temperament in the infant corresponds to Carey's and Cadoret's findings with adopted children cited in the section above. The level of correlation is more significant in Sameroff's sample, perhaps because the maternal contact and interaction with their infants continued after birth, while the mothers in the other groups were separated from their children at birth.

Sarett (25) obtained temperamental data on 31 infants at age 14 weeks, using the Carey questionnaire. She observed the mother's interaction with the child for a 90-minute period in the home and scored the mother's behavior according to frequency of touching, holding, vocalizing, smiling, looking, playing and other ("other" occurred only once in the use of a pacifier). She found that the mothers of Difficult Children engaged in more behaviors related to the infant's crying or fretting, which was a direct correlation with the increased frequency of this latter behavior in temperamentally difficult infants. However, there were no qualitative differences in the pattern of maternal response to the difficult versus easy babies. In terms of overall mother-child interaction, the Difficult Child group

was also not involved in a significantly greater number of interactions than was the easy group.

In the NYLS we have not made quantitative comparisons of the
mothers of the Difficult versus Easy Children. Our most emphatic
qualitative judgments, from contact with the mothers over these
many years, is that we detected no significant personality attributes
or differences in types or severity of psychopathology in those with
Difficult as compared with Easy Children.

Thus, there is some evidence that mothers with prenatal anxiety
and/or from minority lower-class background may have more children with difficult temperament. The negative correlations in Sarett's
sample and in the NYLS probably stem from the middle- and upper-
middle-class composition of both groups and the presumably smaller
percentage of unwanted pregnancies and severe psychopathology in
the mothers.

SOCIOCULTURAL AND SEX COMPARISONS

The extent of parental determination of infant temperament can
also be investigated by comparing groups of different sex or sociocultural background. Korner (26) has recently reviewed the literature indicating "that from a very early age, parents, particularly
mothers, treat boys differently from girls." Parents from different
sociocultural backgrounds will also show significant variations in their
attitudes, expectations and behavior with their children, even in infancy. The NYLS and our longitudinal study of children of Puerto
Rican working-class parents, in which temperamental data in infancy
were obtained and scored by the same method, provided an opportunity to make cross-cultural comparisons. The temperamental scores
for boys versus girls were also examined in the NYLS samples.

The comparisons between the NYLS and Puerto Rican groups
were done when we were using the percent-rank model of rating and
involved 48 children from each group at two to three months of age,
and matched for sex distribution. The statistical comparisons utilized
a 20 percent score as a cut-off point in all categories except mood,
because of the skewed distribution of scores with the percent-rating
method. The comparisons were based on the number of children with

TABLE 2

Comparison of Percent-Scores of Puerto Rican (PR) and NYLS
Middle-Class (MC) Samples, at Two to Three Months
(N is 48 for each sample)

Comparison is made in terms of the number of children above or below the
cut-off point of 20 percent for each category except for mood, where the cut-
off point is 50 percent.

ACTIVITY*				RHYTHMICITY**				ADAPTABILITY		
	0-20%	21+%	total		0-20%	21+%	total		0-20%	21+%	total
PR	12	36	48	PR	43	5	48	PR	25	23	48
MC	22	26	48	MC	20	28	48	MC	25	23	48

APPROACH/ WITHDRAWAL				THRESHOLD*				INTENSITY**		
	0-20%	21+%	total		0-20%	21+%	total		0-20%	21+%	total
PR	18	30	48	PR	27	21	48	PR	26	22	48
MC	16	32	48	MC	19	29	48	MC	9	39	48

MOOD*				DISTRACTIBILIY				PERSISTENCE		
	0-50%	51+%	total		0-20%	21+%	total		0-20%	21+%	total
PR	25	23	48	PR	32	16	48	PR	32	16	48
MC	37	11	48	MC	31	17	48	MC	36	12	48

*Chi Square analysis is significant beyond the .001 level of confidence.
**Chi Square analysis is "borderline significant" between the .10 and .05 level of confidence.

percent scores above, as contrasted to below, this cut-off point. In
mood 50 percent was used as a cut-off point because of the more
normal distribution.

As can be seen from Table 2, the differences between the two
groups are markedly significant for rhythmicity and intensity, of
borderline significance for activity level, mood and threshold, and not
significant for the other four categories. Overall, the differences are
not dramatic. This is especially noteworthy because of the marked
dissimilarity in parental attitudes and practices between the two
groups. The middle-class native-born families in the NYLS had high
educational and career expectations for their children, emphasized
early accomplishment of self-care activities, particularly feeding and
dressing, structured feeding and sleep schedules and were greatly
concerned over any evidence of deviant behavior, even in early infancy. The Puerto Rican parents, by contrast, had more modest goals
for their children, did not press for early self-care achievement, were

very permissive with sleep and feeding schedules in the preschool years and tolerated behavioral deviations with the formulation "he's a baby and he'll outgrow it."

If parental characteristics and functioning were decisive in shaping the infant's temperament, one would expect that the comparisons of these two samples from such markedly different sociocultural and economic backgrounds would have shown much more striking differences than were actually found. Even these differences may be in some part the result of culturally determined biases in the mother's perception in reporting of her infant's behavior.

As indicated in the earlier section on prenatal and perinatal influences, a comparison was also made between the temperamental scores in the NYLS and the children born markedly premature. The distribution curves of the weighted scores in all nine categories for each of the years one to five were virtually superimposable on each other. The minor variations were not statistically significant (27). Most of the mothers of the premature infants were separated from their children for several weeks or more after birth because of the use of a special premature nursery unit. The parents were, in most cases, also realistically concerned and even anxious as to whether their premature baby would develop normally. The similarity in temperament scores with the NYLS, in which these special factors did not exist, is, therefore, especially striking.

Differences in temperamental scores for boys and girls were examined within the NYLS. The mean weighted scores for each of the nine categories for each of the first five years of life were utilized. The means for the boys as a group, with the N varying from 48 to 58 for the nine categories, were compared with the means for the girls, with the N varying from 54 to 66. In the 45 comparisons made—nine categories for five years—significant differences beyond the .05 level of confidence were found only once for activity level, twice for adaptability, three times for threshold, once for distractibility, once for persistence, and not at all for the other four categories. The significant differences were also scattered over the five years.

These very modest sex differences in temperament scores indicate that any differences in parental attitudes and behavior toward male versus female children in the preschool years do not influence tem-

TABLE 3

Socioeconomic Status (SES) and Racial Difference
in Carey Infant Temperament Scores

Race SES	High	White Middle	Low	Black Low
N	48	48	54	70
Activity	.65	.56	.52	.55
Rhythmicity	.55	.53	.67	.92**
Adaptability	.26	.35	.36	.62***
Approach *	.42	.60	.52	.75***
Threshold ***	1.14	1.27	1.48	1.35
Intensity **	1.18	1.04	.94	1.04
Mood	.42	.46	.46	.60**
Distractibility	.56	.65	.63	.65
Persistence	.75	.80	.70	.78

*p < .05
**p < .01
***p < .001

peramental individuality significantly, at least in the NYLS families.

Sameroff and Kelly (28) determined the temperamental characteristics of 220 four-month-old infants, using the Carey questionnaire.
The findings were related to the sex of the infant, birth order, race
and socioeconomic status. No sex differences were found in their
sample of four-month-olds, but two significant differences were found
related to birth order. Firstborn infants were rated as more active
and more adaptable than later-borns.

The sample was subdivided into three socioeconomic status (SES)
groups based on the occupational status and educational achievement of the father. High-SES individuals were primarily administra-
tive personnel, managers and professionals; middle-SES individuals
were primarily clerical workers, technical workers, and small business owners; low-SES individuals included skilled, semi-skilled and
unskilled workers. Since the Blacks in the Rochester sample were
predominantly from lower socioeconomic backgrounds, the racial

comparison was restricted to whites of similar socioeconomic level. Table 3 shows the results of these analyses.

As shown in Table 3, social class differences were primarily reflected in the threshold and intensity categories. The lower the SES of the family, the more likely the child was to be rated as having high intensity and low threshold for stimulation. A puzzling curvilinear relationship was found in the approach category. Both the high- and low-SES infants were rated as being more approaching than the middle-SES group.

In the racial comparison, Black infants were rated as more difficult on four of the five variables contributing to difficult temperament. They were significantly less rhythmic, less adaptable and less approaching, and they showed significantly poorer mood. Such a major difference in temperament raises questions about the effect of possible subculture variables on mother's questionnaire responses.

Sameroff and Kelly recommended that until other data are available to confirm these social status and racial differences in temperament, scores derived from the Carey questionnaire should be compared to subculture norms rather than the total population norms.

DeVries and Sameroff (29) reported temperament data from an African sample of infants in three East African tribes. The Carey questionnaire was translated and administered by deVries. The three tribes all lived in Kenya, a country which straddles the equator and has varied geographical conditions. The current rapid transition of many African cultures from traditional to modernized living styles produces a diversity of cultural patterns within as well as between each of the tribes in the study.

The Kikuyu are a highly modernized tribe with many men leaving the traditional farming life to work for wages. Traditionally the infant is in continuous contact with either one of the wives or an older sibling. In the more modernized homes contact is reduced as the infant, for example, is left to sleep in a cot instead of on the mother's back. The infant is viewed as fragile and helpless during the first few months.

In contrast, the Digo, an agrarian tribe in the coastal plain, view the infant as competent from birth. They begin toilet and motor training during the first few weeks of life. The daily routine and

TABLE 4

Temperament Scores from Kikuyu, Digo, and Maasi Infants

	Kikuyu	Digo	Maasi	Total
N	77	53	48	178
Activity	.53	.83	1.01	.75***
Rhythmicity	1.28	1.61	.86	1.26***
Adaptability	.91	.74	.63	.78***
Approach	.91	.83	.59	.80***
Threshold	1.25	1.16	1.15	1.19
Intensity	.76	.89	.92	.84**
Mood	.89	.82	.74	.83*
Distractibility	.97	.49	.78	.78***
Persistence	.71	1.02	1.22	.94***

*p < .05
**p < .01
***p < .001

family life of the Digo, who dwell in a tropical climate, are similar to that of the Kikuyu, who live in the more temperate highlands.

The nomadic Maasi differ from the two agrarian tribes both in culture and racial background. The Maasi are Nilo-Hamitic, while both the Kikuyu and Digo are Bantu. The Maasi herd cattle on vast inland plateaus and live in igloo-like homes. In their strict traditional life, child-rearing is carried out by a variety of women who interchangeably tend to infant needs, including breast-feeding. After spending the first weeks in a dark smoky hut, the child spends most of his time tied to his mother's back.

Table 4 shows the temperament scores from the three tribes.

Compared to the American norms, there was only one category in which the African sample was in congruence, i.e., threshold. In every other category there were significant differences between the African and American sample, as well as among the three tribes. The cross-cultural data indicate that temperament must be interpreted within a cultural context.

DeVries and Sameroff suggest that the differences among groups may be accounted for in a number of ways. Response bias could account for much of the difference in spite of much effort to make the questionnaire culturally appropriate. Concepts of timing and culture-bound ideas of infant behavior may already have influenced maternal responses. Tribal child-rearing practice as well as genetic differences between the Maasi and two Bantu groups may be influential. Early infant experience differs from tribe to tribe as well as across economic class levels within tribes.

CONCLUSION

This review of the available data suggests an appreciable, but by no means exclusive, genetic role in the determination of temperamental individuality in the young infant. Prenatal or perinatal brain damage does not appear to influence temperament in any striking fashion. The data also indicate that parental attitudes and functioning, as shaped by the sex of the child or special concerns for a premature infant, at the very most have a modest etiological influence on temperament.

The sociocultural factors appear to have some influence, as indicated by the comparisons between the NYLS and Puerto Rican working-class samples and by the data reported by Sameroff and Kelly and deVries and Sameroff. Special idiosyncratic perinatal characteristics such as chronic anxiety preceding or at least starting in pregnancy may also be significant.

Korner has suggested that behavioral sex differences in the neonate may result from the action of hormones in utero in sensitizing the organism's central nervous system (30). It may be that prenatal variations in hormonal activity or other chemical or physiological influences on the developing brain may play a highly significant role in the etiology of temperamental individuality. This hypothesis still remains to be tested.

Brazelton (31) has developed a sensitive scale for measuring the level of sensory and neuromuscular functioning in the newborn and young infant which is now in wide use. It would be of great interest to compare the findings in a sample of newborns on the Brazelton Scale with their temperament scores in later infancy. Such a comparison could illuminate the relationship of temperament to neuro-muscular patterns at birth.

A definitive study of the role of the parent also remains to be done. A promising approach would be to identify parental characteristics and neonatal temperament systematically in an appropriate sample, then determine the infants' temperament two to three months and six months later, and finally correlate changes in temperament during this early infancy period with specific parental attributes.

Temperamental individuality is well established by the time the infant is two to three months old. The origins of temperament must therefore be sought in the factors reviewed in this chapter: genetic, prenatal, and early postnatal parental influences. Intra- and extra-familial influences exclusive of the parent can be considered to be of negligible behavioral significance in the first few months of life.

Once temperamental individuality is established, it cannot be considered immutable as development proceeds, any more than any other characteristic of the growing child. Whatever their role may be in the origin of temperament, environmental influences may very well accentuate, modify, or even change temperamental traits over time. This issue will be examined in the next chapter.

REFERENCES

1. A. M. Torgersen, "Temperamental Differences in Infants: Their Cause as Shown Through Twin Studies." Doctoral dissertation, University of Oslo, Norway, 1973.
2. A. M. Torgersen, "Temperamental Differences in Infants: Illustrated Through a Study of Twins." Paper presented at a conference on Temperament and Personality, Warsaw, Poland, 1974.
3. *Ibid.*
4. M. Rutter, S. Korn and H. G. Birch, "Genetic and Environmental Factors in the Development of Primary Reaction Patterns," *British J. Clin. Soc. Psychol.*, 2:161 (1963).
5. S. Chess, S. Ladimer and A. Thomas, "Behavioral Development of a Pair of Identical Twins Separated at Birth." In preparation.
6. T. Dobzhansky, *Mankind Evolving* (New Haven: Yale University Press, 1962).
7. W. B. Carey, W. L. Lipton and R. A. Meyers, "Temperament in Adopted and Foster Babies," *Child Welfare*, 53:352-359 (1974).
8. A. J. Sameroff and P. Kelly, "Socio-economic Status, Racial and Mental Health Factors in Infant Temperament." Unpublished manuscript.
9. R. J. Cadoret, L. Cunningham, R. Loftus and J. Edwards, "Studies of

Adoptees from Psychiatrically Disturbed Biologic Parents," *J. Pediatrics*, 87:301-306 (1975).

10. A. M. Torgersen, *op. cit.* (1974).
11. M. Hertzig, "Neurologic Findings in Prematurely Born Children at School Age," *Life History Research in Psychopathology, Vol. 3*, eds., D. Ricks, A. Thomas and M. Roff. (Minneapolis: University of Minnesota Press, 1974) pp. 42-52.
12. M. Hertzig, personal communication.
13. P. M. Wender, *Minimal Brain Dysfunction in Children* (New York: John Wiley and Sons, 1971), pp. 43-44.
14. S. Chess and M. Hassibi, "Behavior Deviations in Mentally Retarded Children," *J. Am. Acad. Child Psychiat.*, 9:282-297 (1970).
15. S. Chess, S. Korn and P. Fernandez, *Psychiatric Disorders of Children with Congenital Rubella* (New York: Brunner/Mazel, 1971).
16. S. Chess, "Evaluation of Behavior Disorders in Mentally Retarded Children," *J. Am. Acad. Child Psych.*, in press.
17. B. Birns, W. H. Bridger and S. Barten, "Longitudinal Study of Temperamental Characteristics of Infants," Unpublished data.
18. R. Q. Bell, G. M. Weller and M. F. Waldrop, "Newborn and Pre-schooler: Organization of Behavior and Relations Between Periods," *Monograph of the Society for Research in Child Development*, Vol. 132, No. 142 (1971).
19. A. J. Sameroff, "Infant Risk Factors in Developmental Deviancy," Paper presented at the International Association for Child Psychiatry and Allied Professions, Philadelphia, July, 1974.
20. A. Katcher, unpublished data.
21. P. T. Sarett, "A Study of the Interaction Effects of Infant Temperament on Maternal Attachment." Doctoral dissertation, Rutgers University, New Jersey, 1975.
22. A. F. Korner and M. C. Kramer, "Individual Differences in Spontaneous Oral Behavior in Neonates," *Third Symposium in Oral Sensation and Perception: The Mouth of the Infant*, J. F. Bosma, ed. (Springfield, Ill.: Charles C Thomas, 1972).
23. A. F. Korner and E. B. Thoman, "The Relative Efficiency of Contact and Vestibular-Proprioceptive Stimulation in Soothing Neonates," *Child Development*, 43: 443-453 (1972).
24. A. J. Sameroff, *op. cit.*
25. P. T. Sarett, *op. cit.*
26. A. F. Korner, "Sex Differences in Newborns, with Special Reference to Differences in the Organization of Oral Behavior," *J. Child Psychol. Psychiat.*, 14:19-29 (1973).
27. M. Hertzig, personal communication.
28. A. J. Sameroff and P. Kelly, *op. cit.*
29. M. W. deVries and A. J. Sameroff, "Influences on Infant Temperament in Three East African Cultures." In preparation.
30. A. F. Korner, *op. cit.*
31. Brazelton, T. B., *Neonatal Behavioral Assessment Scale*, Clinics in Developmental Medicine No. 50, Philadelphia: J. B. Lippincott Co., 1973.

12

Consistency and inconsistency of temperament over time

Theories of psychological development, whatever their bias, generally presume a linear predictable sequence from conception or birth onward. As Sameroff points out in his critical review of this concept, "Scientists with viewpoints biased toward either a maturational or an environmentalist position generally make an implicit assumption that behaviors necessarily build on each other to produce a continuity of functioning from conception to adulthood. The continuity seen in the physical identity of each individual is generalized to the psychological identity of each individual. Just as an individual retains the same body throughout the lifespan, so must he have the same mind" (1).

The concepts of continuity and predictability take credence from the multitude of instances in which adults behave as they did in their earlier years, pursue the same interests and express the same values and goals, and resist vigorously attempts by others to change these behaviors and values. The I.Q. score is presumed to remain constant from early childhood on, and so are the psychodynamic mechanisms the individual uses to cope with his environment. If linear continuity exists, then we can predict the course of behavioral development and

155

know where and how to intercede to prevent behavior disorders in the future.

Theories of development may take many forms: preformism on a hereditary and constitutional basis; predetermined stages of instinctual development in Freudian theory; a hierarchy of ideational-behavioral stages in Erikson's formulation; conditioned reflex patterns to avoid anxiety in behavior theory; or sociological theories such as the culture of poverty. But almost all agree in asserting that later behavior derives directly and predictably from childhood patterns.

Where a developmental concept, such as Piaget's, envisions successive stages which are qualitatively different, other theorists will assert that even in such instances the character of functioning at a new stage is determined by the nature of functioning at the preceding stage. This commitment to the continuity-predictability model is well articulated by Bronson: "Along with some others, I see our apparent inability to make empirical predictions about later personality from the early years as so much against good sense, common observation, and the thrust of all developmental theories that I can take it only as an indictment of established paradigms and methods rather than as evidence of a developmental reality" (2).

As we originally began to observe clinically and impressionistically the phenomenon of temperament, we were struck by the many dramatic evidences of continuity in individuals we knew, sometimes from early childhood to adulthood. It was tempting to generalize from these instances to the concept that an adult's temperamental characteristics could be predicted from a knowledge of his behavior style in early childhood. However, such a formulation would be completely at variance with our fundamental commitment to an interactionist viewpoint, in which individual behavioral development is conceived as a constantly evolving and changing process of organism-environment interaction.

All other psychological phenomena, such as intellectual competence, coping mechanisms, adaptive patterns, and value systems, can and do change over time. How could it be otherwise for temperament? Perhaps our inability to predict accurately from earlier behavior does reflect a "developmental reality" and not just "an indictment of established paradigms and methods" (3). Perhaps the continuity that is so frequently observed results not from consistency in the psychological attribute *per se,* but from consistency in the environment-organism interaction. Thus, Bloom states that intelligence loses its plasticity after about four years of age. However, he makes this point: "Our research suggests that although the environment may have its greatest effect on individuals in the first year or so that they are within it, its effect is stabilized and reinforced only when the environment is relatively constant over a period of time" (4).

The NYLS has provided the opportunity to examine a number of issues with regard to continuity or discontinuity in psychological development. The middle childhood period has been studied in relation to Freud's concept of a sexual latency period which was expanded by others to an all-encompassing concept denoting the absence of change during this age period. As Shaw commented, the term came to suggest "that nothing really important is happening and that the child is simply waiting for puberty to begin" (5). Our own findings in the NYLS indicated clearly that the middle childhood period is one of continued development and psychologic change (6). We would suggest that the label "latency" is a confusing and inappropriate way to designate and characterize children between the ages of six and 12, and that the term be abandoned.

The problem of prediction from early to later childhood and adolescence is also highlighted by the cases of behavior disorder in the NYLS (7). Of 42 clinical cases diagnosed in the childhood period and then followed into adolescence, 19 recovered, five improved, three were unchanged, eight became mildly or moderately worse, and seven became markedly worse. In a number of the cases the clinical course could be related to specific factors, such as the effectiveness of parent guidance and the overall nature of the parent-child relationship. In other instances, however, the reasons for favorable outcome are not obvious, despite the extensive longitudinal data available in each case. In addition, five new cases have thus far been identified in the adolescent period. Here, again, our review of the anterospective longitudinal data, while still incomplete, has as yet not revealed any specific characteristics of the five cases or their families in early childhood which could have been predictive of the development of pathology.

In considering the data on the consistency of temperament over time, certain methodological problems should first be mentioned. A number of the difficulties in attempting to predict later psychological development from infancy data have been discussed by Rutter (8). These include: 1) the amount of development still to occur, i.e., the fact that most of psychological development takes place after early infancy; 2) modifiability of psychological development by the child's subsequent experiences; 3) effects of intrauterine environment on the characteristics of the young infant, and disappearance of these effects over time; 4) the effects of differing rates of maturation, which may make for wide variations in different children in levels of correlation between infancy and later measures; and 5) differences in the function being tested in infancy and maturity, so that a test in infancy may not measure the same attribute as a test in later childhood or adult life.

With regard to temperament scores, Rutter points up several specific methodological problems, such as the reliance on adjectives parents use in describing their children's behavior, the possibility of selective bias in determining which episodes of behavior the parent or other observer reports, and the problem of separating the content from the style of behavior. Most important, he feels, is the effect that the changing context of the child's behavior might have on the behavioral ratings.

This last problem raised by Rutter bears on a knotty issue in all developmental research. A specific characteristic may have significant continuity in an individual or a group from one age period to another. Yet the changing context of the child's behavior and the emergence of new forms of behavior at later age-stage levels of development may give the same characteristic very different forms of expression. Kagan (9), in his consideration of this issue, has used the term "homotypic continuity" to refer to stabilities over time in the same response and "heterotypic continuity" to refer "to stabilities between two classes of responses that are manifestly different, but theoretically related." He points out that even if this behavioral phenomenon itself may remain stable over time, it may still be the expression of different motives, standards and expectancies.

The problem, therefore, is one of determining when dissimilar behavior over time reflects the same characteristic—whether it be temperament, motivation, cognition, values and standards, or psychopathology—and when the same behavior reflects different characteristics at different age periods. As regards temperament specifically, the behavioral criteria for any temperamental trait must necessarily change over time as the child's psychological functioning develops and evolves. What remains consistent over time is the *definitional identity* of the characteristic (a term suggested by our co-worker, Dr. Sam Korn). Thus, a two-year-old may have loud temper tantrums, and at 18 years of age be described as "hot tempered." Both behaviors, though phenomenologically different, will fit the definition of intensity of mood. Or a two-month-old may show his withdrawal responses by the first reactions to the bath and a new food, and a ten-year-old by his first reactions to a new peer group or academic subject.

Definitional identity over time, of course, is not self-evident. It involves theoretical concepts of the developmental process, and investigators with different theoretical frameworks will disagree as to whether specific behaviors at different age-periods reflect the same psychological characteristic or not. The validity and heuristic value of any theoretical concept, as well as the internal consistency of its application to specific behavioral phenomena, are then evaluated according to traditional scientific methods.

In addition to these issues raised by Rutter, several other methodological problems regarding the determination of consistency over time have been apparent in the NYLS. A child's characteristic expression of temperament may be blurred at any specific age-period by routinization of functioning. Thus, an infant who shows marked withdrawal reactions to the bath, new foods and new people may, a year or two later, show positive responses to these same stimuli because of repeated exposure and final adaptation. If, at that time he experiences few new situations and stimuli, the withdrawal reaction may not be evident. Adaptation and routinization of activities may, in the same way, blur the expression of other temperamental traits, such as irregularity, slow adaptability and negative mood expression. Limitation of opportunity for physical activity may lead to frequent restless movements which may be interpreted as high activity or even hyperactivity. The procedures for quantitative scores necessarily rely on routine judgments and scoring approaches which can preclude the identification of meaningful subtleties in the developmental course of individual children. Specific single items of behavior may sometimes be significant in indicating temperamental consistency from one age-period to another, but quantitative scoring methods can hardly give proper weight to the importance of such functionally significant items.

Finally, the issue of consistency of temperament over time cannot be studied globally. One or several temperamental traits may show striking continuity from one specific age-period to another and the other attributes may not. At other age-periods the reverse may be true: The originally consistent traits may not show the correlations, whereas other attributes may now do so. The factors affecting the identification of continuity over time are so complex and variable as to create all kinds of permutations in the patterns of correlations.

CONSISTENCY OF TEMPERAMENT OVER TIME:
QUANTITATIVE ANALYSIS

As indicated above, the factors which may make for inconsistency of temperament over time or for the blurring of patterns of consistency which may exist are especially likely to influence the quantitative data analysis. The NYLS quantitative temperament scores for the first five years of life were utilized to calculate inter-year correlations for the nine categories. The scores for an individual child were pooled for each year. Product-moment correlations were calculated based on these pooled weighted scores for years one to five. The correlations are presented in Table 1.

As can be seen from Table 1, there are significant correlations from one year to the next for all categories except approach/withdrawal, distractibility and persistence. As the time span for the comparison is increased, from one year to two, three or four years, the

TABLE 1

Inter-Year Correlations for Each of the Nine Categories
(N = 100-110)

Category	1-2	1-3	1-4	1-5	2-3	2-4	2-5	3-4	3-5	4-5
Activity	.30*	.21*	.26*	.16	.30*	.31*	.23*	.26*	.29*	.31*
Rhythmicity	.44*	.39*	.21*	.15	.32*	.03	.07	.10	.09	.37*
Adaptability	.38*	.22*	.18	.07	.46*	.37*	.25*	.54*	.33*	.51*
Approach/ Withdrawal	.07	.13	.01	—.03	.11	.14	.06	.30*	.07	.33*
Threshold	.39*	.36*	.14	.21*	.25*	—.03	.09	.18	.19	.11
Intensity	.47*	.17	.02	.10	.28*	.01	.13	.30*	.14	.32*
Mood	.45*	.25*	.10	.08	.18	.06	.16	.28*	.11	.25*
Distractibility	—.05	.13	—.12	.12	.15	.05	—.06	.12	.37*	.14
Persistence	.11	.04	.01	.09	.38*	.23*	.16	.24*	.28*	.13

*Correlation is significant beyond the .05 level of confidence for respective N (N varies due to cases with no scored items in particular category for a given year).

number of significant correlations decreases. The number of significant correlations is greatest for the categories of activity level and adaptability.

Approach/withdrawal, distractibility, and persistence, the three categories with the least inter-year correlations, are also the three categories with skewed distribution curves of the group-weighted scores for each of the first five years. The other six categories, with higher inter-year correlations, all approximate normal distribution curves. This suggests that a lack of sufficient differentiation of the subjects by the quantitative scores for approach/withdrawal, distractibility, and persistence may be at least partially responsible for the low level of inter-year correlations.

The dwindling in significant correlations over longer time periods may be due to the cumulative effect of the methodological problems discussed above, to change in the expression of temperament over time, or both. It would be of interest to analyze quantitatively the consistency of temperament over time in individual children. It might be that certain children show marked consistency and others show marked inconsistency. These variations might be correlated with specific environmental influences or events. The coding of data in the NYLS would make such an analysis feasible, but thus far such a project has not been undertaken.

McDevitt has recently reported a longitudinal assessment of continuity in temperamental characteristics from infancy to early childhood (10). The sample consisted of 187 children from primarily white middle-class families. The Carey questionnaire was administered to the mothers when the children were between four and eight months of age, and the Behavioral Style Questionnaire developed by McDevitt and Carey was administered when the children were between three and seven years of age. Quantitative analysis showed that activity level, adaptability, threshold and intensity were stable for children of both sexes up to five years. Rhythmicity was stable for girls, mood for boys. At five to seven years activity level and mood were stable, but only for boys. At each age interval, easy, slow-to-warm-up and difficult temperament types were obtained by cluster analysis, with a significant degree of consistency of cluster assignment from infancy to five years. From infancy to five to seven years, there was little cluster stability. McDevitt takes the position that "temperamental characteristics are influential in personality and behavior throughout development and that periods of instability are reflective of concurrent developmental changes in behavioral competence or major changes in social environment. . . . It is the theoretical definition of the constructs which remains stable" (11).

CONSISTENCY OF TEMPERAMENT OVER TIME:
QUALITATIVE ANALYSIS

As the children in the NYLS have been followed from early infancy through adolescence, a number of qualitative longitudinal studies of the children have been done. These analyses have provided information on a number of issues: responses to environmental events and stresses in the preschool years (12), adaptive patterns in the preschool child (13), development in middle childhood (14), temperament and school functioning and learning (15), temperament and behavior disorders (16), sexual patterns in adolescence (17), and the evolution of behavior disorders into adolescence (18). These qualitative studies also make it possible to trace the consistency of temperamental characteristics in individual children over time.

In general, five patterns can be defined: 1) clear-cut consistency; 2) consistency in some aspects of temperament at one period and in other aspects at other times; 3) distortion of the expression of temperament by other factors, such as psychodynamic patterns; 4) consistency in temperament but qualitative change in temperament-environment interaction; and 5) change in a conspicuous temperamental trait. Any individual child may show a combination of several of these five possibilities, i.e., consistency over time with one or several temperamental traits, distortion in another, change in several others, etc.

These five patterns will be illustrated by brief vignettes from the longitudinal data.

1) *Consistency Over Time*

Karen's responses to new situations and new people were typical of the Slow-To-Warm-Up Child in infancy and childhood. No problems developed because her parents understood and accepted her behavioral patterns and gave her enough time to adapt to new situations in an unpressured way. One incident of interest occurred when the nursery school had a special program for the parents. When Karen came in with her mother and saw the congregation of strange adults, she climbed on her mother's lap, stayed there all evening and refused to join her group. As the mother described it, "All the other parents were looking at me, and I knew they were mentally criticizing me for encouraging my daughter's clinging and dependency." Fortunately for Karen, her mother was amused by the experience, and not threatened by these derogatory judgments of other parents.

Karen, now 16 years old, has pursued this same developmental course throughout. She has responded "warily" (as her mother puts it) to almost all new situations—a change of school, a new summer group program, a new curriculum. However, this initial slow-to-warm-up reaction has never created avoidance or permanent withdrawal from stimulating situations and experiences. A new mathematics course was difficult and distressing at first, but she persisted and now plans to take an elective course next year. Karen still asks her mother to call a new doctor or dentist for the first appointment, but then takes over all the subsequent arrangements. She has many friends and interests and has become one of the student activity leaders. She is assertive and appropriately independent for her age, with no evidence of excessive dependency on her parents or others.

Dorothy's temperamental pattern was characterized by frequent negative reactions of mild intensity, a high degree of persistence and a relatively low activity level. These characteristics were difficult for her parents to understand and accept. They themselves were both intense, positive and energetic people. Dorothy tended to express frustration by whining and fussing—behaviors which irritated her parents considerably. However, once the parents gained insight into Dorothy's normal behavioral style, they were able to make allowance for her slow movements and accept her pattern of expression.

In the middle childhood years Dorothy's persistence became a major asset in mastering academic demands. Though she lacked a superior I.Q. level, her ability to plug away at tasks resulted in a high level of academic achievement and a sense of confidence in her scholastic abilities. She also made friends slowly but successfully. In the early adolescent years, however, she again came into conflict with her mother. Her father had died suddenly, a younger sister had developed serious behavioral problems and the mother was highly pressured by her need to work full-time, maintain the family, and cope with the younger sister's difficulties. The tension in the family increased Dorothy's negative reactions, her mother was now impatient with them because of her own burdens, and frequent antagonistic mother-child interactions developed. However, these never evolved into any significant behavior disorder at home and Dorothy's academic and social functioning outside the home continued satisfactorily.

Dorothy was accepted into an excellent college away from home and did well in the beginning. By the end of the first year, however, she began to be progressively unhappy over her social functioning, dropped out of college after the first semester of the second year and asked for psychiatric consultation with one of us (A.T.). In this interview Dorothy reported increasing dissatisfaction with her peer social relationships, both male and female. She made friends slowly, as always, but this did not disturb her. What did concern her was her difficulty in "opening up" to her friends, in reciprocating their confidences and expressions of positive feeling. This one-sided interchange caused her relationships to drift, with eventual withdrawal and isolation on her part. Her academic work was no problem. In this area she was self-confident and could easily concentrate and work hard, as always.

Psychiatric evaluation showed no evidence of a major mental illness. Dorothy's facial expression was serious, even gloomy, though she did smile brightly though briefly at intervals. Her concerns were expressed in a low, even voice, though she was thoughtful and focused intently on the issues that bothered her. Her major temperamental characteristics were clearly unchanged from childhood: mild negative mood expressions and persistence. Her low activity level was reflected in the sedentary nature of her interests. While it was probable that these temperamental characteristics were playing a major role in the development of her current behavior problems, analytic psychotherapy, which was arranged, was required to define the interplay of temperament with other possible etiological influences.

2) Consistency in Some Aspects of Temperament at One Period and Other Aspects at Other Times

Carl requested a discussion with one of us (S.C.) after his first term in college because of feelings of depression and inability to cope with the academic and social situation at college. He had made virtually no friends and found studying difficult, experiences he could not recall ever having had before. He had done well academically in high school, had many friends, found school enjoyable, and had a wide range of interests, including the piano. In the interview he was alert, articulate and in very good contact. He did not appear depressed, but rather bewildered at what was happening, exclaiming, "This just isn't me!"

The anterospective longitudinal data showed that in earlier life Carl had been one of our most extreme Difficult Child temperamental types, with intense, negative reactions to new situations and slow adaptability only after many exposures. This was true whether it was the first bath or first solid foods in infancy, the beginning of nursery school and elementary school, first birthday parties or the first shopping trip. Each experience evoked stormy responses, with loud crying and struggling to get away. However, his parents learned to anticipate Carl's reactions, knew that if they were patient, presented only one or a few new situations at a time and gave him the opportunity for repeated exposure, Carl would finally adapt positively. Furthermore, once he adapted, his intensity of responses gave him a zestful enthusiastic involvement, just as it gave his initial negative reactions a loud and stormy character. His parents became clear that the difficulties in raising Carl were due to his temperament and not to their being "bad parents." The father even looked on his son's shrieking and turmoil as a sign of "lustiness." As a result of this positive parent-child interaction, Carl never became a behavior problem even though Difficult Children as a group are significantly at risk for disturbed development.

In his later childhood and high school years Carl met very few radically new situations. He lived in the same community and went through the neighborhood school with the same schoolmates and friends. Academic progression was gradual and new subjects were not introduced abruptly. He had sufficient time to adapt to new demands, and generally became enthusiastically involved with a number of activities. As a result, he developed an appropriate positive and self-confident self-image. He played the piano and spoke with animated zest of his pleasure in this activity. He was asked in the interview, "Do you remember what happened when you first started piano lessons?" He thought for a moment and a startled expression came over his face. He described how he had asked his mother if he could take lessons, and she said yes—but she insisted on one condition, that he stick to the lessons for six months, no matter how he felt, and then, if he wanted, he could give them up. He agreed, started, and began by "hating it." But he stuck to the bargain and six months later his mother asked if he wanted to quit. His answer was, "Are you crazy? I love it!"

When Carl went off to college away from home, however, he was suddenly confronted with a whole series of new situations—strange surroundings, an entirely new peer group, new types of faculty approaches, school schedules and curriculum, and a complex relationship with a girl student with whom he was living. Again, as with the many new adaptive demands of early childhood, his temperamental responses of withdrawal and intense negative reactions were expressed. Other possible reasons for his difficulties were explored—dependency needs for his parents, sexual conflict, anxiety over academic demands, peer competition—but no evidence of any of these was elicited.

Only the one discussion was necessary with Carl, and consisted primarily in clarifying for him his temperamental pattern and the techniques he could use for adaptation. Actually, Carl had already begun to take these steps on his own—cutting the number of new subjects, disciplining himself to study each subject daily for a specific time, attenuating his involvement with the girl, and making a point of attending peer social group activities, no matter how uncomfortable he felt. By the end of the academic year his difficulties had disappeared and his subsequent functioning has been on the previous positive level. He was told that similar negative reactions to new experiences might occur in the future. His response was "That's all right. I know how to handle them now."

Carl's behavior showed a number of dramatic shifts over the years, from early childhood to middle childhood and early adolescence, to the onset of college life and then to his subsequent adaptation at college. But these behavioral changes did not constitute change in his temperamental pattern. The phenomenon of shifts in behavioral patterns over time even though underlying psychodynamic patterns remain consistent is well recognized. The same phenomenon can occur with temperament.

3) *Distortion of the Expression of Temperament Over Time*

Norman was seen at age 17 by one of us (S.C.), who had followed him since age four and a half because of persistent behavior disturbance. At age 17 he had already dropped out of two colleges in one year, and was planning to go abroad for a work-study program. He was in good contact, but dejected and depressed. He was extraordinarily self-derogatory, said he couldn't finish anything he started, was lazy, and didn't know what he wanted to do. "My father doesn't respect me, and let's face it, why should he." He talked of "hoping to find myself" in a vague, unplanned way.

Norman had always been a highly distractible child with a short attention span. Intelligent and pleasant, the youngest in his class throughout his school years due to birth date, he started his academic career with good mastery. However, at home his parents were impatient and critical of him even in the preschool years because of his quick shifts of attention, dawdling at bedtime, and apparent "forgetfulness." By his fifth year he showed various reactive symptoms such as sleeping difficulties, nocturnal enuresis, poor eating habits and nail tearing. Year by year his academic standing slipped. His father, a hard-driving, very persistent professional man, became increasingly hypercritical and derogatory of Norman. The father equated the boy's short attention span and distractibility with irresponsibility, lack of character and willpower. He used these terms openly to the boy and stated that he "disliked" his son. The mother grew to understand the issue, but no discussion with the father as to the normalcy of his son's temperament and the impossibility of the boy's living up to his standards of concentrated hard work succeeded in altering the father's attitude. He remained convinced that Norman had an irresponsible character and was headed for future failure—indeed a self-fulfilling prophecy. There were several times when the boy tried to comply with his father's standards and made himself sit still with his homework for long periods of time. This only resulted in generalized tension and multiple tics and Norman could not sustain this effort so dissonant with his temperament—another proof to himself and his father of his failure. Direct psychotherapy was arranged in early adolescence, but Norman entered this with a passive, defeated attitude and the effort was unsuccessful. His subsequent development was all too predictable.

In Norman's case the dissonance between parental standards and demands and his temperamental characteristics led to psychodynamic patterns which then distorted, but did not change, temperament qualitatively. The acceptance of his father's derogatory and hypercritical value judgments on himself led to increasing drifting, shifting quickly from one vague plan to another, grasping at straws —all in all, a caricature of his temperamental characteristics of distractibility and short attention span.

4) Consistency in Temperament, but Qualitative Change in Temperament-Environment Interaction

Nancy, when seen in the routinely scheduled interview at age 17, was bright, alert and lively. She was involved in a number of activities that interested her, and reported an active social life, good school functioning and a pleasant relationship with her parents. She had no symptoms of psychological disturbances. Nancy's report of positive functioning was confirmed in the separate interview with her parents. They did describe her as "hot-headed," but did not consider this a problem.

It would have been very difficult to predict this favorable development into adolescence in Nancy's early years. Like Carl, she was a Difficult Child temperamentally from early infancy onward. But unlike Carl's parents, Nancy's parents responded to her intensity, irregularity in biological functions, negative reactions and slow adaptability so as to produce extreme stress and difficulty in development in the youngster. The father was highly critical of her behavior, rigid in his expectations for quick positive adaptation, and punitive when Nancy did not respond to his demands. The mother was intimidated by both husband and daughter and vacillating and anxious in her handling of her child. By the age of six Nancy developed explosive anger outbursts, fear of the dark, thumb-sucking, hair-pulling and poor peer group relationships. Her symptoms and clinical findings were severe enough to warrant the diagnosis of neurotic behavior disorder, moderately severe. Psychotherapy was instituted with some improvement. But the dramatic change occurred when in the fourth and fifth grades Nancy showed evidence of musical and dramatic talent. This brought increasingly favorable attention and praise from teachers and other parents. This talent also ranked high in her parents' own hierarchy of desirable attributes. Nancy's father now began to see his daughter's intense and explosive personality, not as a sign of a "rotten kid" as heretofore, but as evidence of a budding artist. She was now a child he could be proud of, and he could afford to make allowances for her "artistic" temperament. With this view of Nancy and her temperament the mother was also able to relax and relate positively to her daughter. Nancy was permitted to adapt at her own pace, the positive aspects of her temperament came into evidence, and her self-image improved progressively. By adolescence all evidence of her neurotic symptomatology and functioning had disappeared and she was considered as recovered from her neurotic disorder.

5) *Change in a Conspicuous Temperamental Trait over Time*

David, when seen in the direct interview at age 17 years, was obese and conspicuously apathetic and lethargic. He reported little interest or involvement in any kind of outside activities. The time-related interview with his parents confirmed this observation of David as a very low-active adolescent.

In his early years David had been consistently one of the most motorically active children in our study sample. He was always in motion, with a cheerful and friendly manner. However, David's home environment was not a happy one, but marked by constant discord and destructive competition between his parents. They repeatedly preached to David and others what a superior child he was (David did indeed have a superior I.Q.), and that any difficulties he had in school were due to poor teaching. As time went on David's school performance deteriorated, as did his other activities. The parents held the school and teachers entirely responsible for their son's growing school failure, and over time David internalized his parents' almost paranoid-like projection of blame. Motivation dwindled, any critical self-evaluation was entirely absent, and disinterest and apathy became progressively dominant features of his overall functioning. With these attitudes it was no surprise that resistance to psychotherapy was complete.

In David's case, temperament did not appear to play an influential role in the ontogenesis of his behavior disorder. Furthermore, a conspicuous temperamental characteristic of his early years, high activity level, was no longer in evidence by adolescence. On the contrary, he was apathetic and sluggish and showed a strikingly low activity level. The inertia and inactivity appeared to be psychodynamically determined.

In our original analysis of David's development, we conceived of the possibility that his temperamental attribute of high activity level might not have been changed but only "submerged" by the psychodynamic influences on his behavior. However, temperament is a phenomenologic description of behavioral style at any particular point in time. Whatever the findings are at any time, whether high or low activity level, persistence or non-persistence, etc., and whatever changes may occur, the designation of temperament is based on those findings. In that sense, the concept of "submersion" of a temperamental trait is inapplicable.

DISCUSSION

In the above vignettes, the data and findings have of necessity been selectively culled and reported from the enormous amount of longitudinal information available on each youngster. In each case, however, the essential facts regarding child psychopathology, parental attitudes and practices and special environmental events available in our records have been sketched in. Of course, it is always possible that, even with the mass of data accumulated on each child, significant data have been missed at one point or another in the developmental course from infancy to adolescence. This is one of the inevitable contingencies of any behavioral research and a special hazard of an anterospective longitudinal study.

From the quantitative inter-year correlations of temperament for years one to five, and from the qualitatively derived vignettes, it is clear that temperament does not necessarily follow a consistent, linear course. Discontinuities over time are certainly to some extent the result of the methodological problems in data collection and analysis. Much more important, however, are the functional, dynamic reasons which determine continunity or discontinuity over time.

Temperament is a phenomenologic term in which the categorization of any individual is derived from the constellation of behaviors exhibited at any one age-period. These behaviors are the result of all the influences, past and present, which shape and modify these behaviors in a constantly evolving interactive process. Consistency of a temperamental trait or constellation in an individual over time, therefore, may require stability in these interactional forces, such as environmental influences, motivations and abilities. The vignettes reported above illustrate some of the vicissitudes of temperament over time as one expression of the dynamics of the organism-environment interactional process.

In Carl's case, the Difficult Child pattern was strikingly and consistently in evidence in early childhood in the response to the demands for adaptation to one new situation and expectation after another—the bath, new foods, new people, nursery school, etc. There were withdrawal reactions to the new, irregular biological functions, intense negative reactions to the new with much screaming, and slow adaptation. With patient, consistent and understanding parents and no special new situations to overwhelm him, Carl finally made the necessary adaptations to become a smoothly functioning, relaxed and happy child. He was then largely indistinguishable from the child who started with an easy temperament, except that Carl's positive mood expressions were enthusiastic and lusty—definitely an asset. An occasional special new situation, such as learning to play the piano, again evoked temperamental expressions of initial withdrawal, intense negative mood and slow adaptation. Otherwise, the middle childhood period was serene, with successful progressive mastery of gradually evolving social and academic expectations and opportunities, and proportional development of self-confidence and a positive self-image. It would be inaccurate to say that the difficult temperament was "repressed" or "latent" during this period, and use the occasional short-lived expression of his earlier childhood characteristics as evidence of some "return of the unconscious." Rather, it should be said that at any period the observable temperamental characteristics were the expression of his actual temperament at that time. Any difference from a previous time would be the consequence of modification by the evolving organism-environment interactional process. A temporary change to difficult temperament we would interpret as an actual change due to special environmental influences, not an activation of temperamental characteristics existing in some latent form. Continuity from one period to another was indicated by similarity in temperamental responses at different periods, given the same interactional dynamics. Another youngster, with a different temperamental potential, would, of course, have responded differently to the new.

However, continuity is not identity. Carl's distressing behavioral manifestations in the first year of college were similar to the difficult temperamental reactions in infancy, but not identical. His psychological structure was different at 18 years from one year of age in self-image, self-awareness, self-assurance born out of a succession of successful mastery experiences and in the repertoire of adaptive techniques available to him. As a result, the expression of temperament was different and the sequence of coping activity was also different.

In Karen, Dorothy and Norman, consistency in temperament over time was clearly evident. But this did not mean an identical developmental course for all three. In Karen's case, the environment was uniformly favorable at all times, with smooth, positive progression through childhood and adolescence. For Dorothy, the environment was basically positive, though with periods—in early childhood and the beginning college years—in which excessively stressful demands were made which were dissonant with her temperamental potential. As a result, relatively mild behavior disorders developed at these dissonant interactional periods.

In Norman's case, the environment was consistently unfavorable and dissonant with his temperamental capacities, and served to exaggerate and distort these temperamental traits in a pathological direction. In David's case, the organism-environment interactional process was also pathogenic, but was of such a nature as to change rather than distort a major temperamental trait.

Nancy illustrates most dramatically the difficulty in predicting developmental sequences. An unanticipated emergence of a special talent transformed the basic character of the organism-environment interaction. In other instances, a similar degree of change might occur from an unpredictable change in the environment or some other new emerging feature in the child's own characteristics.

Continuity and predictability can thus not be assumed for a specific attribute or pattern of the child, whether it be temperament, intellectual functioning, motivational attributes or psychodynamic defenses. What is predictable is the process of organism-environment interaction. Consistency in development will come from continuity over time in the organism and significant features of the environment. Discontinuity will result from changes in one or the other which make for modification and change in development.

REFERENCES

1. A. J. Sameroff, "Early Influences on Development, Fact or Fancy?" *Merrill-Palmer Quarterly*, 21:267-294 (1975).
2. W. C. Bronson, "Mother-Toddler Interaction: A Perspective on Studying the Development of Competence," *Merrill-Palmer Quarterly*, 20:275-301 (1974).
3. *Ibid.*
4. B. S. Bloom, *Stability and Change in Human Characteristics* (New York: John Wiley & Sons, 1964).
5. C. R. Shaw, *The Psychiatric Disorders of Childhood* (New York: Appleton-Century-Crofts, 1966).
6. A. Thomas and S. Chess, "Development in Middle Childhood," *Seminars in Psychiatry*, 4:331-341 (1972).
7. A. Thomas and S. Chess, "Evolution of Behavior Disorders into Adolescence," *Am. J. Psychiatry*, 133:5 (1976).
8. M. Rutter, "Psychological Development: Predictions from Infancy," *J. Child Psychiat. and Psychol.*, 11:49-62 (1970).
9. J. Kagan, *Change and Continuity in Infancy* (New York: John Wiley and Sons, 1971).
10. S. C. McDevitt, "A Longitudinal Assessment of Continuity and Stability in Temperamental Characteristics from Infancy to Early Childhood." Doctoral dissertation, Temple University, 1976.
11. S. C. McDevitt, Manuscript in preparation.
12. A. Thomas, H. G. Birch, S. Chess and L. C. Robbins, "Individuality in Responses of Children to Similar Environmental Situations," *Am. J. Psychiatry*, 117:434-441 (1961).
13. M. Hertzig, S. Chess, H. G. Birch and A. Thomas, "Methodology of a Study of Adaptive Functions of the Pre-School Child," *J. Am. Acad. Child Psychiat.*, 2:236-245 (1962).
14. A. Thomas and S. Chess, *op. cit.*, 1972.
15. S. Chess, A. Thomas and M. Cameron, "Temperament: Its Significance for School Adjustment and Academic Achievement," *New York University Educational Review*, 7:24-29 (1976).
16. A. Thomas, S. Chess and H. G. Birch, *Temperament and Behavior Disorders in Children* (New York: New York University Press, 1968).
17. S. Chess, A. Thomas and M. Cameron, "Sexual Attitudes and Behavior Patterns in a Middle Class Adolescent Population," Paper presented at meeting of American Orthopsychiatric Association, March 1976.
18. A. Thomas and S. Chess, *op. cit.*, 1976.

13

Temperament in the older child and the adult

In infancy, the delineation of temperamental individuality is relatively simple. The other major categories of behavior—abilities and talents (the what of behavior), and motives and goals (the why of behavior)—are rudimentary and as yet undeveloped and easy to distinguish from temperament (the how of behavior). The psychoanalytic movement, which emphasizes the role of motivational forces in development, such as drive states and psychodynamic mechanisms, has tended to postulate the existence and significance of such motivational factors even in the young infant. But this has required speculations regarding subjective intrapsychic states which cannot be validated by objective behavioral data (1), and assumption of a level of conceptual ability which is not consonant with the infant's immaturity of cerebral development and functioning (2).

By contrast, temperament in the infant past the age of two to three months can be clearly defined, scored and categorized from objective behavioral data. Temperament, in this early age-period, can also be easily separated from the simple behavioral manifestations of abilities and motivations.

As the child grows older, the task of identifying and categorizing the separate elements of behavior—temperament, abilities and moti-

175

vations—becomes more and more complex. Increasingly elaborate repertoires of abilities and talent mature, become evident and influence the developmental course. This is true in all areas—neuromuscular, perceptual, linguistic, cognitive, social and artistic. Motivational patterns become conceptualized as brain functioning develops and matures, as life experiences become cumulative in their effects, and as coping and psychodynamic mechanisms become elaborated. Motivations, abilities and temperament enter into increasingly complex interactional processes so that individual items and patterns of behavior begin to reflect this interplay of influences. Thus, it may be relatively simple in a two-year-old to determine whether slow achievement in task performance, such as feeding and dressing, is due primarily to short attention and non-persistence, avoidance because of anxiety, immaturity in neuromuscular or perceptual development, or a simple combination of these factors. In an adolescent or an adult the isolation of the factor or combination of factors responsible for difficulty in task achievement in school or work may be much more difficult.

The identification of the category or categories of characteristics responsible for any specific behavioral phenomena must also be distinguished from the developmental processes and dynamics involved in the evolution of behavior. The nature of the parent-child interaction, other intra- and extrafamilial environmental influences, and the impact of special life experiences may all play significant roles in shaping behavior and modifying temperament, motivations and abilities. These factors interact with each other and with temperament, motivations and abilities so that the analysis of developmental course requires the consideration of all these interactional possibilities. An adolescent's difficulties in school or an adult's problems with a job may, for example, be the result of the constantly evolving interplay between parental expectations and pressures, sibling and peer competition, characteristics of schools attended, socioeconomic problems of the family, cognitive and perceptual abilities, self-image and self-judgments, and various temperamental characteristics such as activity level, approach or withdrawal to the new, distractibility, persistence and attention span. The determination of parental attitudes and behavior, in such an instance, may be essential to the analysis of the ontogenesis and evolution of the problem in school or on the job. But it does not eliminate the necessity to also identify the temperamental traits and cognitive and perceptual characteristics which may also have been influential.

The problem of identifying and rating temperament in the older child and adult is further compounded by the increasing individual variations in activities of all kinds which emerge as children grow older. In the early years of life, there is similarity and comparability in the major activities and environmental demands and expectations at any age-period. There are, of course, some variations depending on the sociocultural group, such as the age of toilet-training, expectations for level of self-care, attendance at nursery school, etc. But for each group, protocols and questionnaires for temperament can be developed which cover the important areas of behavior and sequences of new demands and expectations for children through infancy, the preschool period and the early school years. Scoring criteria can also be standardized with relative ease.

As the child grows older, however, similarity and comparability of behavior are increasingly replaced by differences and individual variation. Athletic activities, hobbies and other special interests, social life, school curriculum and schedules, and work experiences all become diversified in their form and content, prominence in the individual's life, and their sequence of development. As a result, the standardization of protocols, questionnaires and scoring criteria for temperament becomes increasingly complex for the older child, adolescent, and adult.

We ourselves have explored the possibility of developing a standard interview form for temperament in the adult. Our pilot project confirmed the complexity of the issues involved in obtaining reliable behavioral data comprehensive enough to permit quantitative rating of temperament. Adults vary widely in their activities of daily living, reflecting differences in jobs, family life, social functioning, hobbies and other special interests, economic and health limitations, and special idiosyncratic life-style patterns. These have to be identified in each individual and the basic daily routines of life delineated. Only then can descriptive behavioral data be obtained on the characteristics of everyday routines, the response of the individual to interfer-

TABLE 1

Correspondence of NYLS and TDOT Temperament Variables

Thomas, Chess, Birch Infant Temperament Variables	Scales on Thorndike Dimensions of Temperament
1. Activity Level	Active-Lethargic
2. Regularity and Rhythmicity	Responsive-Casual
3. Approach-Withdrawal	Social-Solitary Ascendent-Withdrawing
4. Adaptability	Accepting-Critical Placid-Irritable
5. Intensity	Active-Lethargic Placid-Irritable
6. Sensory Threshold	Placid-Irritable
7. Mood	Cheerful-Gloomy Placid-Irritable
8. Distractibility	Impulsive-Planful
9. Attention Span	Reflective-Practical Responsible-Casual

ences with these routines, and the initial reaction and subsequent adaptation to new events and experiences—data which are essential for rating temperament. The development of a standard temperament interview protocol is feasible and important, but will require a substantial and demanding research effort.

To date, one effort has been made to develop a simple short questionnaire evaluation of temperament in the adult (3). Scholom utilized the Thorndike Dimensions of Temperament questionnaire (TDOT) which has an extensive reliability and validation history. He empirically assumed a correspondence between the scales of the TDOT and the temperament variables of the NYLS. His assumed correlations are shown in Table 1.

Scholom also employed a brief questionnaire with a global five-point rating scale for each of the nine NYLS temperamental categories. He gave both this questionnaire and the TDOT to 264 adults (132 married couples). A few of the scales of the two instruments compared quite well, especially activity level. As Scholom points out, reliability and validation studies of this global temperament questionnaire are required before its usefulness can be assessed.

QUALITATIVE ASSESSMENT OF ADULT TEMPERAMENT

Even in the absence of systematic protocols for determining temperament, it is possible to estimate most temperamental attributes in older children and adults qualitatively. In fact, it was our impressionistic identification of temperamental patterns in the adults as well as the children we know that stimulated our original interest in studying this behavioral phenomenon.

The delineation of temperament empirically and qualitatively in an older child or adult is essentially similar methodologically to the process of identifying individual motivations, purposes, and psychodynamic defenses. Just as with temperament, we categorize motivations from behavioral data. These include the individual's expressions of attitudes, feelings and thoughts, as well as reports and observations of descriptive concrete items of behavior. We utilize the individual's expressions of intrapsychic states as significant data, not to be taken as *prima facie* evidence, but to be weighed and correlated with other information. Inasmuch as any one situation or context from which data are gathered may be typical or atypical, information from a number of incidents and situations is required. This applies to the categorization of motivation as well as temperament.

Thus, for example, an individual reports or is observed to perform a job assignment carefully and thoroughly. This single instance of behavior may be the result of a number of different motivational or temperamental influences operating singly or in combination. He may have a healthy personal standard of work performance; he may be ambitious; he may have compulsive needs for perfectionism; he may be motivated by competitive goals; he may be trying to compensate for real or fancied inadequacy in ability and intelligence. Several of these factors may also be operating simultaneously. He may also be temperamentally persistent with a long attention span.

The determination of which motivation or motivations are responsible for this pattern of work performance will require data from other life situations. Does this individual show this same work pattern in all job situations, or only in those where it gains him some competitive advantage? Does he insist on finishing every task meticulously even when it interferes with his overall level of functioning? Does he express self-confidence with a new demand or display anxiety that he will be exposed as inadequate? Once the motivation is identified through the analysis of the behavioral data, etiology and psychodynamic mechanisms can be explored—early intrafamilial influences, peer and other extrafamilial experiences, temperament, special abilities, the interaction over time among these factors, etc.

A similar approach can lead to the identification of functionally significant temperamental traits. Thus, for example, an individual may be observed to react with intense anger to criticism. This may reflect the temperamental attribute of intensity of reaction. The anger may also be stimulated by the nature of the situation or the content of the criticism. Finally, the individual's relationship to the critic may create an intense response to someone who otherwise shows mild intensity of affective expression. Data on the individual's intensity level in a variety of situations in which criticism or this critic is not involved will serve to determine whether the marked anger does, in fact, reflect a general temperamental trait.

To take another example, a college student may report that he has difficulty studying because of distraction by the various sounds in his dormitory. This may reflect the temperamental trait of either distractibility or high activity level with restlessness while sitting still for any length of time. Or the student may have a problem with academic demands or studying as such. Again, data on the individual's distractibility and activity in other situations—social, athletic, spectator experiences, etc.—will serve to determine whether the difficulty in concentration in the dormitory is a manifestation of a general temperamental attribute.

In general, the ability to identify temperament by this empirical qualitative approach rests first of all on the recognition that a behavioral phenomenon may reflect temperament, just as it may reflect motivations or abilities, or all three. It then requires an inventory of which specific temperamental traits or motivations or abilities could account for the behavior. Finally, with a knowledge of the individual's activities and routines of life, the inquiry and observations can be shaped which will differentiate among the various possibilities.

It is our impression that temperament and its significance in the older child and adult are most often overlooked because of a one-sided attention to motivational factors. It is a common human tendency to assume that any behavioral phenomenon is the result of an underlying purpose and goal. Even the functioning of animals and plants is commonly designated by motivations. A bee "seeks" food in a flower, a caged bird "wants" its freedom, the roots of a plant spread out "in search" of water. Human behavior is ubiquitously formulated as purposively determined, a conviction buttressed by concepts of free will. Psychiatrists easily fall in with this ideology. Twenty years ago David Levy observed that "The motivational viewpoint. . . . has become ascendent. It is represented by a variety of patterns in the different schools of thought. Essentially, however the patterns may differ, the basic question is the same. What are the motives? The question is directed to the needs of the individual, to his striving, his goals. The point of view is that of the individual as goal-seeker" (4).

The assumption that goals and purposes necessarily underlie behavioral phenomena obscures the role not only of temperament, but also of other functionally significant characteristics. A reading lag due to a learning disability is frequently ascribed to avoidance of academic demands because of anxiety and insecurity. The realistic demoralization of a black youngster and his mother overwhelmed by economic privation in the ghetto is interpreted as intrapsychically determined depression. Racist prejudices are traced to idiosyncratic psychosexual conflicts or to paranoid mechanism (5).

With regard to temperament, the misjudgment of behavior as motivational in origin is an all too frequent occurrence in clinical practice, both by patient and practitioner. Patients constantly formulate explanations of the obscurities of their own behavior, and that of other people with whom they are involved, in terms of some underlying purpose. All too frequently, when the therapist challenges the patient's interpretation, it is not to call into question the motivational bias but to present an alternative purpose and goal as the "correct" explanation. Once the possibility of a non-motivational alternative is considered, it is indeed impressive how often and how easily additional meaningful data can be gathered and analyzed.

One example will suffice. A man complains angrily that his wife is deliberately trying to make him uncomfortable. He cites as evidence the fact that his wife insists on closing their bedroom windows even in warm weather so that he becomes uncomfortable. The therapist agrees that the behavior is purposive but suggests that it may be unconsciously motivated, perhaps as reactive hostility to her treatment by the husband. Neither patient nor therapist gives thought to the possibility of a difference in sensory threshold to cool air, so that the wife is rendered uncomfortable by a lower temperature which is congenial to the husband, and vice versa for a higher temperature. Only if this possibility is considered will data be sought as to the reaction of each to variations in temperature in situations which do not in any way involve the spouse.

To summarize, the development of systematic, reliable and valid protocols for defining temperament in the older child and adult is a complex but important project which still remains to be achieved. In individual instances, however, professionals in the health and educational fields can usually categorize temperament empirically and qualitatively if they focus on this task in addition to searching for motives and abilities.

REFERENCES

1. R. Spitz, "Relevancy of Direct Infant Observations," *Psychoanalytic Study of the Child*, 5:66 (1950).
2. A. Thomas and S. Chess, "The Importance of Non-motivational Behavior Patterns in Psychiatric Diagnosis and Treatment," *Psychiatric Quarterly*, 33:326 (1959).
3. A. H. Scholom, "The Relationship of Infant and Parent Temperament to the Prediction of Child Adjustment." Doctoral dissertation, Michigan State University, 1975.
4. D. Levy, "Capacity and Motivation," *Amer. J. Orthopsychiat.*, 27:1 (1957).
5. A. Thomas and S. Sillen, *Racism and Psychiatry* (New York: Brunner/Mazel, 1972).

14

Practical
implications

The importance of temperament for the developmental process has been detailed in the individual chapters of this volume. The child's temperament influences his responses to parental practices and attitudes and helps to shape his parents' judgments and feelings toward him. Sib and peer group relationships, school functioning and academic achievement, behavioral responses to illness or other special stress—all can be significantly affected by specific temperamental traits. Temperament plays a part in the ontogenesis and evolution of behavior disorders and in the developmental course of the brain-damaged, mentally retarded and physically handicapped child.

For the adult, also, temperamental characteristics frequently play an important role in determining personal and social functioning, work patterns, and adaptation to change. For the mother who is led to believe that she is responsible for any deviation of her child's behavior from a conventional norm, the knowledge of the part played by temperament may relieve her of an oppressive burden of guilt and anxiety.

For the teacher, as well as for the mother, inappropriate burdens of responsibility can be lifted by the awareness that the child's school functioning can be influenced by his temperament. No matter how competent and committed the teacher may be, he will not be able to make a high activity child sit quietly or a distractible child concentrate for long periods of time.

The relief from inappropriate responsibility and guilt does not necessarily mean that the parent's and teacher's tasks will be simpler. It will be so in some regards, as clear-cut objective insight into the child's temperament and its implications is substituted for speculative assumptions of complex psychodynamic mechanisms. At the same time, the parent and teacher must develop a familiarity with temperamental traits and the optimal approach for each temperamental pattern, instead of relying on global characterizations and blanket judgments applied to all children indiscriminately.

Furthermore, the concept that optimal development necessitates consonance between the child's temperament and other attributes and environmental demands and expectations does not mean the acceptance and encouragement of any and all behavioral manifestations of the child's temperament characteristics. Negative mood, withdrawal tendencies, high motor activity, marked distractibility, extreme persistence, etc., may be normal for a particular youngster but may still interfere with desirable peer relations, school and play activities and academic achievement. A parent or teacher may also tolerate or even be pleased with a child's behavior, such as the quiet peaceful withdrawal tendencies of the Slow-To-Warm-Up Child; yet this behavior may interfere with the child's development of constructive social experiences. In such instances, where a child's temperament may have undesirable consequences if allowed unrestrained expression, appropriate guidance and structuring are necessary. Thus, the distractible, nonpersistent child cannot sit and concentrate on homework for long periods of time. But he can be told he must return to his work after each short break. The Slow-To-Warm-Up Child may not be able to become an active part of a peer group immediately, but complete withdrawal should not be tolerated or encouraged. Or, as another example, the persistent child who is pulled away from an activity that absorbs him can learn to express his frustration without the violent tantrums which could alienate him from peers and adults.

Parents and teachers can now be helped to carry out their responsibility to interact appropriately with temperament characteristics by the availability of short questionnaire forms for the infancy and three-to-seven-year age periods which expedite the delineation of temperament.

The same situation applies to the pediatrician, nurse and mental health professional. The mechanical application of conventional formulae may incorrectly pigeonhole a child. Shyness with new people becomes anxiety and insecurity, night-awakening and crying become the response to a rejecting mother, explosive anger when frustrated becomes aggression and opposition, and a mother's guilt and anxiety with a Difficult Child become the expression of a deep-seated neurosis. The knowledge that temperamental individuality and its consequences may also contribute to these behaviors makes such blanket judgments untenable. The health care professional now has the responsibility of gathering and analyzing additional data before interpreting behavior and offering advice and treatment.

There is increased simplicity for the health care professional in the substitution of concrete, descriptive behavioral categories for speculative interpretations of subjective attributes. There is also increased complexity in the introduction of an additional structure of variables, making the analysis of the organism-environment interaction more demanding.

As has been emphasized throughout this volume, considerations of temperament and its functional significance do not in any way negate the importance of other developmental influences. Nor do they mean that all temperamental attributes are *always* important in the developmental process. Each case has to be studied and analyzed individually to determine which factors are influential and to delineate the specific dynamics of the sequential patterns of child-environment interactional process. Only if this is done does the formulation "Know and treat each child as an individual" become a meaningful concept instead of a mechanical cliché.

The identification of an individual's temperamental pattern requires concrete descriptive data from a wide variety of life situations. Information regarding behavior in any one setting may be suggestive and provide leads as to the most promising directions for further inquiry. However, behavioral data from one life situation cannot in themselves reveal whether the behaviors are typical and therefore adequate for rating temperament, or equivocal or atypical and therefore unsatisfactory for identifying temperament.

The necessary data can be obtained by the use of a systematic interview protocol, a brief interview which focuses on clinical material by a series of direct observations, or by a questionnaire. The approach that appears least reliable is the utilization of global questions, in which the individual is asked to rate himself or his child on each of the temperamental characteristics as such. This methodology may be of some value when other techniques are unavailable or impractical. But our experiences and those of Carey indicate that any data obtained by such global self-rating scales must be assessed with great caution.

Behavioral information should be obtained not only from a wide variety of life situations, but also within the context in which behavior occurs. Loud crying or a tantrum may have very different significance if it occurs as a response to a frequent mild frustration versus a reaction to an exceptional and severe frustration. A child's restlessness and fussing during a short automobile ride may not have the same implications as if the behavior occurs during a long trip with enforced inactivity. Actually, the necessity to evaluate behavior within its context applies not only to the rating of temperament, but equally to judgments of motivations, goals, cognitive functioning and perceptual levels.

PARENT GUIDANCE

The concept of "goodness of fit" between the child's characteristics and environmental demands and expectations offers a valuable basis for parent guidance procedures when a child presents evidence of a behavior disorder.

Parent guidance involves first the identification of those elements of parental behavior and overtly expressed attitudes that appear to be exerting a harmful influence on the child's development. This is followed by the formulation of a program of altered parental functioning which will modify or change the interactive pattern between child and parent in a healthy direction. In those instances in which clinical evaluation indicates the presence of a disorder in the child requiring special treatment or management procedures, parent guidance may still be helpful but not sufficient. Where the child's problem behavior or symptoms reflect a reactive disorder, alteration in parent functioning is not only helpful but usually sufficient.

The rationale of the guidance program is explained to the parents in terms of the necessity of a "goodness of fit" between the child's characteristics and the parent's functioning. The specific area or areas of undesirable parent-child interaction are identified, the specific temperamental traits and other pertinent attributes of the child involved in this interaction are described, and the parental behaviors which are creating excessive stress are pointed out. Throughout this discussion, the parents are assured that no judgment is being made or warranted that they are "bad parents," and that the same behavior with a child with different characteristics might be positive instead of negative in its consequences. It is simultaneously emphasized that the child's disturbed responses to their benign intentions and efforts do not mean that he is "bad" or "sick" or "willfully disobedient."

References to concrete incidents in the child's life are made to illustrate each suggestion. For example, the initial intense negative responses to new situations and slow adaptability of a Difficult Child are documented by details of the child's history with new foods, new people, new activities, new school situations, etc. These reactions are distinguished from anxiety or motivated negativism. Harmful parental attitudes, such as guilt, anxiety and hostility, and undesirable management practices, such as impatience, inconsistency, and rigidity in unreasonable demands, are identified, again with concrete illustrations. As another example, the restlessness and shifts in attention of a highly active and distractible youngster are distinguished from "laziness," willful inattention and lack of interest. Parental demands that the child sit still on a long trip or concentrate for long periods without distraction on homework are identified, and their inappropriateness and undesirable consequences explained.

This discussion of the parental attitudes and practices which are inimical to the child's healthy development emphasizes throughout the specificity of the harmful effects for the particular temperamental constellation. Wherever possible, it is emphasized that the same parental functioning might be satisfactory for a child with different temperamental traits, with concrete illustrations. This helps to clarify a basic issue in parent guidance, namely that the necessity for change in attitude and behavior does not mean that the parent in some way "wants" to wrong the child.

The parents are then offered specific suggestions and advice for changing the identified undesirable attitudes and practices. Even with parents who are eager and able to carry through the program of behavioral change recommended to them, more than one discussion is usually necessary for this to be fully implemented. Several sessions may be required for them to grasp adequately the concept of temperamental individuality and its influence on the child's ability to cope with parental and other environmental demands and expectations. It is important, at these follow-up discussions, to review the parents' behavior in a number of specific incidents which have occurred in the interim period. This review, which should be done in detail, is often required for the parents to become adept at identifying those situations in the child's daily life in which modification of their techniques of management is required.

As indicated above, a constructive approach by the parents to the child's temperament does not mean an acceptance or encouragement of all this youngster's behavior in all situations. The parent's goal should be to ameliorate or prevent any undesirable temperament-environment interaction. This involves two considerations: the avoidance of demands or expectations that are substantially dissonant with the child's temperament, and the encouragement and even insistence on those activities and schedules which will minimize any undesirable consequences of the child's temperament. As an example of the latter goal, the high activity child should be guided to channel his motor activity into acceptable directions. The mildly expressive child should be taught to articulate his desires clearly and repetitively until they are noticed. Or, as another of the many possible contingencies, the non-persistent child should be encouraged to take breaks and breathers with a difficult task as often as necessary until mastery is achieved, rather than just giving up.

In these parent guidance procedures no attempt is made to define or change any hypothetical underlying conflicts, anxieties or defenses in the parent that may be presumed to be the cause of the noxious behavior or overtly expressed attitudes. Inevitably, the guidance sessions do reveal misconceptions, confusions, defensiveness, anxiety or guilt in a number of parents which impede their ability to understand the issues and carry through the necessary changes in behavior. In such instances additional discussions are required for clarification of misconceptions and confusions or for explication of the inappropriateness of defensiveness, anxiety or guilt.

In some instances, psychopathology in the parents may be so severe as to prevent their making the necessary changes in behavior. This will usually become evident quickly in the course of the guidance sessions. In fact, the parent guidance procedure is an effective technique for differentiating those instances in which inappropriate and undesirable parental functioning is the result of substantial and fixed psychopathology from those in which it reflects more easily remediable causes, such as ignorance, poor advice or transient situational difficulties. In the former cases, psychotherapy for the parent will be necessary. In our experience, the failure of the parent guidance program will often make the necessity for such treatment clear to the parent and provide the necessary motivation for engaging in psychotherapy, whether it be individual, group, or family therapy. In some cases the nature of the psychopathology may make the parent resistant to psychotherapy as well as to the guidance recommendations. When this occurs, direct treatment of the child will be the only alternative therapeutic approach. Direct treatment of the child may sometimes be desirable even if the parents cooperate in the guidance program. This is especially true if there is a severe degree of psychopathology in the child.

The results of parent guidance in the NYLS have been detailed in a previous volume (1) and will be summarized here. There were 42 children with behavior disorders where parent guidance was attempted. An estimate was made of the degree to which the parents modified their functioning with the child in the desired direction following the guidance sessions. This was then compared with the outcome in the child's behavior disorder on follow-up. A marked relationship was evident between degree of change in parental functioning and change in the child. In eight cases in which there was marked positive parental change, four children with behavior disorders recovered, two improved markedly and two moderately. In 12 instances of moderate parental change, one child recovered, five improved markedly, five moderately and one became slightly worse. The outcome in the 14 cases in which no favorable change in parental functioning was effected was strikingly different. In this group, no child recovered or showed marked improvement, only two improved moderately and three slightly. One child was unchanged, four became moderately worse and four markedly worse. In the case of four of the five children who showed some improvement even with failure of parent guidance, there appeared to be especially benign and constructive extrafamilial influences. The fifth child improved after a course of psychotherapy.

A comparison was also made between the results of parent guidance and the child's temperamental pattern. No differences were found, except that guidance failed in all four cases in which the children were distractible and non-persistent. For the parents in this middle- and upper-middle-class group, great importance is attached to educational achievement for both sexes and to success in professional careers or business for the males. The characteristic of persistence is highly valued. It was, therefore, hard for these parents to accept the fact that the child's attributes of low persistence and distractibility were normal, and, more distressingly, could not be changed by pressure or persuasion. It is of interest that all four children in this group were boys, in whom the qualities of persistence and non-distractibility were especially prized.

All other temperamental patterns were much more acceptable to these parents. Thus, most of the parents were able to be patient with the initial nonadaptive reactions of the Difficult or Slow-To-Warm-Up Child in new situations, once they were convinced that with a change in their approach the child would finally achieve behavioral standards congenial to their own standards. For the parents of these children, as for the easy, persistent, high or low activity child, a change in their handling could bring the outcome they desired. For the parents of the distractible, non-persistent children, however, a change in their handling could still leave the child functioning in a fashion uncongenial to them.

An overall estimate is that the parent guidance procedure, without direct treatment of the child, was markedly or moderately successful in approximately 50 percent of the children with behavior disorders. Furthermore, only a few sessions with the parents were usually required, averaging 2.3 with successful cases and 2.7 for the failures. It is true that the special long-term relationship of these parents with the NYLS staff may have made them more responsive to a guidance program. However, one of us (S.C.) has applied this same approach over many years to private and clinic child patients and found it to be an extremely useful procedure with all types of psychiatric problems and with parents of diverse sociocultural backgrounds. Whether utilized alone or combined with modifications of school or other environmental factors, or with direct treatment of the child, parent guidance is an effective and efficient therapeutic modality in many cases. But its usefulness depends on the specificity with which undesirable areas of parent-child interaction are identified.

Parent guidance, as here formulated, presumes that parental dysfunction with a child is not necessarily the result of fixed psychopathology in the parent. Also, even in those cases where psychiatric disturbance in the parent is the prime cause of unhealthy influence on the child, parent guidance may sometimes be successful despite the absence of change in the parent's personality structure. This formulation stands in contrast to the approach in which a behavior problem in a child is considered *ipso facto* evidence of substantial psychopathology in the parent requiring extensive direct treatment. It also stands in contrast to the more recent concepts in which the child's behavior disturbance is viewed as a sign of pathology in the nuclear family unit. Typical of this latter view is Ackerman's statement that the primary patient, the child, represents "a symptomatic expression of family pathology," and not just an "individual in distress" (2).

Behavior disorder in a child may be the result of pathology in a parent or in the family unit—or it may not. Even if parental or family pathology does exist, the long and expensive treatment of this pathology, with all the uncertainties as to outcome, should not be undertaken if simpler approaches can be effective. Anna Freud put it well when she stated that she refused to believe "That mothers need to change their personalities before they can change the handling of their child" (3).

There is one issue which has impressed us deeply as we have pursued our research studies and clinical activities. It provided the basis of the final peroration of a previous volume and we have also elaborated on it in various sections of this book. We feel that it still bears repetition as a concluding statement here. "The recognition that a child's behavioral disturbance is not necessarily the direct result of maternal pathology should do much to prevent the deep feelings of guilt and inadequacy with which innumerable mothers have been unjustly burdened as a result of being held entirely responsible for their children's problems. Mothers who are told authoritatively that child raising is a 'task not easily achieved by the average mother in our culture' (4) are not likely to approach this responsibility with the relaxation and confidence that would be beneficial to both their own and their child's mental health. It is our conviction, however, that the difficulties of child raising can be significantly lightened by advocating an approach of which the average mother is capable— the recognition of her child's specific qualities of individuality, and the adoption of those child-care practices that are most appropriate to them" (5).

REFERENCES

1. A. Thomas, S. Chess and H. G. Birch, *Temperament and Behavior Disorders in Children* (New York: New York University Press, 1968).
2. N. Ackerman, *The Psychodynamics of Family Life* (New York: Basic Books, 1958), p. 107.
3. A. Freud, "The Child Guidance Clinic as a Center of Prophylaxis and Enlightenment," *Recent Development in Psychoanalytic Child Therapy* (New York: International Universities Press, 1960), p. 37.
4. M. Mahler, "Thoughts About Development and Individuation," *Psychoanalytic Study of the Child*, 18:307 (1963).
5. H. Birch, "Parent Education or the Illusion of Omnipotence," *Amer. J. Orthopsychiat.*, 24:723 (1954).

15

Theoretical

issues

The previous chapters of this volume have considered a number of theoretical issues relevant to the developmental process. A basic concept throughout has been the interactionist view of behavior. This concept demands that all behavioral attributes, including temperament, must at all times be considered simultaneously in their reciprocal relationship with other characteristics of the organism, and in their interaction with environmental opportunities, demands, and stresses. This process produces consequences which may modify or change behavior (1). The new behavior will then affect the influence of recurrent and new features of the environment. The latter may develop independently or as a consequence of the organism-environment interactive process. At the same time other characteristics of the organism, either talents and abilities, goals and motives, behavioral stylistic characteristics, or psychodynamic defenses, may be modified or altered as the result of this continually evolving reciprocal organism-environment influence.

Development thus becomes a fluid, dynamic process which continually possesses the possibility of modification and change of pre-existing psychological patterns. At the same time the potential for reinforcement of the old exists with the same or even greater strength as does the possibility for change. Continuity over time does not imply that a reified structure insulated from change exists intrapsychically. Such continuity can be better conceptualized as the result of consistency in the organism-environment interaction (2).

An hypothesis suggested by the above view is that continuity in behavior and personality structure may reflect consistency in the environment and in the organism-environment interaction process, rather than some *a priori* unchangeability of an intrapsychic state. The alternative view of fixity of psychological attributes, whether at birth or by three to five years of age, has been a dominant theme of developmental theory. The attributes which are considered to be immutable and decisively influential may vary in different theoretical formulations, but the concept is a similar one.

PSYCHOLOGICAL IMMUTABILITY

Perhaps the earliest and most recurrent view of the immutability of human personality stems from the hereditary-constitutional bias. In this formulation, the essential and decisive aspects of personality structure are already determined by birth, either by inheritance from the parental genes, by the influence of prenatal events, or both. This view is reflected in diagnostic labels such as "constitutional psychopath" or "constitutional inferiority," and in such popular aphorisms as "the bad seed" or "the apple does not fall far from the tree." More sophisticated variations keep cropping up from time to time, such as Sheldon's proposition that physical typology is correlated with personality structure (3), or the current proposition of Jensen and others that intelligence is inherited not only individually but racially (4). In these hereditary-constitutional views, the infant is seen as a *homunculus,* an organism which contains within itself in minute form the characteristics which will come to full expression by the process of linear growth and expansion with age.

One of the major achievements of the psychoanalytic movement has been the demonstration of how much of such presumed hereditary-constitutional determinants is really the result of the interaction between the young child and his effective environment. Paradoxically, however, psychoanalytic theory did not make a qualitative break with this concept of fixation and immutability of personality. What it did, in effect, was to move the point of immutability from the gene and the prenatal environment to the first five years of life. Personality structure, in this view, is set in the preschool years in the form of oral, anal or genital characters, depending on the vicissitudes of instinctual development. The environment is influential, but primarily in terms of reinforcing or shaping this evolution of instincts and creating points at which they become fixated. Later and more complex behavioral phenomena then reflect the continued basic influence of these unconscious repressed instinctual drives. The environment may modify the form in which these drive-states come to conscious expression but cannot eliminate or transform them.

Other alternatives to this psychoanalytic view of the developmental process have been formulated which have minimized or denied this primary role of instinct. But, whatever their conceptual emphasis, they have in the main accepted the view that individual psychological characteristics and structures are determined in the first few years of life. The psychosocial life cycle concepts of Erikson emphasize the decisive characteristics that are laid down in the preschool child (5). Family pathology and dynamics are considered by others to determine the ontogenesis of schizophrenia in the young child as well as other pathological developments (6, 7, 8). Concepts of minimal brain dysfunction (9) and a continum of reproductive casualty (10) focus on the later and permanent consequences of brain damage. Early malnutrition is seen as producing irreversible psychological consequences (11, 12). Socioeconomic influences on the young child are presumed to cause profound, permanent behavioral and cognitive consequences, usually subsumed under the labels of "cultural deprivation" (13) and the "culture of poverty" (14). The ethologists have emphasized the decisive permanent effects of early life experience through the concepts of "imprinting" and "critical periods" (15, 16). The importance of early conditioning and learning led Watson to his well-known assertion that he could take any healthy infant and train him to become any type of adult he wanted (17). The newest statement of the all-important role of early childhood is one of the most sweeping. Burton White's report on his Brookline Early Education Project goes even further than the psychoanalysts' emphasis on the first five years of life. White would have it that it is the first three years that are crucial to all subsequent psychological development (18).

Since the theory of early fixation of psychological characteristics recurs with such frequency, it might be argued that this theme reflects an important reality. Like the blind men groping at the elephant, we may find that each concept may reflect only a fragment, and we may even misinterpret that fragment, but maybe the elephant does exist. And certainly, similarities between the young child and the adult are often noticeable and even striking. In physiognomy, musculoskeletal structure, aptitudes, and interests, I.Q. level, cognitive style, perceptual skills or difficulties, temperamental characteristics, psychodynamic defense mechanisms—consistency from early childhood into adult life may be apparent and measurable. The child often does seem to be "father to the man."

In addition, the influential psychodynamic developmental concepts make it possible to identify later behavior with earlier behavior even when they appear to be strikingly dissimilar. The passive, clinging three-year-old has not really changed if he becomes an aggressive adult who refuses all help. He is only displaying a reaction formation against the same unconscious dependency needs which determine his behavior now as they did in the past. The youngster who behaves cruelly toward his younger sibs and peers and then becomes a dedicated surgeon is only sublimating his sadistic drives. Within this closed conceptual scheme, continuity over time is guaranteed. Similarity in behavior from childhood to adult is *ipso facto* evidence. Change in behavior is interpreted as the effect of a psychodynamic mechanism, and not as a qualitative alteration in psychological characteristics. If the I.Q. level changes, this does not mean that the individual's intellectual capacities have changed. These capacities are the same, fixed from infancy, but modified in their expression by anxiety, avoidance reactions, or compulsive needs for "overachievement."

IS HUMAN BEHAVIOR FIXED?

It may be tempting to assume that human psychological characteristics show a basic continuity over time. Linear prediction becomes possible, counseling and therapy become simplified, and there is no need to identify new variables which may complicate the analysis of behavior. But how well do the facts support concepts of invariable continuity over time? What is the evidence from the increasing body of developmental and longitudinal research studies?

Our own data from the NYLS suggest that no simplistic conclusion is possible. As reported in Chapter 12, in some individuals continuity of specific temperamental characteristics over time was dramatically evident, though the actual behavior in later childhood or adolescence was no mere replica of earlier childhood functioning. Maturation in perceptual cognitive and neuromuscular levels affected the behavioral expression of temperament, as did changes in environmental demands and expectations. In other individuals there appeared to be significant distortions or actual change over time in a conspicuous temperamental characteristic.

Torgersen's work suggests a significant genetic factor in the determination of temperament (19). However, this does not preclude phenotypic dissimilarity as the result of organism-environment interaction, as with any other genetically influenced characteristic (20).

Sameroff has recently made two comprehensive reviews of the research literature bearing on this issue of continuity from infancy to later childhood (21, 22). The first, co-authored with M. J. Chandler, deals with the relationship between pregnancy and delivery complications and later deviancy, a relationship reported in various retrospective studies and conceptualized in the phrase "continuum of reproductive casualty." From their review, however, Sameroff and Chandler conclude, "Prospective studies . . . have, however, not succeeded in demonstrating the predictive efficiency of these supposed risk factors. Most infants who suffer perinatal problems have proven to have normal developmental outcomes." They emphasize the crucial role of the environment in minimizing or maximizing early developmental difficulties, and suggest a concept of "continuum of caretaking casualty" to describe the range of deviant outcomes which can result from such environmental variation.

In his second review Sameroff examines the evidence in general for the implicit assumption that "behaviors necessarily build on each other to produce a continuity of functioning from conception to adulthood." Here, again, he concludes, "Despite the reasonableness of the notion that one should be able to make long-range predictions based on the initial characteristics of a child or his environment, the above review has found little evidence for the validity of such predictions. One view of the inadequacy of developmental predictions sees their source in the scientist's inability to locate the critical links in the causal chain leading from antecedents to consequence. A second view, propounded above, is that such linear sequences are non-existent and that development proceeds through a sequence of regular restructuring of the relations within and between the organism and his environment."

A number of recent reports have buttressed this overall judgment by Sameroff. Winick, Meyer and Harris have studied the development of a group of adopted Korean children who suffered early malnutrition (23). They found that the effects of such malnutrition, even when severe, could be overcome by the environmental enrichment resulting from adoption. The successful nutritional rehabilitation was documented by measures of physical growth, school achievement and I.Q. The authors suggest that previous findings of the permanent effects of early malnutrition may have resulted from the persistence of an unfavorable environment, or the failure to provide an enriched environment for a sufficiently long period.

The early studies of the ethologists on animal behavior which suggested that very early life experiences may have fixed permanent effects have also come into question recently. One issue concerns imprinting, described by Lorenz and Hess as a unique form of early learning from one experience which had irreversible and permanent effects (24, 25). In a recent review of Hess' latest volume, Bateson comments that for Hess to maintain this concept of imprinting "he must either ignore or misrepresent strong evidence indicating that the length of the period of sensitivity greatly depends on the nature of the young bird's experience" (26). Bateson also points out: "Assertions about the uniqueness of imprinting are preceded in the book by sections containing much of the evidence incompatible with these claims."

The other issue posed by the ethologists concerns the critical period hypothesis, which asserts that the young organism must be exposed to a given learning opportunity or forever suffer some degree of deficit (27). In a recent review, Peter Wolff, a most distinguished student of early child development, concludes that the "available evidence does not support" the critical period concept (28). He further points out that this concept "may hamper the development of a soundly based approach to the learning difficulties of deprived children." In another review, Connolly also advocates that the term "critical period" be abandoned (29). He emphasizes that "early experience has far-reaching consequences for an organism's development" but that "development is an extremely complex set of processes which are often oversimplified."

Early studies on I.Q. also tended to view the psychometric test score as a measure of an innate, unchangeable entity. Intelligence was considered "inherited, or at least innate, not due to teaching or training; it is intellectual, not emotional or moral, and remains uninfluenced by industry or zeal" (30). In recent years, however, it has become increasingly evident that the I.Q. score can change significantly over time (31). Furthermore, such change cannot be considered to be the result of methodological problems of measurement, but rather to reflect actual modification in levels of intellectual functioning at different ages. A few quotes from the recent literature illustrate the current view. Lewis and McGurk conclude from their studies that "we have found no evidence to support the view that intelligence is a capacity which unfolds at a steady rate throughout the process of development and which increases only quantitatively from one age to the next" (32). McClelland observes, "It is difficult, if not impossible, to find a human characteristic that cannot be modified by training or experience. . . . To the traditional intelligence tester this fact has been something of a nuisance because he has been searching for some unmodifiable, infallible index of innate mental capacity. . . . It seems wiser to abandon the search for pure ability factors and to select tests instead that are valid in the sense that scores on them change as the person grows in experience, wisdom, and ability to perform effectively on various tasks that life presents to him" (33).

In the past few years an attempt has been made to revive the discredited concept that intelligence is not only innate but inherited on a racial basis. Scrutiny of these claims has exposed their unscientific and unsubstantiated basis and reaffirmed the conclusion that intellectual functioning is decisively influenced by life experience (34).

As indicated above, the psychoanalytic movement discredited certain simplistic views of the fixation of individual psychological structure in the newborn or young child by the demonstration of the vital influence of early child-environment interactions. Mechanistic theories linking adult psychological characteristics in a linear fashion to early conditioned reflex patterns were also challenged by the demonstration of the subtleties and complexities which determined adult behavior. However, psychoanalytic theories of predetermined evolution of instinctual drives in the first five years of life and the permanent persistence and influence of these drive states in the "unconscious" provided a new rationale for the concept that individual personality was determined in the first five years of life. However, these psychoanalytic formulations, which offered an attractive comprehensive and predictive schedule for explaining behavioral development at sequential age-stage levels of development, could never meet the acid test of anterospective predictability, as was pointed out by Freud himself (35).

At the opposite extreme from those formulations of immutability which derive from concepts of fixed intrapsychic processes—whether they be genetic, neurophysiological, instinctual or psychodynamic—are the assertions that early life experiences are all-decisive because of the influence of the family or sociocultural environment. Protagonists of these views emphasize that the young child can take many different directions of psychological development, but once the family or society, or both, set him on one road, there is no turning back. The particular formulations which propagate this idea vary as to the specific influences they consider crucial, but agree in the concept that the future is determined in the early years of life.

The familiar assertion that schizophrenia is produced by the impact of a particular kind of family environment on the young child is the most dramatic expression of this view of the all-important role of the family. In a recent review (36), Rosenthal and his group utilize their extensive study of naturally occurring adoptions to ex-

amine this issue of parent-child relationship as the cause of schizophrenia. They conclude that the "quality of rearing and hereditary
input both affect the development of psychopathological disorder,
but the amount of variance explained by rearing tends to be low."
Their criticism of the methodological flaws in those studies which
have reported high correlations between parent characteristics and
schizophrenia in the child is trenchant and incisive.

The studies that assert an all-important and permanent psychological effect of sociocultural influences on the young child have, in
the main, concentrated on underprivileged, deprived and minority
group youngsters. Formulations such as "cultural deprivation," "the
culture of poverty," and "the mark of oppression" have emerged
from these studies and offered attractive alternative ideas to predetermination by heredity, constitution or biological instinctual drives.
A close scrutiny of these formulations, however, has exposed serious
methodological and conceptual flaws, and the inability to explain
healthy as well as pathological outcomes in these youngsters. Beyond
this, these theories, while they deplore the injustices of society, infer
that the children are permanently crippled psychologically and, in
effect, have to be written off.

The latest prophet of doom for young children suffering from im-
proper care is Burton White. To the questions "Is it all over by the
time we are three years old? Are the limits of our capacity for future
achievement irrevocably fixed during the first 36 months of our
lives?" White gives the answer "To some extent, I do believe that it
is all over by three." He further asserts that the child's own family is
obviously central to the child's developmental outcome, and that if
the family does a poor job in the first years of life, "there may be
little the professional can do to save the child from mediocrity" (37).
But these sweeping and truly frightening judgments are based on
data accumulated in the first three years of life, *with no reports of
follow-up into later life*. Without such follow-up to relate outcome to
early care and functioning, White's conclusions have to be labeled
as unproved speculations, which ignore the profound influence of life
experiences in later childhood and adulthood.

There can be little doubt that environmental influences can be
especially and even profoundly important in the infancy and early

childhood years. Any organism is most sensitive and responsive during the period of most rapid growth. Both physical growth and psychological development are greatest in early childhood, and both can be deeply affected by environmental or intra-organismic change during this period. But this is entirely different from an assertion that the influence and experiences of these early years—or for that matter, any other single period of life—are all-decisive for the individual's future life course. Edward Zigler, former director of Head Start, puts it well: "I, for one, am tired of the past decade's scramble to discover some magic period during which interventions will have particularly great pay-offs. Some experts emphasize the nine months *in utero;* Pines and White, the period between eight and 18 months; others, the entire preschool period; and yet others emphasize adolescence. My own predilection is that we cease this pointless search for magic periods and adopt instead the view that the developmental process is a continuous one, in which every segment of the life cycle from conception through maturity is of crucial importance and requires certain environmental nutrients" (38).

CONTINUITY AND CHANGE

The above brief review suggests that the search for early behavioral determinants which fix the individual's psychological development in some permanent form has been a futile enterprise. This should hardly be a surprise. A prime characteristic of the healthy mind, whether in childhood, adolescence or adulthood, is its flexibility, its ability to respond to new challenges, opportunities and stresses with new ideas, feelings and behavior. Creativeness and imaginativeness, among the most highly prized of human characteristics, would be impossible without this fundamental mental attribute of qualitative change and adaptation to new situations.

At the same time, human personality structure does have stability and continuity. Flexibility does not mean that an individual's responsiveness to change or new demands is haphazard or capricious.

Perhaps the wrong questions are being posed. The issue may not be an either-or one: Does behavioral development show continuity or does it not? Do early life experiences have a profound influence on the young child or do they not? Perhaps development can be both continuous and discontinuous, and the effects of early life experience can be both permanent and modifiable. The meaningful questions may then concern the conditions and developmental dynamics which promote behavioral continuity and those which promote discontinuity from early to later age-periods.

Along these lines, Escalona and Heider (39) have advanced the hypothesis that "infantile patterns or schemata of behavior are most likely to continue into later childhood (in overtly identical or very similar forms) among children who experience significant developmental irregularity and maladaptation. In optimal circumstances, early forms of behavior tend to be dissolved during transition stages of development so that reintegration and the formation of new schemata can take place at each new level of maturity." Korner has similarly suggested that the persistence of a trait in an infant, or the derivative of a trait, may largely depend on its original strength (40). She feels that "the average expectable child in an average expectable environment will show developmental outcomes that are apt to express a successful amalgamation between the child's original tendencies and these environmental influences." Bloom emphasizes that stability of a trait is reinforced "only when this environment is relatively constant over time" (41).

These formulations are consonant with the interactionist view that behavioral development reflects a constantly evolving process of organism-environment interaction. Sameroff, who prefers the term *transactional model,* emphasizes the idea of process, rather than end product. "Any truly transactional model must stress the plastic character of both the environment and the organism as it actively participates in its own growth. In this model the child's behavior is more than a simple reaction to his environment. Instead, he is actively engaged in attempts to organize and structure his world. The child is in a perpetual state of active re-organization and cannot properly be regarded as maintaining inborn characteristics as static qualities. In this view, the constants in development are not some sets of traits but rather the processes by which these traits are maintained in the transactions between organism and environment" (42).

The processes of psychological development take place on many

levels simultaneously—neurochemical, neurophysiological, psychophysiological, perceptual, affective, cognitive and behavioral. It is
not within the scope of this discussion to examine the various theories
of developmental process. We can emphasize, however, the importance of the "goodness of fit" concept in the organism-environment
interaction at various sequential developmental stages. As discussed
in various chapters of this volume, goodness or poorness of fit between the individual's temperament, capacities, abilities and motivations and the demands and expectations of the environment influences
profoundly the ability to master the tasks of a given age-period.

This concept does not imply a necessity or even a desirability of
temperamental similarity between parent and child for optimal psychological development. Whether a parent has expectations and
makes demands which are consonant or dissonant with the child's
temperament will depend on many considerations, which may vary
from parent to parent. The parent's response to the child's temperament can also be influenced by many factors. Similarity in temperament may contribute to goodness of fit in parent-child interaction in
some instances, to poorness of fit in others, and may be insignificant
in its influence in still other instances.

Goodness of fit, or consonance between the individual and the
environment, can change even qualitatively from one developmental
stage to another, as new features of the environment affect the individual's responses. The process of development at later periods is
influenced as in earlier stages by the degree of consonance or dissonance between individual and environment, but changes in the goodness or poorness of fit will make for changes in temperament, behavior, motivation, cognition, etc. Murphy and Moriarty put it well in
their study of coping styles from infancy to adolescence, "The relations between earlier and later forms of experience and behavior are
too complex to warrant our thinking of simple causal relations between what came first and what came later. . . . Our conclusion is
that development is not merely due to the effect of either simple
hereditary or environmental forces; at any time the child's response
to and ways of coping with these and their complex interactions
involves unpredictable emergents" (43).

TEMPĒRAMENT AS AN INDEPENDENT VARIABLE

The role of temperament at sequential age-stage levels of development in childhood and with specific environmental demands and expectations has been detailed in the different chapters of this volume. As is the case when any significant variable is identified, there is a temptation to make temperament the core of a general theory of development. To do so, however, would be to repeat a frequent tendency in psychology and psychiatry to base general theories upon fragments rather than the totality of interacting mechanisms. A one-sided emphasis on temperament would repeat such an approach and run contrary to the necessary view of temperament as only one attribute of the organism. The relevance of the concept of temperament for general developmental and psychiatric theory does not lie in any attempt to substitute it for other conceptualizations. Rather, the phenomenon of temperament and its dynamic interplay with other influential variables must be incorporated into any general theory of normal and aberrant behavioral development if the theory is to be complete. A central conclusion from the NYLS is that existing theories, whether they emphasize motives and drive states, learned tactics of adaptation, environmental patterns of influence or primary organic determinants, must focus on the individual and his uniqueness. The same motive, the same adaptive tactic, the same structure of objective influence, or the same neurophysiological or biochemical mechanism will have different functional meaning in accordance with the temperamental style of the specific child. Moreover, in such an individualization of the study of the dynamics of behavior and its evolution over time, temperament must be considered as an independent determining variable in itself, and not as an *ad hoc* modifier used to fill in the gaps left unexplained by other mechanisms.

All too often, when a psychological phenomenon has been identified as an independent variable in the developmental process, it has been reified and given an absolute status. It has furthermore been assumed that this variable must have the same basic influence on all individuals at all times. Thus, the identification of the etiological significance of sociocultural factors has led to generalizations as to their impact on *all* members of the class, racial or sex group affected by these environmental phenomena. As an example, all Blacks are presumed to suffer "the mark of oppression" and all poor children to be afflicted with "cultural deprivation" and the "culture of poverty." Hypotheses concerning the existence in the organism of spontaneous forms of energy and drive states, as postulated in psychoanalytic and ethologic theory, assume their existence prior to and independently of life experiences. Environmental forces are then considered to influence psychological organization by determining the directions taken by these primary drives and energies, by specifying the objects on which they come fixed, and by delineating the concrete forms in which they appear through environmental facilitation or inhibition. But these environmental forces, in these formulations, serve at best to shape the expression of the primary, reified drive states, and do not enter into the dynamics of development as an independent variable.

As another example, where "mothering" is given this kind of primary, absolute influence, then the child's own characteristics are necessarily assigned secondary subordinate importance. Thus, a discussion of autism by a prominent research worker in child development states "Children who suffer from this illness have in common the lack or distortion of a mutual relationship with a mother person . . . in some instances this deficiency arises because there was no mother who responded to the baby as normal mothers do. . . . But the illness also occurs in children who were raised by normally responsive mothers. . . . But the child is so constituted that he cannot participate in the usual patterns of interaction, probably due to an inborn deficit yet to be specified. The child deficient in the capacity to respond is just as motherless as is the normally equipped child without a mother" (44). Leaving aside the dubious evidence for the decisive importance of the mothering process in the etiology of autism, this formulation assigns to this variable an absolute significance. Other variables which may be influential then contribute only to the extent that they produce or intensify a deficiency in mothering.

By contrast, an interactionist view does not assume any *a priori* hierarchy in which different variables are then assigned greater or lesser positions of importance. In this approach, consequently, no variable has any absolute reified significance. Each must at all times be considered in relationship to the simultaneous operation of other influential variables. For temperament, a variable which reflects the organism's own behavioral traits, this means that its significance must at all times be considered in the context of other characteristics of the organism and the environment. The importance of temperament for the developmental process can, therefore, be estimated only if the other attributes of the individual and the nature of the environment are delineated as comprehensively as are the details of the temperamental traits. This is why we insist at all times that temperament can be defined only in the context within which the behavior occurs. The temperamental significance of a specific withdrawal reaction may be different if it is the first exposure to that stimulus, or the recurrence and repetition of withdrawal to a similar situation. It is also necessary to know whether the withdrawal response occurs consistently to new situations, or whether this specific reaction is an exception. As another example, temperamental characterization of an intense positive reaction may be different if this emotional expression occurs only when the individual is gratified by success in a highly meaningful activity or if it occurs even when the achievement is modest or relatively unimportant.

We have emphasized throughout this volume, as well as in our other writings, that the meaningful characterization of temperament in any individual requires concrete descriptive data derived from a variety of functionally significant life situations. Actually, the same type of data is also required for the accurate delineation of other organismic characteristics, whether they be motivations and purposes, cognitive levels, or perceptual characteristics. It may be important, and even necessary, to supplement such information by subjective, introspective data, especially in the older child and adult, but the descriptive objective material is always crucial. Thus, for example, if any individual's behavior consistently has a self-defeating end result, this result may reflect his actual motive and purpose. On the other hand, he may actually have an opposite motive, to achieve success, but his behavioral style and coping mechanisms may be so ineffectual and contradictory that his actions have consequences which are opposite to his actual purposes. Only the analysis of the detailed concrete sequences of his interaction with others in a number of such episodes will serve to clarify the issue.

The delineation of a temperamental or other organismic attribute in the environmental context within which it occurs also necessitates the avoidance of global, sweeping labels. A mother may be nurturing and affectionate in one context and rejecting and hostile in another. A father may be permissive and flexible with his child in certain contexts and authoritarian and rigid in others. A Difficult Child temperamentally may display intense negative responses to some life situations and demands and lively ebullient pleasure in others. Motivations and cognitive and perceptual patterns may also vary dramatically with different expectations, opportunities and demands. To label a parent globally as "permissive" or "rejecting" and a child as "difficult" temperamentally, "dependent" or "verbally deficient" may have an element of truth, but will run the risk of missing the nuances, subtleties and variabilities which characterize psychological functioning in different life situations. Assertions that we should look at the "whole individual," that each person is "unique" are valid generalizations only when this uniqueness is not conceptualized in global categories and labels.

FINAL COMMENTS

The opportunity to follow the youngsters in the NYLS from early infancy through adolescence has provided us with a wealth of data on many issues in developmental psychology. The present volume has touched on some of these. Overall, we have been impressed by the range and variety of the behavioral repertoire of the young infant. We have seen how this behavior makes it possible for the child to play an active role in his development from birth onward. Any global concept of "personality" becomes untenable as one identifies the many different behaviors in different interactions that each child and adolescent exhibits. All of us play many roles as we go back and forth from one life situation to another. All our roles are interrelated, all are parts of our individuality, and no one can be entitled "the real self" at the expense of the others, and endowed with some mystique of personality.

Above all, we have been deeply impressed at the breadth and scope of individual differences in behavior of even the youngest infants. Recently, Bryan Clarke (45), the biologist, has reviewed the evidence which shows that most natural populations of plants and animals are genetically heterogeneous, to an extent not previously appreciated. Moreover, he emphasizes, "there is strong evidence that the diversity of forms exists because natural selection favors it, that is, because the variants themselves affect the survival and reproduction of the individuals carrying them." He points out that human beings show wide diversity genetically and biochemically and that polymorphism not only characterizes the human species, but is desirable. This is the theme which we hope this volume has dramatized with regard to behavior.

Clarke leaves the last word to Sir Thomas Browne and so do we (45). "It is the common wonder of all men, how among so many millions of faces, there should be none alike: now contrary, I wonder as much how there should be any. He that shall consider how many thousand several words have been carelessly and without study composed out of 24 letters; withal how many hundred lines there are to be drawn in the Fabrick of one man, shall find that this variety is necessary."

·REFERENCES

1. A. Thomas, "Purpose and Consequence in the Analysis of Behavior," *Am. J. Psychotherapy*, 24:49-64 (1970).
2. B. S. Bloom, *Stability and Change in Human Characteristics* (New York: John Wiley and Sons, 1964).
3. W. H. Sheldon and S. S. Stevens, *The Varieties of Temperament* (New York: Harper and Bros., 1942).
4. A. R. Jensen, "How Much Can We Boost I.Q. and Scholastic Achievement?" *Harvard Educational Review*, 39:1-23 (1969).
5. E. H. Erikson, *Childhood and Society* (New York: W. W. Norton, 1950).
6. N. Ackerman, *The Psychodynamics of Family Life* (New York: Basic Books, 1958).
7. T. Lidz, S. Fleck and A. R. Cornelison, *Schizophrenia and the Family* (New York: International Universities Press, 1965).
8. L. C. Wynne and M. T. Singer, "Thought Disorder and Family Relations of Schizophrenia," *Arch. Gen. Psychiat.*, 9:191-206 (1963).
9. P. Wender, *Minimal Brain Dysfunction in Children* (New York: John Wiley and Sons, 1971).
10. Pasamanick and H. Knobloch, "Retrospective Studies on the Epidemiology of Reproductive Casualty: Old and New," *Merrill-Palmer Quarterly*, 12:7-26 (1966).

11. M. B. Stoch and P. M. Smythe, "Does Undernutrition during Infancy Inhibit Brain Growth and Subsequent Intellectual Development?" *Archives of Diseases of Children*, 38:546-552 (1963).
12. H. G. Birch, "Malnutrition, Learning and Intelligence," *Am. J. Public Health*, 62:773-785 (1972).
13. R. D. Hess, "Social Class and Ethnic Influences on Socialization," *Carmichael's Manual of Child Psychology*, ed., P. M. Mussen (New York: John Wiley and Sons, 1970).
14. O. Lewis, "The Culture of Poverty," *Scientific American*, 215:19-25, (1966).
15. K. Lorenz, *King Solomon's Ring: New Light on Animal Ways* (New York: Thomas Y. Crowell, 1952).
16. R. Hinde, *Animal Behavior: A Synthesis of Ethology and Comparative Psychology* (New York: McGraw Hill, 1966).
17. J. B. Watson, *Behaviorism* (New York: W. W. Norton, 1924).
18. B. L. White, *The First Three Years of Life* (Englewood Cliffs, N. J.: Prentice Hall, 1975).
19. A. M. Torgersen, "Temperamental Differences in Infants: Illustrated Through A Study of Twins." Presented at Conference on Temperament and Personality, Warsaw, Poland, 1974.
20. T. Dobzhansky, *Mankind Evolving* (New Haven: Yale University Press, 1962).
21. A. J. Sameroff and M. J. Chandler, "Reproductive Risk and the Continuum of Caretaking Casualty," *Review of Child Development Research*, eds., S. Scarr-Salapatek and G. Siegel (Chicago: University of Chicago Press, 1975), IV:187-245.
22. A. J. Sameroff, "Early Influences on Development: Fact or Fancy?" *Merrill-Palmer Quarterly*, 20:275-301 (1975).
23. M. Winick, K. K. Meyer and R. C. Harris, "Malnutrition and Environmental Enrichment by Early Adoption," *Science*, 190:1173-1175 (1975).
24. K. Lorenz, *op. cit.*
25. E. H. Hess, " 'Imprinting' in Animals," *Scientific American*, 198:81-90 (1958).
26. P. O. G., Bateson, Book review of *Imprinting* by E. H. Hess, *Science*, 183:740-741 (1974).
27. R. Hinde, *op. cit.*
28. P. H. Wolff, "Critical Periods in Human Cognitive Development," *Hospital Practice*, 11:77-87 (1970).
29. K. Connolly, "Learning and the Concept of Critical Periods in Infancy," *Develop. Med. and Child Neurol.*, 14:705-714 (1972).
30. C. Burt, E. Jones, E. Miller and W. Moodie, *How the Mind Works* (New York: Appleton-Century-Crofts, 1934), p. 29.
31. L. B. Murphy and A. E. Moriarty, *Vulnerability, Coping and Growth* (New Haven: Yale University Press, 1976), p. 158.
32. M. Lewis and H. McGurk, "Evaluation of Infant Intelligence," *Science*, 178:1174-1177 (1972).
33. D. C. McClelland, "Testing for Competence Rather Than for Intelligence," *American Psychologist*, 28:1-14 (1973).
34. A. Thomas and S. Sillen, *Racism and Psychiatry* (New York: Brunner/Mazel, 1972).
35. S. Freud, *Collected Papers*, Second Edition (London: Hogarth Press, 1950), p. 226.
36. D. Rosenthal, P. H. Wender, S. S. Kety, F. Schulsinger, J. Welner and

R. O. Rieder, "Parent-Child Relationships and Psychopathological Disorder in the Child," *Arch. Gen. Psychiat.*, 32:466-476 (1975).

37. B. L. White, *op. cit.*, p. 4.
38. E. Zigler, Letter to the Editor, *New York Times Magazine*, January 18, 1975.
39. S. K. Escalona and G. M. Heider, *Prediction and Outcome: A Study in Child Development* (New York: Basic Books, 1959).
40. A. F. Korner, personal communication, 1976.
41. B. S. Bloom, *op. cit.*
42. A. J. Sameroff, *op. cit.*
43. L. B. Murphy and A. E. Moriarty, *op. cit.*, p. 150.
44. S. K. Escalona, "Patterns of Infantile Experience and the Developmental Process," *Psychoanalytic Study of the Child*, 18:243 (1963).
45. B. Clarke, "The Causes of Biological Diversity," *Scientific American*, 233:50-60 (1975).

Appendix A. Carey

questionnaire

SLEEP

1. (a) Generally goes to sleep at about same time for night and naps (within ½ hour).
   (b) Partly the same times, partly not.
   (c) No regular pattern. Times vary 1-2 hours or more.

2. (a) Generally wakes up at about same time from night and naps.
   (b) Partly the same times, partly not.
   (c) No regular pattern. Times vary 1-2 hours or more.

3. (a) Generally happy (smiling, etc.) on waking up and going to sleep.
   (b) Variable mood at these times.
   (c) Generally fussy on waking up and going to sleep.

4. (a) Moves about crib much (such as from one end to other) during sleep.
   (b) Moves a little (a few inches).
   (c) Lies fairly still. Usually in same position when awakens.

5. With change in time, place or state of health:
   (a) Adjusts easily and sleeps fairly well within 1-2 days.

Reprinted with permission from Carey, W. B. "Measurement of Infant Temperament in Pediatric Practice," in *Individual Differences in Children*, ed., J. C. Westman, New York, 1973, pp. 298-306.

(b)   Variable pattern.

(c)   Bothered considerably. Takes at least 3 days to readjust sleeping routine.

FEEDING

6. (a)   Generally takes milk at about same time. Not over 1 hour variation.

    b)   Sometimes same, sometimes different times.

    (c)   Hungry times unpredictable.

7. (a)   Generally takes about same amount of milk, not over 2 oz. difference.

    (b)   Sometimes same, sometimes different amounts.

    (c)   Amounts taken unpredictable.

8. (a)   Easily distracted from milk feedings by noises, changes in place, or routine.

    (b)   Sometimes distracted, sometimes not.

    (c)   Usually goes on sucking in spite of distractions.

9. (a)   Easily adjusts to parents' efforts to change feeding schedule within 1-2 tries.

    (b)   Slowly (after several tries) or variable.

    (c)   Adjusts not at all to such changes after several tries.

10. (a)   If hungry and wants milk, will keep refusing substitutes (solids, water, pacifier) for many minutes.

    (b)   Intermediate or variable.

    (c)   Gives up within a few minutes and takes what is offered.

11. (a)   With interruptions of milk or solid feedings, as for burping, is generally happy, smiles.

    (b)   Variable response.

    (c)   Generally cries with these interruptions.

12. (a)   Always notices (and reacts to) change in temperature or type of milk or substitution of juice or water.

    (b)   Variable.

    (c)   Rarely seems to notice (and react to) such changes.

13. (a)   Suck generally vigorous.

    (b)   Intermediate.

    (c)   Suck generally mild and intermittent.

14. (a) Activity during feedings—constant squirming, kicking, etc.
    (b) Some motion: intermediate.
    (c) Lies quietly throughout.

15. (a) Always cries loudly when hungry.
    (b) Cries somewhat but only occasionally hard or for many minutes.
    (c) Usually just whimpers when hungry, but doesn't cry loudly.

16. (a) Hunger cry usually stopped for at least a minute by picking up, pacifier, putting on bib, etc.
    (b) Sometimes can be distracted when hungry.
    (c) Nothing stops hunger cry.

17. (a) After feeding, baby smiles and laughs.
    (b) Content but not usually happy (smiles, etc.) or fussy.
    (c) Fussy and wants to be left alone.

18. (a) When full, clamps mouth closed, spits out food or milk, bats at spoon, etc.
    (b) Variable.
    (c) Just turns head away or lets food drool out of mouth.

19. (a) Initial reaction to new foods (solids, juices, vitamins) acceptance. Swallows them promptly without fussing.
    (b) Variable response.
    (c) Usually rejects new foods. Makes face, spits out, etc.

20. (a) Initial reaction to new foods pleasant (smiles, etc.), whether accepts or not.
    (b) Variable or intermediate.
    (c) Response unpleasant (cries, etc.), whether accepts or not.

21. (a) This response is dramatic whether accepting (smacks lips, laughs, squeals) or not (cries).
    (b) Variable.
    (c) This response mild whether accepting or not. Just smiles, makes face or no expression.

22. (a) After several feedings of any new food, accepts it.
    (b) Accepts some, not others.
    (c) Continues to reject most new foods after several tries.

23. (a) With changes in amounts, kinds, timing of solids does not seem to mind.
    (b) Variable response. Sometimes accepts, sometimes not.

(c) Does not accept these changes readily.

24. (a) Easily notices and reacts to differences in taste and consistency.
    (b) Variable.
    (c) Seems seldom to notice or react to these differences.

25. (a) If does not get type of solid food desired, keeps crying till gets it.
    (b) Variable.
    (c) May fuss briefly but soon gives up and takes what offered.

SOILING AND WETTING

26. (a) When having bowel movement, generally cries.
    (b) Sometimes cries.
    (c) Rarely cries though face may become red. Generally happy (smiles, etc.) in spite of having bowel movement (b.m.)

27. (a) Bowel movements generally at same time of day (usually within 1 hour of same time).
    (b) Sometimes at same time, sometimes not.
    (c) No pattern. Usually not same time.

28. (a) Generally indicates in some way that is soiled with b.m.
    (b) Sometimes indicates.
    (c) Seldom or never indicates.

29. (a) Usually fusses when diaper soiled with b.m.
    (b) Sometimes fusses.
    (c) Usually does not fuss.

30. (a) Generally indicates somehow that is wet (no b.m.).
    (b) Sometimes indicates.
    (c) Seldom or never indicates.

31. (a) Usually fusses when diaper wet (no b.m.).
    (b) Sometimes fusses.
    (c) Usually does not fuss.

32. (a) When fussing about diaper, does so loudly. A real cry.
    (b) Variable.
    (c) Usually just a little whimpering.

33. (a) If fussing about diaper, can easily be distracted for at least a few minutes by being picked up, etc.
    (b) Variable.
    (c) Nothing distracts baby from fussing.

DIAPERING AND DRESSING

34. (a) Squirms and kicks much at these times.
    (b) Moves some.
    (c) Generally lies still during these procedures.

35. (a) Generally pleasant (smiles, etc.) during diapering and dressing.
    (b) Variable.
    (c) Generally fussy during these times.

36. (a) These feelings usually intense: vigorous laughing or crying.
    (b) Variable.
    (c) Mildly expressed usually. Little smiling or fussing.

BATHING

37. (a) Usual reaction to bath: smiles or laughs.
    (b) Variable or neutral.
    (c) Usually cries or fusses.

38. (a) Like or dislike of bath is intense. Excited.
    (b) Variable or intermediate.
    (c) Like or dislike is mild. Not excited.

39. (a) Kicks, splashes and wiggles throughout.
    (b) Intermediate—moves moderate amount.
    (c) Lies quietly or moves little.

40. (a) Reaction to very first tub (or basin) bath. Seemed to accept it right away.
    (c) At first protested against bath.

41. (a) If protested at first, accepted it after 2 or 3 times.
    (b) Sometimes accepted, sometimes not.
    (c) Continued to object even after two weeks.

42. (a) If bath by different person or in different place, readily accepts change first or second time.
    (b) May or may not accept.
    (c) Objects consistently to such changes.

PROCEDURES—NAIL CUTTING, HAIR BRUSHING, WASHING FACE AND HAIR, MEDICINES

43. (a) Initial reaction to any new procedure: generally acceptance.
    (b) Variable.
    (c) Generally objects; fusses or cries.

44. (a) If initial objection, accepts after 2 or 3 times.
    (b) Variable acceptance. Sometimes does, sometimes does not.
    (c) Continues to object even after several times.

45. (a) Generally pleasant during procedures once established—smiles, etc.
    (b) Neutral or variable.
    (c) Generally fussy or crying during procedures.

46. (a) If fussy with procedures, easily distracted by game, toy, singing, etc., and stops fussing.
    (b) Variable response to distractions.
    (c) Not distracted. Goes on fussing.

VISITS TO DOCTOR

47. (a) With physical exam, when well, generally friendly and smiles.
    (b) Both smiles and fusses: variable.
    (c) Fusses most of time.

48. (a) With shots cries loudly for several minutes or more.
    (b) Variable.
    (c) Cry over in less than a minute.

49. (a) When crying from shot, easily distracted by milk, pacfier, etc.
    (b) Sometimes distracted, sometimes not.
    (c) Goes right on crying no matter what is done.

RESPONSE TO ILLNESS

50. (a) With any kind of illness, much crying and fussing.
    (b) Variable.
    (c) Not much crying with illness. Just whimpering sometimes. Generally his usual self.

SENSORY—REACTIONS TO SOUNDS, LIGHT, TOUCH

51. (a) Reacts little or not at all to unusual loud sound or bright light.
    (b) Intermediate or variable.
    (c) Reacts to almost any change in sound or light.

52. (a) This reaction to light or sound is intense—startles or cries loudly.
    (b) Intermediate—sometimes does, sometimes not.
    (c) Mild reaction—little or no crying.

53. (a) On repeated exposure to these same lights or sounds, does not react so much any more.
    (b) Variable.
    (c) No change from initial negative reaction.

54. (a) If already crying about something else, light or sound makes crying stop briefly at least.
    (b) Variable response.
    (c) Makes no difference.

RESPONSES TO PEOPLE

55. (a) Definitely notices and reacts to differences in people: age, sex, glasses, hats, other physical differences.
    (b) Variable reaction to differences.
    (c) Similar reactions to most people unless strangers.

56. (a) Initial reaction to approach by strangers positive, friendly (smiles, etc.).
    (b) Variable reaction.
    (c) Initial rejection or withdrawal.

57. (a) This initial reaction to strangers is intense: crying or laughing.
    (b) Variable.
    (c) Mild—frown or smile.

58. (a) General reaction to familiar people is friendly—smiles, laughs.
    (b) Variable reaction.
    (c) Generally glum or unfriendly. Little smiling.

59. (a) This reaction to familiar people is intense—crying or laughing.
    (b) Variable.
    (c) Mild—frown or smile.

REACTION TO NEW PLACES AND SITUATIONS

60. (a) Initial reaction acceptance—tolerates or enjoys them within a few minutes.
    (b) Variable.
    (c) Initial reaction rejection—does not tolerate or enjoy them within a few minutes.

61. (a) After continued exposure (several minutes) accepts these changes easily.

(b)   Variable.

(c)   Even after continued exposure, accepts changes poorly.

PLAY

62. (a)   In crib or play pen can amuse self for half-hour or more looking at mobile, hands, etc.

(b)   Amuses self for variable length of time.

(c)   Indicates need for attention or new occupation after several minutes.

63. (a)   Takes new toy right away and plays with it.

(b)   Variable.

(c)   Rejects new toy when first presented.

64. (a)   If rejects at first, after short while (several minutes) accepts new toy.

(b)   Variable.

(c)   Adjusts slowly to new toy.

65. (a)   Play activity involves much movement—kicking, waving arms, etc. Much exploring.

(b)   Intermediate.

(c)   Generally lies quietly while playing. Explores little.

66. (a)   If reaching for toy out of reach, keeps trying for 2 minutes or more.

(b)   Variable.

(c)   Stops trying in less than $\frac{1}{2}$ minute.

67. (a)   When given a toy, plays with it for many minutes.

(b)   Variable.

(c)   Plays with one toy for only short time (only 1-2 minutes).

68. (a)   When playing with one toy, easily distracted by another.

(b)   Variable.

(c)   Not easily distracted by another toy.

69. (a)   Play usually accompanied by laughing, smiling, etc.

(b)   Variable or intermediate.

(c)   Generally fussy during play.

70. (a)   Play is intense: much activity, vocalization or laughing.

(b)   Variable or intermediate.

(c)   Plays quietly and calmly.

CAREY TEMPERAMENT QUESTIONNAIRE—SCORING SHEET

(x = no score; * = score in two categories). The responses on the questionnaire are transposed to this score sheet providing a total score of high, medium, or low for each dimension of temperament.

Activity			Rhythmicity			Adaptability			Approach			Threshold			Intensity			Mood			Distractibility			Persistence		
H	M	L	R	V	I	A	V	N	A	V	W	H	M	L	I	Y	M	P	V	N	D	V	N	P	V	N
4 a	b	c	1 a	b	c	5 a	b	c										3 a	b	c	8 a	b	c			
			2 a	b	c	9 a	b	c																			
			6 a	b	c																					
			7 a	b	c																					
13 a	b	c							19 a	b	c	12 c	b	a	15 a	b	c	11 a	b	c	16 a	b	c	10 a	b	c
14 a	b	c													18 a	b	c	17 a	b	c						
			27 a	b	c	22 a	b	c				24 c	b	a	21 a	b	c	20 a	b	c				25 a	b	c
						23 a	b	c				28 c	b	a	26* a	b	c	26* c	b	a						
																		29 x	b	a						
34 a	b	c				35* a	b	c				30 c	b	a	32 a	b	c	31 x	b	a	33 a	b	c			
															36 a	b	c	35* x	b	c						
39 a	b	c													38 a	b	c	37 a	b	c						

CAREY TEMPERAMENT QUESTIONNAIRE—SCORING SHEET

(x = no score; * = score in two categories). The responses on the questionnaire are transposed to this score sheet providing a total score of high, medium, or low for each dimension of temperament. (*Continued*)

	Activity			Rhythmicity			Adaptability			Approach			Threshold			Intensity			Mood			Distractibility			Persistence		
	H	M	L	R	V	I	A	V	N	A	V	W	H	M	L	I	V	M	P	V	N	D	V	N	P	V	N
40							41 a	b	c	40 a	x	c	42* a	b	c	48 a	b	c	45 a	b	c	46 a	b	c			
							42* a	b	c	43 a	b	c							47* a	b	c	49 a	b	c			
							44 a	b	c																		
							47* a	b	c																		
50							53 a	b	c	56* a	b	c	51 a	b	c	52 a	b	c	50 c	b	a	54 a	b	c			
													55 c			57 a	b	c	56* a	b	c						
																59 a	b	c	58 a	b	c						
60	65 a	b	c				61 a	b	c	60* a	b	c							60* a	b	c	68 a	b	c	62 a	b	c
							64 a	b	c	63 a	b	c				70 a	b	c	69 a	b	c				66 a	b	c
																									67 a	b	c
TOTAL																											

Appendix B. Parent and teacher temperament questionnaire for children 3-7 years of age

PARENT QUESTIONNAIRE
(from the NYLS of Thomas, Chess and Korn)

This questionnaire is designed to gather information on the way your child behaves in different situations of everyday life. Each statement asks you to judge whether that behavior occurs *hardly ever, infrequently, once in a while, sometimes, often, very often* or *almost always*. Before each statement, please circle the number from 1 to 7 that best describes your child's behavior. The statements often involve making judgments (such as whether your child does something "quickly" or "slowly," for a "long time" and so on). Please try to make these judgments to the best of your ability, based on how you think your child compares to other children of about the same age.

Some statements may seem similar to each other because they ask about the same situation. However, each one looks at a different area of the child's behavior. Therefore, your answers may be different in each case. Should you feel that some of the choices you make need more explanation because you are uncertain about that particular choice, or because you feel that your child's behavior in that area is special enough to call for more information, *please circle the choice that seems to fit best,* and then write a brief note under "comments" at the end of the questionnaire. For example, if you feel that on some specific item your child's behavior "never" occurs or "always" occurs, circle the "almost always" or "hardly ever" and indicate that it is "always" or "never" in the comment.

A few items may not apply to your child (such as questions about school for those children not yet in school). In that case, please write "NA" (not applicable) next to the item.

1	2	3	4	5	6	7
hardly ever	infrequently	once in a while	sometimes	often	very often	almost always

1. My child splashes hard in the bath and plays actively.   hardly ever 1 2 3 4 5 6 7 almost always

2. When with other children, my children seems to be having a good time.   hardly ever 1 2 3 4 5 6 7 almost always

3. My child quickly notices odors and comments on unpleasant smells.   hardly ever 1 2 3 4 5 6 7 almost always

4. My child is shy with adults he/she does not know.   hardly ever 1 2 3 4 5 6 7 almost always

5. When my child starts a project such as model, puzzle, painting, he/she works at it without stopping until completed, even if it takes a long time.   hardly ever 1 2 3 4 5 6 7 almost always

6. My child has a bowel movement at about the same time every day.   hardly ever 1 2 3 4 5 6 7 almost always

7. My child now eats food that she/he used to dislike.

    hardly ever 1 2 3 4 5 6 7 almost always

8. My child shows strong enthusiasm for food he/she likes or strong dislike for food he/she does not like.

    hardly ever 1 2 3 4 5 6 7 almost always

9. If my child is in a bad mood, he/she can easily be "joked" out of it.

    hardly ever 1 2 3 4 5 6 7 almost always

10. When first meeting new children, my child is bashful.

    hardly ever 1 2 3 4 5 6 7 almost always

11. My child ignores loud noises. For example, he/she is the last to complain about music being too loud, sirens, etc.

    hardly ever 1 2 3 4 5 6 7 almost always

12. If my child is not permitted to wear an item of clothing he/she selects, he/she accepts wearing mother's choice after a short discussion.

    hardly ever 1 2 3 4 5 6 7 almost always

13. My child asks for or takes a snack at approximately the same time every day.

    hardly ever 1 2 3 4 5 6 7 almost always

14. My child is happy and pleased when telling about something that has happened during the day.

    hardly ever 1 2 3 4 5 6 7 almost always

15. My child is at ease within a few visits when visiting at someone else's home.

    hardly ever 1 2 3 4 5 6 7 almost always

16. When upset or annoyed with a task my child may throw it down, cry, yell or slam door, etc.

hardly ever 1 2 3 4 5 6 7 almost always

17. If my child wants a toy or candy (while shopping) he/she will easily accept something else offered instead.

hardly ever 1 2 3 4 5 6 7 almost always

18. When my child moves about in the house or outdoors, he/she runs rather than walks.

hardly ever 1 2 3 4 5 6 7 almost always

19. My child enjoys going shopping with parents.

hardly ever 1 2 3 4 5 6 7 almost always

20. After my child is put to bed at night it takes about the same length of time to fall asleep.

hardly ever 1 2 3 4 5 6 7 almost always

21. My child likes to try new foods.

hardly ever 1 2 3 4 5 6 7 almost always

22. When mother is busy and cannot do what child wants, he/she goes away and does something else instead of keeping after mother.

hardly ever 1 2 3 4 5 6 7 almost always

23. My child quickly notices colors (for example, may comment on how pretty or ugly they are).

hardly ever 1 2 3 4 5 6 7 almost always

24. In the playground, my child runs, climbs, swings and is constantly on the go.

hardly ever 1 2 3 4 5 6 7 almost always

25. If my child resists some procedure, such as having hair cut, brushed or washed, he/she will continue to resist it for at least several months.

hardly ever   1   2   3   4   5   6   7   almost always

26. If there is a sudden noise or activity nearby when my child is playing with a favorite toy, he/she ignores it, or at most, looks up briefly.

hardly ever   1   2   3   4   5   6   7   almost always

27. When taken away from an activity that my child really enjoys, he/she protests only mildly, with a little bit of fussing or some whining.

hardly ever   1   2   3   4   5   6   7   almost always

28. When my child is promised something in the future, he/she keeps reminding parents constantly.

hardly ever   1   2   3   4   5   6   7   almost always

29. When playing with other children, my child argues with them.

hardly ever   1   2   3   4   5   6   7   almost always

30. When in the park, at a party or visiting, my child will go up to strange children and join in their play.

hardly ever   1   2   3   4   5   6   7   almost always

31. My child sleeps more one night and less another night, rather than the same number of hours each night.

hardly ever   1   2   3   4   5   6   7   almost always

32. My child ignores the temperature of foods (hot or cold).

hardly ever   1   2   3   4   5   6   7   almost always

33. If my child is shy with a strange adult he/she quickly (within a half-hour or so) gets over this.

hardly ever   1   2   3   4   5   6   7   almost always

34. My child sits still to have a story told or read, or a song sung.

hardly ever   1   2   3   4   5   6   7   almost always

35. When scolded or reprimanded by parents, my child reacts mildly, such as whining or complaining rather than strongly with crying or screaming.

hardly ever   1   2   3   4   5   6   7   almost always

36. When my child becomes angry about something, it is difficult to sidetrack him/her.

hardly ever   1   2   3   4   5   6   7   almost always

37. When learning a new physical activity (such as hopping, skating, bike riding) my child will spend long periods of time practicing.

hardly ever   1   2   3   4   5   6   7   almost always

38. My child gets hungry at different times each day.

hardly ever   1   2   3   4   5   6   7   almost always

39. My child is highly sensitive to changes in the brightness or dimness of light.

hardly ever   1   2   3   4   5   6   7   almost always

40. When away from home with parents, my child has a problem (even after a few nights) in falling asleep in a new bed.

hardly ever   1   2   3   4   5   6   7   almost always

41. My child looks forward to going to school.

hardly ever   1 2 3 4 5 6 7   almost always

42. When the family takes a trip, my child immediately makes self at home in the new surroundings.

hardly ever   1 2 3 4 5 6 7   almost always

43. When shopping together and mother does not buy candy, toys or clothing that child wants, he/she cries and yells.

hardly ever   1 2 3 4 5 6 7   almost always

44. If my child is upset, it is hard to comfort him/her.

hardly ever   1 2 3 4 5 6 7   almost always

45. When the weather is bad and my child is confined to the house, he/she runs around and cannot be entertained by quiet activities.

hardly ever   1 2 3 4 5 6 7   almost always

46. My child is immediately friendly with and approaches unknown adults who visit our home.

hardly ever   1 2 3 4 5 6 7   almost always

47. My child eats a lot one day and very little the next day, rather than the same amount each day.

hardly ever   1 2 3 4 5 6 7   almost always

48. When a toy or game is difficult, my child will turn quickly to another activity.

hardly ever   1 2 3 4 5 6 7   almost always

49. My child ignores differences in temperature, indoors or outdoors.

hardly ever   1 2 3 4 5 6 7   almost always

50. If a favorite toy or game is broken, my child gets noticeably upset.

hardly ever   1 2 3 4 5 6 7   almost always

51. In a new situation, such as a nursery, day care center, or school my child is still uncomfortable even after a few days.

hardly ever   1 2 3 4 5 6 7   almost always

52. Although my child dislikes some procedures (such as nail cutting or hair brushing), he/she will easily allow it if watching television or being entertained while it is done.

hardly ever   1 2 3 4 5 6 7   almost always

53. My child can sit quietly through an entire children's movie, baseball game, or a long TV program.

hardly ever   1 2 3 4 5 6 7   almost always

54. When my child objects to wearing certain clothing, he/she argues loudly, yells, cries.

hardly ever   1 2 3 4 5 6 7   almost always

55. On weekends and holidays my child wakes himself/herself up at the same time each morning.

hardly ever   1 2 3 4 5 6 7   almost always

56. My child complains to own parents about other children if anything goes wrong.

hardly ever   1 2 3 4 5 6 7   almost always

57. My child is sensitive and complains about clothing being tight, itchy or uncomfortable.

hardly ever   1 2 3 4 5 6 7   almost always

58. If my child is angry or annoyed, he/she gets over it quickly.

    hardly ever 1 2 3 4 5 6 7 almost always

59. When there is a change in daily routine, such as not being able to go to school, change of usual daily activities, etc., my child goes along with the new routine easily.

    hardly ever 1 2 3 4 5 6 7 almost always

60. When outdoors, in a playground or park, my child plays quietly with toys or dolls.

    hardly ever 1 2 3 4 5 6 7 almost always

61. My child complains quietly when another child takes his/her toy away.

    hardly ever 1 2 3 4 5 6 7 almost always

62. The first time my child is left in a new situation without mother (such as school, nursery, music lesson, camp), he/she gets upset.

    hardly ever 1 2 3 4 5 6 7 almost always

63. If my child starts to play with something and I want him to stop, it is hard to turn his attention to something else.

    hardly ever 1 2 3 4 5 6 7 almost always

64. My child gets involved in quiet activities such as crafts, watching television, reading or looking at picture books.

    hardly ever 1 2 3 4 5 6 7 almost always

65. My child becomes easily upset when he/she loses a game.

    hardly ever 1 2 3 4 5 6 7 almost always

66. My child would rather wear familiar clothes than new clothes.

hardly ever 1 2 3 4 5 6 7 almost always

67. If my child gets dirty or wet, he/she ignores this and appears quite comfortable.

hardly ever 1 2 3 4 5 6 7 almost always

68. My child has difficulty in adjusting to rules of another household, if they are different from those at home.

hardly ever 1 2 3 4 5 6 7 almost always

69. My child seems to take things matter of factly. Accepts events in stride without getting very excited.

hardly ever 1 2 3 4 5 6 7 almost always

70. If meals are delayed for an hour or more, my child easily waits without seeming to mind.

hardly ever 1 2 3 4 5 6 7 almost always

71. My child can be stopped from pestering if he/she is given something else to do.

hardly ever 1 2 3 4 5 6 7 almost always

72. When assistance is offered in doing a task, my child continues to do it on his/her own.

hardly ever 1 2 3 4 5 6 7 almost always

FINDER'S KEY

Category for Each Question of Parent Temperament Questionnaire

ACTIVITY	1	18	24	34	45	53	60	64
RHYTHMICITY	6	13	20	31	38	47	55	70
ADAPTABILITY	7	15	25	33	40	51	59	68
APP/WITH	4	10	21	30	42	46	62	66
THRESHOLD	3	11	23	32	39	49	57	67
INTENSITY	8	16	27	35	43	54	61	69
MOOD	2	14	19	29	41	50	56	65
DISTRACTIBILITY	9	17	26	36	44	52	63	71
PERSISTENCE	5	12	22	28	37	48	58	72

QUESTION	CATEGORY	Q	CAT	Q	CAT	Q	CAT	Q	CAT
1	ACT (U) *	16	INT (U)	31	RHY (L)	46	APP (U)	61	INT (L)
2	MOOD (U)	17	DIST (U)	32	THR (U)	47	RHY (L	62	APP (L)
3	THR (L)	18	ACT (U)	33	ADA (U)	48	PERS (L)	63	DIST (L)
4	APP (L)	19	MOOD (U)	34	ACT (L)	49	THR (U)	64	ACT (L)
5	PERS (U)	20	RHY (U)	35	INT (L)	50	MOOD (L)	65	MOOD (L)
6	RHY (U)	21	APP (U)	36	DIST (L)	51	ADA (L)	66	APP (L)
7	ADA (U)	22	PERS (L)	37	PERS (U)	52	DIST (U)	67	THR (U)
8	INT (U)	23	THR (L)	38	RHY (L)	53	ACT (L)	68	ADA (L)
9	DIST (U)	24	ACT (U)	39	THR (L)	54	INT (U)	69	INT (L)
10	APP (L)	25	ADA (L)	40	ADA (L)	55	RHY (U)	70	RHY (L)
11	THR (U)	26	DIST (L)	41	MOOD (U)	56	MOOD (L)	71	DIST (U)
12	PERS (L)	27	INT (L)	42	APP (U)	57	THR (L)	72	PERS (U)
13	RHY (U)	28	PERS (U)	43	INT (U)	58	PERS (L)		
14	MOOD (U)	29	MOOD (L)	44	DIST (L)	59	ADA (U)		
15	ADA (U)	30	APP (U)	45	ACT (U)	60	ACT (L)		

"U" Signifies Upper Extreme Of Category Range
"L" Signifies Lower Extreme Of Category Range

For each temperament category there are eight questions; four each in the upper and lower extremes of the behavioral range involved (e.g., High and Low Activity, Adaptive and Non-Adaptive, etc.). These, together with the rated frequency of occurrence of the behavioral item, yield a score.

Thus, an upper extreme question (High Activity) rated "7—almost always" is assigned a weighted score of 7. A lower extreme question (Low Activity) rated "7—almost always" is assigned a weighted score of 1. The total sum of all weighted scores in a category (e.g., Activity) is divided by the total number of questions answered—eight, if all the questions in the category are answered.

The score range is 1 to 7, and reflects the relative frequency of the two types of behavioral items in the particular category. For example, a weighted score of 7 in Activity would signify an almost always occurrence of High Activity and a hardly ever occurrence of Low Activity for the child. On the other hand, a weighted score of 1 would signify an almost always occurrence of Low Activity, and a hardly ever occurrence of High Activity.

In order to obtain the weighted score, the procedure for each question involves the following:

1) Identification of the temperament category;

2) Location of the position in the range—upper or lower extreme;

3) Recording the rating assigned by the informant;

4) Multiplying by the appropriate weighted score;

5) Summing the weighted scores within the category;

6) Dividing the sum of weighted scores by the number of questions answered in the category.

In the scoring key reproduced, many of these operations are consolidated. Questions are already organized by category, and into upper and lower levels. This key is obviously for hand scoring and is cumbersome. Computer scoring is clearly recommended where possible.

For each category in the key, the following symbols are used:

N—the number of questions rated as 1, 2, etc.

XW—multiply N by the denoted Weighted Score

WS—sum these weighted scores across the set of questions.

This is done for the four upper extreme questions and for the four lower extreme questions. The two sets of "WS" (Weighted Scores) are then added together, and divided by the number of questions answered in the category, yielding the category score.

To facilitate the recording of responses, the "finders' keys" are useful.

SCORING KEY:

PARENT TEMPERAMENT QUESTIONNAIRE FOR CHILDREN
3-7 YEARS OF AGE

Name .... Date ....

Birthdate .... Age ....

Completed by ....

MOOD

Q#							
2:	1	2	3	4	5	6	7
14:	1	2	3	4	5	6	7
19:	1	2	3	4	5	6	7
41:	1	2	3	4	5	6	7
N	•	•	•	•	•	•	•
	x	x	x	x	x	x	x
xw	7	6	5	4	3	2	1
WS	+	+	+	+	+	+	+

Q#							
29:	1	2	3	4	5	6	7
50:	1	2	3	4	5	6	7
56:	1	2	3	4	5	6	7
65:	1	2	3	4	5	6	7
N	•	•	•	•	•	•	•
	x	x	x	x	x	x	x
xw	7	6	5	4	3	2	1
WS	+	+	+	+	+	+	+

Category Total* _____
MOOD SCORE _____

Q# DISTRACTABILITY

Q#							
9:	1	2	3	4	5	6	7
17:	1	2	3	4	5	6	7
52:	1	2	3	4	5	6	7
71:	1	2	3	4	5	6	7
N	•	•	•	•	•	•	•
	x	x	x	x	x	x	x
xw	1	2	3	4	5	5	7
WS	+	+	+	+	+	+	+

Q#							
26:	1	2	3	4	5	6	7
36:	1	2	3	4	5	6	7
44:	1	2	3	4	5	6	7
63:	1	2	3	4	5	6	7
N	•	•	•	•	•	•	•
	x	x	x	x	x	x	x
xw	7	6	5	4	3	2	1
WS	+	+	+	+	+	+	+

Category Total* _____
DISTRACT SCORE _____

Q# PERSISTENCE

Q#							
5:	1	2	3	4	5	6	7
28:	1	2	3	4	5	6	7
37:	1	2	3	4	5	6	7
72:	1	2	3	4	5	6	7
N	•	•	•	•	•	•	•
	x	x	x	x	x	x	x
xw	1	2	3	4	5	6	7
WS		+	+	+	+	+	+

Q#							
12:	1	2	3	4	5	6	7
22:	1	2	3	4	5	6	7
48:	1	2	3	4	5	6	7
58:	1	2	3	4	5	6	7
N	•	•	•	•	•	•	•
	x	x	x	x	x	x	x
xw	7	6	5	4	3	2	1
WS	+	+	+	+	+	+	+

Category Total* _____
PERSIST SCORE _____

* Divide by 8, or the number of questions in the category answered.

ACTIVITY

Q#							
1:	1	2	3	4	5	6	7
18:	1	2	3	4	5	6	7
24:	1	2	3	4	5	6	7
45:	1	2	3	4	5	6	7
N	.	.	.	.	.	.	.
xW	x	x	x	x	x	x	x
	1	2	3	4	5	6	7
WS	+	+	+	+	+	+	=

Q#							
34:	1	2	3	4	5	6	7
53:	1	2	3	4	5	6	7
60:	1	2	3	4	5	6	7
64:	1	2	3	4	5	6	7
N	.	.	.	.	.	.	.
xW	x	x	x	x	x	x	x
	7	6	5	4	3	2	1
WS	+	+	+	+	+	+	=

Category Total* _____
ACTIVITY SCORE _____

RHYTHMICITY

Q#							
6:	1	2	3	4	5	6	7
13:	1	2	3	4	5	6	7
20:	1	2	3	4	5	6	7
55:	1	2	3	4	5	6	7
N	.	.	.	.	.	.	.
xW	x	x	x	x	x	x	x
	1	2	3	4	5	6	7
WS	+	+	+	+	+	+	=

Q#							
31:	1	2	3	4	5	6	7
38:	1	2	3	4	5	6	7
47:	1	2	3	4	5	6	7
70:	1	2	3	4	5	6	7
N	.	.	.	.	.	.	.
xW	x	x	x	x	x	x	x
	7	6	5	4	3	2	1
WS	+	+	+	+	+	+	=

Category Total* _____
RHYTHMIC SCORE _____

ADAPTABILITY

Q#							
7:	1	2	3	4	5	6	7
15:	1	2	3	4	5	6	7
33:	1	2	3	4	5	6	7
59:	1	2	3	4	5	6	7
N	.	.	.	.	.	.	.
xW	x	x	x	x	x	x	x
	1	2	3	4	5	6	7
WS	+	+	+	+	+	+	=

Q#							
25:	1	2	3	4	5	6	7
40:	1	2	3	4	5	6	7
51:	1	2	3	4	5	6	7
68:	1	2	3	4	5	6	7
N	.	.	.	.	.	.	.
xW	x	x	x	x	x	x	x
	7	6	5	4	3	2	1
WS	+	+	+	+	+	+	=

Category Total* _____
ADAPTAB SCORE _____

*Divide by 8, or the number of questions in the category answered.

Q# APPROACH/WITHDRAWAL

Q#							
21:	1	2	3	4	5	6	7
30:	1	2	3	4	5	6	7
42:	1	2	3	4	5	6	7
46:	1	2	3	4	5	6	7
N	.	.	.	.	.	.	.
xW	x	x	x	x	x	x	x
	1	2	3	4	5	6	7
WS	+	+	+	+	+	+	=

Q#							
4:	1	2	3	4	5	6	7
10:	1	2	3	4	5	6	7
62:	1	2	3	4	5	6	7
66:	1	2	3	4	5	6	7
N	.	.	.	.	.	.	.
xW	x	x	x	x	x	x	x
	7	6	5	4	3	2	1
WS	+	+	+	+	+	+	=

Category Total* _____

APPROACH SCORE _____

Q# THRESHOLD

Q#							
11:	1	2	3	4	5	6	7
32:	1	2	3	4	5	6	7
49:	1	2	3	4	5	6	7
67:	1	2	3	4	5	6	7
N	.	.	.	.	.	.	.
xW	x	x	x	x	x	x	x
	1	2	3	4	5	6	7
WS	+	+	+	+	+	+	=

Q#							
3:	1	2	3	4	5	6	7
23:	1	2	3	4	5	6	7
39:	1	2	3	4	5	6	7
57:	1	2	3	4	5	6	7
N	.	.	.	.	.	.	.
xW	x	x	x	x	x	x	x
	7	6	5	4	3	2	1
WS	+	+	+	+	+	+	=

Category Total* _____

THRESHOLD SCORE _____

Q# INTENSITY

Q#							
8:	1	2	3	4	5	6	7
16:	1	2	3	4	5	6	7
43:	1	2	3	4	5	6	7
54:	1	2	3	4	5	6	7
N	.	.	.	.	.	.	.
xW	x	x	x	x	x	x	x
	1	2	3	4	5	6	7
WS	+	+	+	+	+	+	=

Q#							
27:	1	2	3	4	5	6	7
35:	1	2	3	4	5	6	7
61:	1	2	3	4	5	6	7
69:	1	2	3	4	5	6	7
N	.	.	.	.	.	.	.
xW	x	x	x	x	x	x	x
	7	6	5	4	3	2	1
WS	+	+	+	+	+	+	=

Category Total* _____

INTENSITY SCORE _____

* Divide by 8, or the number of questions in the category answered.

TEACHER TEMPERAMENT QUESTIONNAIRE
FOR CHILDREN 3-7 YEARS OF AGE

(From the NYLS of Thomas, Chess and Korn)

This questionnaire is designed to gather information on the way a child behaves in different situations of everyday school life. Each statement asks you to judge whether that behavior occurs hardly ever, infrequently, once in a while, sometimes, often, very often or almost always. For each statement, please circle the number from 1 to 7 that best describes the child's behavior. The statements often involve making judgments (such as whether the child does something "quickly" or "slowly," for a "long time" or a "short time," and so on.) Please try to make these judgments to the best of your ability, based on how you think the child compares to other children of about the same age.

Some statements may seem similar to each other because they ask about the same situation. However, each one looks at a different area of the child's behavior. Therefore, your answers may be different in each case. Should you feel that some of the choices you make need more explanation because you are uncertain about the particular choice, or because you feel that the child's behavior in that area is special enough to call for more information, *please circle the choice that seems to fit best,* and then write a brief note under "comments" at the end of the questionnaire. For example, if you feel that on some specific item the child's behavior "never" occurs or "always" occurs, circle the "almost always" or "almost never" and indicate that it is "always" or "never" in the comment.

A few items may not apply to the child. In that case, please write "NA" (not applicable) next to the item.

1	2	3	4	5	6	7
hardly ever	infrequently	once in a while	sometimes	often	very often	almost always

1. Child seems to have difficulty sitting still, may wriggle a lot or get out of seat. hardly ever 1 2 3 4 5 6 7 almost always

2. When with other children, this child seems to be having a good time. hardly ever 1 2 3 4 5 6 7 almost always

3. Child is very conscious of odors, comments on pleasant or unpleasant smells.   hardly ever   1 2 3 4 5 6 7   almost always

4. Child is shy with adults he/she doesn't know.   hardly ever   1 2 3 4 5 6 7   almost always

5. If child's activity is interrupted, he/she tries to go back to the activity.   hardly ever   1 2 3 4 5 6 7   almost always

6. Child seems to take things matter-of-factly (such as a visitor to class, trips or other special events), without getting very excited.   hardly ever   1 2 3 .4 5 6 7   almost always

7. When teacher establishes safety rule (such as behavior during fire drill), child learns to obey quickly.   hardly ever   1 2 3 4 5 6 7   almost always

8. When telling a story, such as what happened on the weekend or during a vacation, the child talks about it loudly, with enthusiasm and excitement.   hardly ever   1 2 3 4 5 6 7   almost always

9. Child is easily drawn away from his/her work by noises, something outside the window, another child's whispering, etc.   hardly ever   1 2 3 4 5 6 7   almost always

10. Child will initially avoid new games and activities, preferring to sit on the side and watch.   hardly ever   1 2 3 4 5 6 7   almost always

11. Child does not notice colors, and does not comment on how pretty or ugly they are.

hardly ever   1   2   3   4   5   6   7   almost always

12. Child quickly becomes impatient with a task he/she cannot grasp, and goes on to something else.

hardly ever   1   2   3   4   5   6   7   almost always

13. If child is in a bad mood, he/she can easily be "joked" out of it.

hardly ever   1   2   3   4   5   6   7   almost always

14. Child enjoys going on errands for the teacher.

hardly ever   1   2   3   4   5   6   7   almost always

15. If initially hesitant about entering into new games and activities, child gets over this quickly.

hardly ever   1   2   3   4   5   6   7   almost always

16. Child's responses are loud.

hardly ever   1   2   3   4   5   6   7   almost always

17. If another child has a toy he/she wants, this child will easily accept a substitute.

hardly ever   1   2   3   4   5   6   7   almost always

18. Child runs rather than walks.

hardly ever   1   2   3   4   5   6   7   almost always

19. Child smiles, laughs.

hardly ever   1   2   3   4   5   6   7   almost always

20. After an absence of many days or after a long holiday, it takes time for this child to readjust to school routine.

hardly ever   1   2   3   4   5   6   7   almost always

21. Child gets involved immediately in new learning situations.

hardly ever   1   2   3   4   5   6   7   almost always

22. If teacher is busy when child wants teacher's attention, child goes away, instead of keeping after the teacher.

hardly ever   1   2   3   4   5   6   7   almost **always**

23. Child remarks if teacher or classmates wear new clothes.

hardly ever   1   2   3   4   5   6   7   almost **always**

24. In outdoor play, child is active and energetic, rough and tumble, compared to other children.

hardly ever   1   2   3   4   5   6   7   almost **always**

25. Child takes a long time to become comfortable in a new physical location (e.g., different classroom, new seat, etc.).

hardly ever   1   2   3   4   5   6   7   almost **always**

26. If another child tries to interrupt when this child is engaged in an activity, he/she will ignore them.

hardly ever   1   2   3   4   5   6   7   almost **always**

27. Child will show little or no reaction when another child takes his/her toy or possession away.

hardly ever   1   2   3   4   5   6   7   almost **always**

28. When class is promised something in the future (trip, party, etc.), this child keeps reminding the teacher of it.

hardly ever   1   2   3   4   5   6   7   almost **always**

29. When playing with other children, this child argues with them.

hardly ever   1   2   3   4   5   6   7   almost **always**

30. Child plunges into new activities and situations without hesitation.

hardly ever   1   2   3   4   5   6   7   almost **always**

31. Child can continue at the same activity for an hour.

hardly ever 1 2 3 4 5 6 7 almost always

32. Child has to be seriously hurt before he/she comments or cries about cuts or bruises.

33. If he/she initially does not get along well with another child, this child's relationship with them improves quickly.

hardly ever 1 2 3 4 5 6 7 almost always

34. Child is able to sit quietly for a reasonable amount of time (as compared to classmates).

hardly ever 1 2 3 4 5 6 7 almost always

35. It is hard to tell what this child is feeling (either positive or negative) as there is little change in facial expression.

hardly ever 1 2 3 4 5 6 7 almost always

36. Child cannot be distracted when he/she is working (seems able to concentrate in the midst of bedlam).

hardly ever 1 2 3 4 5 6 7 almost always

37. When assistance is offered in doing a task, child prefers to do it on his/her own.

hardly ever 1 2 3 4 5 6 7 almost always

38. Child becomes easily upset when he/she loses a game.

hardly ever 1 2 3 4 5 6 7 almost always

39. Child is sensitive to temperature and likely to comment on classroom being hot or cold.

hardly ever 1 2 3 4 5 6 7 almost always

40. Child takes a long time to become comfortable in a new situation.

hardly ever   1 2 3 4 5 6 7   almost always

41. Child enjoys listening to stories.

hardly ever   1 2 3 4 5 6 7   almost always

42. Child will get up and perform before the class (sing, recite, etc.) with no hesitation, even the first time.

hardly ever   1 2 3 4 5 6 7   almost always

43. Child over-reacts (becomes very upset) in a stressful situation.

hardly ever   1 2 3 4 5 6 7   almost always

44. If other children are talking or making noise while teacher is explaining a lesson, this child remains attentive to the teacher.

hardly ever   1 2 3 4 5 6 7   almost always

45. If recess must be skipped so child doesn't have usual physical outlet, he/she becomes restless.

hardly ever   1 2 3 4 5 6 7   almost always

46. When given a new school assignment, child responds with immediate interest.

hardly ever   1 2 3 4 5 6 7   almost always

47. Child is bashful when meeting new children.

hardly ever   1 2 3 4 5 6 7   almost always

48. Child starts an activity and does not finish it.

hardly ever   1 2 3 4 5 6 7   almost always

49. Child doesn't react if accidently touched or lightly brushed by another child.

hardly ever   1 2 3 4 5 6 7   almost always

50. Child complains to teacher about other children.

hardly ever   1 2 3 4 5 6 7   almost always

51. Child adjusts to changes in school routine, rules or procedures, only after a long time.   hardly ever   1   2   3   4   5   6   7   almost always

52. This child is easily sidetracked.   hardly ever   1   2   3   4   5   6   7   almost always

53. Child's movements are slow.   hardly ever   1   2   3   4   5   6   7   almost always

54. Child lets other children know when he/she does not like something by yelling or fighting.   hardly ever   1   2   3   4   5   6   7   almost always

55. Child is not bothered by loud noises (for example, fire alarm, siren, etc.)   hardly ever   1   2   3   4   5   6   7   almost always

56. When child can't have or do something he/she wants, child becomes annoyed or upset.   hardly ever   1   2   3   4   5   6   7   almost always

57. Child is highly sensitive to changes in the brightness or dimness of light.   hardly ever   1   2   3   4   5   6   7   almost always

58. During free play, child will stick to any one activity for only a short time.   hardly ever   1   2   3   4   5   6   7   almost always

59. Child will adjust quickly to a game if others want to play in a different way.   hardly ever   1   2   3   4   5   6   7   almost always

60. During free play time, child prefers quiet activities (such as reading or coloring) over play involving more movement (such as ball, jump-rope, tag, etc.)   hardly ever   1   2   3   4   5   6   7   almost always

61. When child loses a game,   hardly   1   2   3   4   5   6   7   almost
     he/she takes it lightly.   ever   always

62. Child prefers familiar toys   hardly   1   2   3   4   5   6   7   almost
     and games to new play   ever   always
     equipment.

63. Teacher may have to speak   hardly   1   2   3   4   5   6   7   almost
     to child several times be-   ever   always
     fore child hears or re-
     sponds if he/she is en-
     gaged in a task.

64. Child sits still when a   hardly   1   2   3   4   5   6   7   almost
     story is being told or read.   ever   always

FINDER'S KEY

NYLS-Teachers Questionnaire for Children
3-7 Years of Age

1. ACTIVITY	33. ADAPTABILITY
2. MOOD	34. ACTIVITY
3. THRESHOLD	35. INTENSITY
4. APPROACH/W	36. DISTRACTIBILITY
5. PERSISTENCE	37. PERSISTENCE
6. INTENSITY	38. MOOD
7. ADAPTABILITY	39. THRESHOLD
8. INTENSITY	40. ADAPTABILITY
9. DISTRACTIBILITY	41. MOOD
10. APPROACH/W	42. APPROACH/W
11. THRESHOLD	43. INTENSITY
12. PERSISTENCE	44. DISTRACTIBILITY
13. DISTRACTIBILITY	45. ACTIVITY
14. MOOD	46. APPROACH/W
15. ADAPTABILITY	47. APPROACH/W
16. INTENSITY	48. PERSISTENCE
17. DISTRACTIBILITY	49. THRESHOLD
18. ACTIVITY	50. MOOD
19. MOOD	51. ADAPTABILITY
20. ADAPTABILITY	52. DISTRACTIBILITY
21. APPROACH/W	53. ACTIVITY
22. PERSISTENCE	54. INTENSITY
23. THRESHOLD	55. THRESHOLD
24. ACTIVITY	56. MOOD
25. ADAPTABILITY	57. THRESHOLD
26. DISTRACTIBILITY	58. PERSISTENCE
27. INTENSITY	59. ADAPTABILITY
28. PERSISTENCE	60. ACTIVITY
29. MOOD	61. INTENSITY
30. APPROACH/W	62. APPROACH/W
31. PERSISTENCE	63. DISTRACTIBILITY
32. THRESHOLD	64. ACTIVITY

Appendix C.

Temperamental

characteristics schedule

INTERVIEWING NOTES

(From P. Graham, M. Rutter and S. George)

The aim of the interview is to obtain information about the everyday behaviour of the child in question. The information is then used to categorise the child in terms of a number of personality dimensions or temperamental characteristics, namely: mood, intensity of emotional expression, activity, fastidiousness, malleability, regularity and approach/withdrawal behaviour.

The interview is divided into three parts. In the first the mother is asked to describe how the child behaved in a variety of situations during the previous 24 hours, this information being used mainly to rate mood, intensity and activity. The second part is concerned with the eating, sleeping and bowel habits of the child—the mother being asked to describe the pattern of the child's behaviour in these areas over the last fortnight. This section is primarily used to rate regularity. Finally, the mother is asked to describe how the child has behaved in certain less frequently occurring situations over the past six months in order to rate the remaining categories.

Personal communication from Dr. P. Graham. For more information on the work of this group, see P. Graham, M. Rutter, and S. George, "Temperamental Characteristics as Predictors of Behavior Disorders in Children," *Am. J. Orthopsychiatr.*, 43:3:328-339, 1973.

The techniques of interviewing and of rating are somewhat different in each of the three sections, and they will therefore be dealt with separately. However, there are certain common points to be made, and these will be dealt with first.

The interview is not a structured questionnaire. Although where this is specified the initial question should be asked in the form laid down, it is up to the interviewer to obtain information which is both rateable and, as far as possible, an accurate reflection of the behavior in question. The interviewers should persist in questioning until satisfied that this has been done.

In general, mothers appear to enjoy answering these questions and do not object to being pressed to give specific instances, but it is important not to sacrifice rapport with the informant by being too demanding and asking her to remember events that appear not to be within her powers of recall. It is better to rate an item as 'not applicable' than to rate it on the basis of an answer which has been invented by the mother to satisfy or placate the interviewer.

At all points of the interview, it is important to obtain descriptions of actual behaviour, rather than generalisations, attitudes, or assumptions. Thus statements that a child on a particular occasion was 'happy' or 'angry' should not be accepted without obtaining a description of the child's behaviour that led the mother to make these inferences. Similarly, general remarks such as 'He is always fussy about his hair' or 'He is very shy with children he has not met before' cannot be utilised unless they are accompanied by descriptions of what the child has done on occasions when his hair has become ruffled or (in the case of shyness) when he has actually been confronted by another child.

It is preferable to obtain spontaneous descriptions of the child's temperamental style from the mother and, indeed, most mothers can give very adequate descriptions of their child's behaviour with little prompting. Where, however, the mother uses adjectives which are unhelpful because they are imprecise or ambiguous, the interviewer should offer a wide choice of descriptions from which the mother can take her pick. Thus, for example, if a mother replied 'He was just ordinary' in reply to a question about how a child was showing his feelings while having his breakfast, the interviewer should probe on the following lines. . . . 'Was he grizzling a bit, or laughing. . . . or just talking?' It is important to offer a wide range of possibilities as, for example, a mother's description of her child as 'just happy' can cover a wide range of emotional expression from loud laughter to quiet preoccupation or even silent misery.

Recent Routine Activities

The mother is asked to describe very recent specific instances of various routine activities. Most children will have been observed by their mothers while engaged in these situations during the previous 24 hours, but if for some reason this is not the case, then the mother should be asked to describe the last such occasion at which she was present.

Each 'recent routine activity' (rising from bed, getting washed and dressed, eating two meals, watching a television programme, playing with a friend, going to bed, playing with an adult and going for a walk) is rated for mood, intensity, and activity.

Each of these categories should be rated twice for each activity or item, the ratings being made on the two extremes of behaviour shown. Therefore, if for example a child roars with laughter during part of a meal and sits quietly talking for the rest, he should receive one rating of positive mood and one of neutral mood. In addition, he should receive one rating for very high intensity of emotional expression (average mood is not rated for intensity).

For convenience, some information relevant to the rating of malleability, fastidiousness, sensitivity and assertiveness is collected during this section, but points relating to this will be dealt with later.

If the mother has not observed the child getting out of bed and spending the first five minutes of the day, then she should be asked to give an account of the first five minutes in which she did have an opportunity of observing him. If the mother's description does not include sufficient material to rate mood or intensity, she should be asked 'How was he showing his feelings?', this being followed by further probes as necessary. If insufficient information is forthcoming to rate activity, then probes such as 'Did he come running into your room, or trudging in, or just walking ordinarily?' may be helpful.

The probe 'How was he showing his feelings?' or some variant of this, will always be useful in eliciting mood and intensity, but the probes for eliciting level of activity will usually have to be tailored to the situation. Thus, for example, with respect to the child's behaviour at meals the mother may be asked 'Was he sitting very still, or jumping up and down, or just fidgeting a little?'

Habits

In the section concerned with the child's habits, the mother is asked about the timing and frequency of certain events associated with the child's sleep and bowel activity over the past fortnight. In addition, she is asked to describe the child's recent appetite in terms of its conformity or non-conformity to a general pattern.

In obtaining information about sleeping and waking it is convenient to find out how the child usually behaves in this area both at weekends and during the week, and then to establish any deviations from this pattern in the last two weeks. A similar approach should be used for bowel habits.

Constancy of amount eaten at each meal should be approached by asking the mother whether she always knows beforehand how much the child will eat or whether she is frequently surprised by his eating more or less than she expected. Ratings should be tied particularly to any examples that she can give. Regularity of times when the child gets hungry should be approached by asking the mother if she always knows beforehand when he is going to be hungry, or if he often asks for food at odd times of the day. The child's behaviour on occasions when the meal has had to be put forward or delayed for any reason is important here, and in any event the rating should again be tied to examples.

Appetite away from home should be obtained by asking the mother about the last occasion when this situation occurred.

Non-routine Events

This final section deals with events which are rarer in the child's life, and experience has shown that, too commonly, mothers do not remember these unless orientating questions which enable them to express their attitudes are asked first. So the mother is first asked in general how the child behaves in these situations. Some mothers will have been affected by the behaviour slant of the interview up to this point to such an extent that they give descriptions of actual behaviour in answer to the attitudinal questions. These descriptions are, of course, immediately rateable. On the other hand, where mothers give a general account, they must be asked to describe the last occasion on which the child was observed by the mother in the situation in question. The mother's description of the child's behaviour may contradict the attitude she has expressed about him. For example, she may say that the child is very shy, but only be able to give descriptions of approaching behaviour to strangers. In this event, ratings should be made on the basis of the actual behaviour, although the mother should be given every opportunity to provide examples to substantiate her attitude.

Where a particular type of behaviour is invariable, it is often difficult for the mother to remember a concrete instance when it occurred. It is, in fact, easier for her to remember exceptions, and although these may be important, for the purposes of this interview it is the *usual* pattern of behaviour in which we are interested. For this reason if the mother cannot remember an actual occasion when a particular type of behaviour occurred, but can assure the interviewer that in this situation the child has *always* behaved in the specified manner during the past month, then her description can be accepted as rateable.

Actual examples of behaviour in this section can be rated if they occurred up to six months prior to interview, but not if they occurred before this.

As far as possible each item in this section should be rated in addition for mood and intensity of emotional expression, and information relevant for these ratings should be obtained throughout.

Mood

As far as possible *all* items should be rated for mood, 'Recent routine activity' items may be rated twice for mood, depending on the range of emotional expression demonstrated.

Mood should be rated as positive or negative regardless of the appropriateness of the response, e.g., it should be rated as negative even if the child cries when he falls down and hurts himself.

Examples of mood:

Positive: Laughing, smiling, giggling.
              Grinning, beaming, looking pleased.

Neutral: Chattering, just ordinary, looking serious.

Negative: Crying, sobbing, looking worried.
              Looking tense, pouting, looking annoyed.
              Looking angry, frowning.

Some items, such as 'shouting, excited, happy' cannot be rated in this category without further elaboration by the mother making it quite clear what mood the child is showing.

Intensity of Emotional Expression

Wherever a rating of positive or negative mood is made anywhere in the schedule, a rating of intensity should be made in addition.

Ratings should not be made on this scale when mood is rated as neutral. Where, in the same item, two different levels of intensity are described, then rate the highest level expressed, e.g., rate 'high' for the description 'He was smiling and laughing.'

Again the ratings should be summed at the bottom of the page. In addition an overall rating of intensity of emotional expression on a five point scale should be made.

Examples of intensity of emotional expression:

Very low: Face dropped, gave a slight smile.

Low: Beaming, moaning, smiling, whining, grizzling, grinning, looking annoyed.

Average: Giggling, quietly crying.

High: Laughing out loud, crying out loud.

Very high: Roaring with laughter, screaming with anger, crying his eyes out.

Activity

All the recent routine activities apart from the last two occasions on which the child was reprimanded should be rated on this scale. The scale refers to the tempo of physical activity in relation to the type of behaviour in which the child is engaged. Thus a child who moves about while doing a jigsaw puzzle would be rated high, and a child who dawdled about in a game of football low even though the latter might be more physically active in an absolute sense.

Again, the individual ratings should be summed at the bottom of the page, and, in addition an overall rating of physical activity on a five point scale should be made.

Examples of ratings of activity:

Very low: Glued to the chair, standing completely still.

Low: Dawdling, lagging behind, sitting quietly, just sitting, strolling around.

Average: Just walking, moving about a bit (when playing with doll's house), fidgeting a little (at meals), rocking quietly.

High: Running, wriggling and squirming (at meals), jumping around (while playing), swinging as high as he could, running ahead.

Very high: Restrict this rating to situations where the child repeatedly moves around the room in situations where he might be expected to stay still, e.g., when watching a favourite TV programme, or after being sat down to a meal.

Malleability

This category refers to the ease or difficulty with which another person (usually the parent) can alter the child's behaviour. Malleability or its absence is shown when the parent intrudes upon an activity and attempts to get the child to do something else.

The category should not be scored when the child changes activity without intervention by the parents, e.g., comes in for lunch without being called.

The parent must repeat his attempt to persuade at least once before a rating of average or low can be made, i.e., if a parent tries to get the child to do something once, and the child refuses, this item cannot be rated on malleability.

Three types of rating of malleability are made—one on the basis of the behaviour of the child in different situations in which the parent tries to get the child to do something, one on the basis of the mother's response to the direct probes on malleability, and finally on overall assessment.

The first should be rated using the following rules:

0—Very low —Child does not change activity despite frequent attempts by parents.

1—Low   —Child does not change activity after two parental attempts.

2—Average —Child does as required on the second parental attempt.

3—High   —Child does as required on first occasion.

4—Very high—Restrict to occasions when the child acts promptly even though against his own clear inclinations.

Regularity

Individual ratings are made for each of the aspects of the child's habits that are probed. These ratings are made on a three point scale—low regularity, average, and high regularity.

Note that ratings must be made about behaviour which is directly independent of parental imposition. Thus, for example, the time that the child goes to bed and the time that he goes to the lavatory are irrelevant in rating. What is important is the time he goes to sleep and the time he has his bowels open.

Examples:

a) Going to sleep:

    0—Low   Asleep or showing signs of wanting to go to sleep within one hour of same time each night in past two weeks. More than four deviations .

    1—Average As above but 2-3 deviations.

    2—High   As above but 0-1 deviations.

b) Waking in night:

    0—Low   More than 3 deviations from pattern described in 2 (high)

    1—Average 1-3 deviations from pattern described in 2 (high)

    2—High   No waking in night or regular waking at same time of the night within one hour.

c) Morning waking:
Rate on same principles as a) going to sleep.

d) Sleep after day when kept up beyond usual sleep time:

    0—Low   No signs of sleep at normal bedtime, or does not go to sleep immediately when put to bed.

    1—Average Shows a few signs of sleep at usual bedtime, but not really bothered.

    2—High   Shows sleepiness or other signs (e.g., increase in irritability at normal sleep-time, or falls asleep straightaway when gets to bed).

e) Bowel habits:

    0—Low   Less regular than 1.

    1—Average 1-2 deviations from regular daily pattern.

    2—High   Unvarying daily pattern of bowel activity in last fortnight, i.e., open every day or every other day, etc. The time of day is unimportant in rating.

f) Appetite—time of hunger:

0—Low   Does not seem to matter if meal presented to him late or early by half-hour or more.
Asks for snacks irregularly.

1—Average   Will usually come and ask if meal delayed by half-hour or more, but makes no fuss.

2—High   Will not eat meal if half-hour or more earlier than usual, or makes a fuss if meal delayed by this amount. Regularly snack-taking.

g) Appetite—amount eaten:

0—Low   Mother rarely knows how much he will eat—it might be a lot or a little.

1—Average   Mother usually knows how much he will have, but is sometimes surprised.

2—High   Mother always knows how much he will have—either always a lot or always a little.

h) Appetite away from home:

0—Low   Definitely eats more or less.

1—Average   Eats about the same.

2—High   Eats exactly the same as when at home.

Fastidiousness

This category takes account of the child's tolerance of mess. Individual ratings should be made with respect to this aspect of the child's behaviour at meal times, at play, when his hair ruffled or his clothes get dirty, when his underpants get soiled, and in any other relevant situation that may arise. In addition, an overall rating of fastidiousness on a five point scale is made.

Example of individual ratings:

0—Very low   No precautions taken against mess and tends to actively resist attempts to clean or tidy himself up.

1—Low   No precautions against mess, but will go and clean or clean or tidy himself if asked.

2—Average   No precautions against mess, but will go and clean or tidy self up spontaneously.

3—High   Some precautions against mess, and will go and clean or tidy self up spontaneously. Sometimes upset if gets self messed up.

4—Very high   Careful not to get dirty or mess self up. Usually upset if he does.

Approach/Withdrawal Behaviour

This refers to the child's *initial* behaviour when confronted with new adults, new places, new children, people seen only rarely, and behaviour when the door bell rings and he can have no idea who is there. For this purpose 'new people' are adults or children that the child has not seen for a year or more. Babies who have not yet started to walk do not count as 'new children.' People seen rarely are people who have been seen less than a year before, but not in the previous month.

Approach refers to verbal approach as well as physical, so that if a child speaks first to an adult (and shows no physical withdrawal) this rates as approach even though the child does not go up to the adult. If, however, the verbal approach is associated with physical vacillation or withdrawal, the latter are rated.

Examples:

0—Approach   Child goes up to person unprompted or speaks first without shyness.

1—Modified approach   Child smiles in friendly fashion before being spoken to or approached. Speaks readily when spoken to. Shows no shyness.

2—Average or stationary Child speaks when spoken to without hesitation but does not make first verbal or physical approach.

3—Modified withdrawal   Child speaks when spoken to but may look at mother for reassurance, or look worried.

4—Withdrawal   Child does not speak when spoken to or withdraws physically or definitely looks frightened or cries.

Note that although in the examples given the mood of the child is described, mood should be rated separately and should not be taken into account when rating approach/withdrawal behaviour. If the child moves towards the stranger and cries at the same time, this should be rated as approach and negative mood. Usually, of course, where a child shows negative mood he/she will also show withdrawal behaviour. Where a child vacillates, the most withdrawing aspect of his behaviour should be rated.

An overall assessment of approach/withdrawal behaviour is made on the basis of the same definitions using the impression gained from all the examples that have been obtained.

Appendix D. Obtaining data on temperament in clinical practice

An accurate diagnostic judgment requires that data on the child's temperamental characteristics be gathered with the same care and regard for detail that are considered essential for the evaluation of parental attitudes and practices, family relationships and sociocultural influences. Naturally, the clinician does not have anterospectively gathered behavioral descriptions of a child's developmental course available to him. But neither does he have available such antereospective data on intra- and extrafamilial environmental influences. With all information gathered retrospectively, whether it be on temperament, the attainment of developmental landmarks, the medical history, the patterns of parental functioning or special environmental events, the clinician must assess the accuracy, completeness and pertinence of the data reported to him. In the authors' experience, the collection of behavioral data from which evaluations of temperament can be made has presented no greater difficulties than gathering information on other aspects of the clinical history. Some informants are able to give detailed, factual and precise descriptions of their children's past and present behavior. Others give vague, general and subjective reports. In all cases, it is desirable to confirm the accuracy of the data by directly observing the

Extracted from A. Thomas, S. Chess and H. G. Birch, *Temperament and Behavior Disorders in Children*, New York: New York University Press, 1968.

259

child and, wherever possible, by obtaining information from multiple sources.

A number of items in the basic clinical history, such as the course of the child's development and the history of the presenting complaints, will often in themselves elicit clues as to significant issues relating to the child's temperament. For example, the parents of a 12-year-old boy reported that he was unable to study or do homework at an academic level appropriate to his intellectual capacity and his grade placement, and that he started many endeavors, such as music lessons or rock collections, but seemed to lose interest in them rapidly. The parents also complained that routines took an inordinate amount of time to be accomplished although the child was cheerful and apparently well-intentioned. He would start on his way to bed but might be found 15 minutes later puttering with some game which attracted his attention, playing with a brother or involved in a discussion with his grandmother. The composite of presenting problems in this case suggested that the temperamental quality of distractibility might be an important factor in causing the child's difficulties.

As another example, the parents of a nine-year-old girl reported that she found it difficult to undertake new endeavors and to join new groups of children her own age and that she tended to avoid new situations whenever she could. This presenting complaint suggested the possibility that a temperamentally based tendency to make initial withdrawal reactions to new experiences might be relevant to the reported behavioral difficulty.

Following the taking of a basic clinical history, systematic inquiry can be made into the child's temperamental characteristics during infancy, keeping in mind the necessity to investigate similarly other possible causes for the problem behaviors. The inquiry can be started with the general question, "After you brought the baby home from the hospital and in the first few weeks and months of his life, what was he like?"

First answers to such questions are usually very general ones: "He was wonderful." "He cried day and night." "He was a bundle of nerves." "He was a joy."

The next question is still open-ended: "Would you give me some details that will describe what you mean?"

The replies to this second general question often include useful descriptions of behaviors from which judgments of temperament may be made. Further information requires specific inquiry, which is most economically pursued by taking up areas of behavior relevant to defining each of the temperamental attributes one at a time. The questions asked should be directed at obtaining a number of descriptive behavioral items from which the interviewer can then make an estimate of the child's temperamental characteristics. A list of questions appropriate to each of the nine categories can be suggested at this point.

ACTIVITY LEVEL

How much did your baby move around? Did he move around a lot, was he very quiet or somewhere in between? If you put him to bed for a nap and it took him 10 or 15 minutes to fall asleep, would you have to go in to rearrange the covers, or would he be lying so quietly that you knew they would be in their proper place and not disarranged? If you were changing his diaper and discovered that you had left the powder just out of reach, could you safely dash over to get it and come right back without worrying that he would flip over the surface and fall? Did you have trouble changing his diaper, pulling his shirt over his head or putting on any other of his clothing because he wiggled about, or could you count on his lying quietly to be dressed?

RHYTHMICITY

How did you arrange the baby's feedings? Could you tell by the time he was six weeks (two months, three months) old about when during the day he would be hungry, sleepy, or wake up? Could you count on this happening about the same time every day or did the baby vary from day to day? If he varied, how marked was it? About when during the day did he have his bowel movements (time and number) and was this routine variable or predictable?

Parents can generally recall such events. They will say, "He was regular as clockwork;" "I could never figure out when to start a long job because one day he would have a long nap and the next day he wouldn't sleep more than 15 minutes;" or, "I used to try to take him out for his airing after I cleaned him from his bowel movement, but I never could figure it right because his time changed every day."

ADAPTABILITY

How would you describe the way the child responded to changed circumstances? For example, when he was shifted from a bathinette to a bathtub, if he didn't take to the change immediately, could you count on his getting used to it quickly or did it take a long time? (Parents should be asked to define what they mean by "quickly" and what they mean by "a long time" in terms of days or weeks.) If his first reaction to a new person was a negative one, how long did it take the child to become familiar with the person? If he didn't like a new food the first time it was offered, could you count on the child's getting to like it and most other new foods sooner or later? If so, how long would it take if the new food was offered to him daily or several times a week?

APPROACH/WITHDRAWAL

How did the baby behave with new events, such as when he was given his first tub bath, offered new foods or taken care of by a new person for the first time? Did he fuss, did he do nothing or did he seem to like it? Were there any changes during his infancy that you remember, such as a shift to a new bed, a visit to a new place or a permanent move? Describe the child's initial behavior at these times.

THRESHOLD LEVEL

How would you estimate the baby's sensitivity to noises, to heat and cold, to things he saw and tasted and to textures of clothing? Did he seem to be very aware of or unresponsive to these things? For example, did you have to tiptoe about when the baby was sleeping lest he be awakened? If he heard a faint noise while awake, would he tend to notice the sound by looking toward it? Did bright lights or bright sunshine make him blink or cry? Did the baby's behavior seem to show that he noticed the difference when a familiar person wore glasses or a new hair style for the first time in his presence? If he didn't like a new food and an old food that he liked very much was put with it on the spoon, would the baby still notice the taste of the new one and reject it? Did you have to be careful about clothing you put on him because some textures were too rough? If so, describe the kind of things he disliked.

INTENSITY OF REACTION

How did you know when the baby was hungry? Did he squeak, did he roar or were his sounds somewhere in between? How could you tell that he didn't like a food? Did he just quietly turn his head away from the spoon or did he start crying loudly? If you held his hand to cut his fingernails and he didn't like it, did he fuss a little or a lot? If he liked something, did he usually smile and coo or did he laugh loudly? In general, would you say he let his pleasure or displeasure be known loudly or softly?

QUALITY OF MOOD

How could you tell when the baby liked something or disliked something? After a description of the infant's behavior in these respects is obtained, the parents should be asked if he was more often contented or more often discontented and on what basis they made this judgment.

DISTRACTIBILITY

If the child were in the midst of sucking on the bottle or breast, would he stop what he was doing if he heard a sound or if another person came by, or would he continue sucking? If he were hungry and fussing or crying while the bottle was being warmed, could you divert him easily and stop his crying by holding him or giving him a plaything? If he were playing, for example, gazing at his fingers or using a rattle, would other sights and sounds get his attention very quickly or very slowly?

PERSISTENCE AND ATTENTION SPAN

Would you say that the baby usually stuck with something he was doing for a long time or only momentarily? For example, describe the longest time he remained engrossed in an activity all by himself. How old was he and what was he doing? (Examples might be playing with the cradle gym or watching a mobile.) If he reached for something, say a toy in the bathtub, and couldn't get it easily, would he keep after it or give up very quickly?

After completing the inventory of the child's temperamental characteristics in infancy, the next step is to identify those attributes which appear extreme in their manifestations and/or those which seem clearly related to the child's current pattern of deviant behavior. This is followed by an inquiry into the characteristics of these temperament attributes at succeeding age-stage periods of development. Thus, if the history of the infancy period suggests a pattern of marked distractibility, it would be desirable to gather data on behavior related to distractibility at succeeding age periods and in varied life situations, such as play, school, homework, etc. Similarly, if the presenting complaints indicate that the child currently finds it difficult to undertake new endeavors or to join new groups of age-mates, and if the early temperamental history suggests a characteristic pattern of initial withdrawal coupled with slow adaptation, it would be important to obtain descriptions of the child's patterns of initial responses to situations and demands that arose at different points in his developmental course.

The final step in the assessment of the child's temperament is the evaluation of his current temperamental characteristics. The behavioral information obtained for current functioning is usually more valid than that obtained for behavioral patterns in the past, since the problems of forgetting and retrospective distortion are minimized. The inquiry into current behavior will attempt to cover all temperamental categories but should concentrate on those which appear most pertinent to the presenting symptoms.

Activity level may be estimated from a child's behavior preferences. Would he rather sit quietly for a long time engrossed in some task or does he prefer to seek out opportunities for active physical play? How well does he fare in routines that require sitting still for extended periods of time? For example, can he sit through an entire meal without seeking an opportunity to move about? Must a long train or automobile ride be broken up by frequent stops because of his restlessness?

Rhythmicity can be explored through questions about the child's habits and their regularity. For instance, does he get sleepy at regular and predictable times? Does he have any characteristic routines relating to hunger, such as taking a snack immediately after school or during the evening? Are his bowel movements regular?

Adaptability can be identified through a consideration of the way the child reacts to changes in environment. Does he adjust easily and fit quickly into changed family patterns? Does he have difficulty adapting to the routines of a new classroom or a new teacher? Is he willing to go along with other children's preferences or does he always insist on pursuing only his own interests?

Approach/withdrawal, or the youngster's pattern of response to new events or new people, can be explored in many ways. Questions can be directed at the nature of his reaction to new clothing, new neighborhood children, a new school and a new teacher. What is his attitude when a family excursion is being planned? Will he try new foods or new activities easily or not?

Threshold level is more difficult to explore in an older child than in a young one. However, it is sometimes possible to obtain information on unusual features of threshold such as hypersensitivity to noise, to visual stimuli or to rough clothing, or remarkable unresponsiveness to such stimuli.

The intensity of reactions can be ascertained by finding out how the child displays disappointment or pleasure. If something pleasant happens does he tend to be mildly enthusiastic, average in his expression of joy or ecstatic? When he is unhappy, does he fuss quietly or bellow with rage or distress?

Quality of mood can usually be estimated by parental descriptions of their offspring's overall expressions of mood. Is he predominantly happy and contented or is he a frequent complainer and more often unhappy than not?

Distractibility, even when not a presenting problem, will declare itself in the parent's descriptions of ordinary routines. Does the child start off to do something and then often get sidetracked by something his brother is doing, by his coin collection or by any number of several circumstances that catch his eye or his ear? Or, on the contrary, once he is engaged in an activity is he impervious to what is going on around him?

Data on persistence and attention span are usually easier to obtain for the older child than for the infant. The degree of persistence in the face of difficulty can be ascertained with regard to games, puzzles, athletic activities, such as learning to ride a bicycle, and school work. Similarly, after the initial difficulty in mastering these activities has been overcome, the length of the child's attention span for and concentration on these same kinds of activities can be ascertained.

In many instances, additional data on temperamental organization can be obtained by querying teachers or other adults familiar with the child's behavior. For such inquiry, the history-taking protocol for the parents can be utilized if it is appropriately modified to permit a focus on the areas of the child's functioning with which the adult is acquainted. Observation of the child's behavior during a clinical play interview or in the course of psychological testing can also supply useful information on activity level, approach/withdrawal, intensity of reactions, quality of mood, distractibity and persistence and attention-span. Temperamental characterizations which require information on the child's behavior over time, namely rhythmicity and adaptability, cannot be made from such single observations over a short time span and the nature of the clinical observation and testing situations is such that behaviors referable to the sensory threshold characteristic of the child are usually not observable.

Index